*The Royal Navy in European Waters
during the American Revolutionary War*

STUDIES IN MARITIME HISTORY

William N. Still Jr., Series Editor

THE ROYAL NAVY IN EUROPEAN WATERS DURING THE AMERICAN REVOLUTIONARY WAR

David Syrett

UNIVERSITY OF SOUTH CAROLINA

© 1998 University of South Carolina

Published in Columbia, South Carolina, by the
University of South Carolina Press

Manufactured in the United States of America

02 01 00 99 98 5 4 3 2 1

Library of Congress Cataloging-in-Publication Data

   Syrett, David.
   The Royal Navy in European waters during the American
Revolutionary War / David Syrett.
     p. cm. — (Studies in maritime history)
   Includes bibliographical references and index.
   ISBN 1-57003-238-6
   1. United States—History—Revolution, 1775–1783—Naval
operations, British. 2. Great Britain. Royal Navy—History–
Revolution, 1775–1783. 3. Europe–History, Naval. I. Title.
II. Series.
E271.S97 1998
973.3'5—dc21   97-45362

For Eleni

CONTENTS

ILLUSTRATIONS

PREFACE

From the beginning of the fighting in America in 1775, the Royal Navy in European waters combated American blockade runners and cruisers. From 1778 to 1782, they were joined by the navies of France, Spain, and the Netherlands. For the Royal Navy, with its tradition of victory, the naval war in European waters is a saga of single-ship actions, blockades, cruises by great fleets and fleet actions, and, above all, failures and lost opportunities.

The inability of the Royal Navy in the American Revolution to decisively defeat American, French, Spanish, and Dutch naval power in European waters was due to a great extent to the failure of Lord North's ministry as a war government. North, the first lord of the Treasury and head of the government, was a brilliant parliamentary tactician, but he was totally unsuited to lead a government at war. Because of North's skill as a parliamentarian, the government enjoyed a comfortable majority in the House of Commons; however, they were unable to grapple successfully with the problems of the American war. North, who freely admitted that the war's conduct was beyond his capabilities, confined his activities for the most part to matters of finance and parliamentary politics, leaving the conduct of the war to individual members of the cabinet. In the absence of leadership from North or from any other member of the cabinet, the war was run by departments, with little coordination among the various ministers, and no one person, to coordinate policy, strategy, and the activities of various ministers and governmental departments. This was in marked contrast to the Seven Years' War, when William Pitt's leadership led the British to victory and established Great Britain as the world's chief colonial empire. Although Lord George Germain, secretary of state for America, was responsible for military operations in America and the West Indies, there was little or no coordination or cooperation between him and Lord Sandwich, the first lord of the Admiralty, who was responsible for naval operations.

Because of divisions of responsibility and lack of leadership within the North government, British policy vacillated between objectives, depending on which minister or group of ministers prevailed in the cabinet. There was no overarching strategy for the conduct of the American war. British strategy was, for the most part, a series of contradictions and paradoxes formulated in response to events. From the beginning of the fighting in America, it was never clear whether the government's policy was one of crushing the American rebels by force of arms or one of inducing through conciliation submission to royal authority. After France's entry into the conflict in 1778, the government could never decide if the major enemy was the American rebels or the Bourbon powers, or whether the main British effort should be made in America, the West Indies, or Europe. Strategic swings and fluctuations during the American Revolutionary War dispersed British strength between the eastern and western Atlantic, resulting in the Royal Navy's inability to meet effectively the challenge of Bourbon naval power in European waters.

The Royal Navy in the American war, unlike other eighteenth-century naval wars, such as the Seven Years' War, the French Revolutionary, and the Napoleonic Wars, was unable to decisively defeat Britain's enemies' navies in European waters. In the Seven Years' War, French sea power was defeated by the Royal Navy at the battles of Lagos and Quiberon Bay, and the remainder of the French fleet was bottled up in port. With the enemy fleet neutralized, Britain dispatched expeditions across the Atlantic, conquering the French empire in North America and the West Indies. British victory in the Seven Years' War was to a great extent made possible by the defeat of the French fleet in European waters. In the French Revolutionary and Napoleonic Wars, the Royal Navy smashed French and Spanish naval power and, through a system of blockades, confined the fleets of her enemies to European ports.

In the American war, with British military and naval power scattered in America, the West Indies, and Europe, there were no decisive victories for the Royal Navy similar to those in Quiberon Bay and Trafalgar in European seas during the Seven Years' and Napoleonic Wars. The Royal Navy's inability to defeat the naval forces of America and her European allies directly affected the course of the war in America, the West Indies, and India. In the first years of the American war, the Royal Navy's failure to hunt down and destroy American blockade runners and commerce raiders resulted in American rebels' easy access to arms and munitions in Europe, turning European waters into a major theater of war. After French entry into the conflict in 1778, the inability of the British to smash French and Spanish naval power off the Continent gave those Bourbon monarchies the means to intervene with naval forces in America, and to conduct naval operations against the British in areas such as the West Indies and Indian Ocean.

History is littered with missed opportunities, and victory for the British in a conflict as complex as the American war was elusive at best. But if the Royal Navy had been able to prevail over Britain's enemies in European waters, the course of the uprising in America, if not its eventual outcome, would have been quite different.

This book is an operational history. As such, it deals with events that affected the operations of the British navy during the years 1775–82, and its narrative thrust follows the sound of the guns. Subjects such as the workings of the British government, British parliamentary politics, and diplomatic affairs are explored only when necessary to understand the operations of the Royal Navy. With the advantages of hindsight, modern historians can see all sides of a question, while policy makers and commanders in wartime usually make decisions based on information that is fragmentary at best: intelligence of the enemy is always imperfect in wartime. Thus this study's view of the other side of the hill— American, French, Spanish, and Dutch motives and actions—is, for the most part, limited to what British policy makers and commanders knew at the time.

This book would not have been possible without the assistance of a number of people and institutions in Great Britain and the United States. I wish to thank the staffs of the University of London's Institute of Historical Research; the Public Record Office; British Library; William L. Clements Library of the University of Michigan; and the Rosenthal Library of Queens College, CUNY. I also wish to thank Dr. Mary Ellen Condon of the U.S. Army's Center for Military History for providing me with microfilm of the Keppel Papers; Dr. Mary Jo Kline of the John Hay Library, Brown University; Professor I. R. Christie for giving me the opportunity to consult his transcripts of the Grantham Papers; and the Combat Studies Institute of the U.S. Army Command and General Staff College for permitting me to republish portions of my study *Neutral Rights and the War in the Narrow Seas, 1778–82*. The maps and diagrams were made by Matthew D. Syrett. Research for this book was supported in part by the City University of New York-PSC-CUNY Research Award Program.

I am, of course, responsible for any sins of commission or omission.

*The Royal Navy in European Waters
during the American Revolutionary War*

Chapter 1

THE FAILURE TO
MOBILIZE FOR WAR,
1775-77

On 17 June 1775 the British army fought a bloody action with Massachusetts militia at Bunker Hill. The political crisis in America had exploded into armed conflict. When news of the fighting at Bunker Hill arrived in London during the last week of July 1775, the British government realized that it was confronted with a war in America. This war began as one between American militia and the British army but spread outward from Massachusetts to involve not only America and Britain but also France, Spain, and the Netherlands. The engagement on land at Bunker Hill led to one of the great naval wars of the eighteenth century in which fleets and warships of the belligerents battled each other, not only in American waters but also in European seas, eventually involving the naval forces of the new United States of America and, after 1778, the insurgent republic's European allies. However, in 1775, authorities in London foresaw none of this, for the government perceived the rebellion in America as a conflict which would be fought in America.

At its onset, that insurrection was seen by the British government as primarily a military problem that could and should be solved by the dispatch of an army to America. It was assumed that fighting would be limited to America and that the rebellion would be quickly ended when the British army crushed the American rebels with overpowering force.[1] If this strategy was successful, a major naval mobilization would not be required and the role of the Royal Navy would be one of supporting military operations in America. In 1775–76, the Royal Navy, rather than being mobilized to confront the battle fleet of a major European power, would be required to transport the British army across the Atlantic and to support it logistically.[2] A cost-conscious government believed that the policy of crushing the rebellion in America by force of arms would not require placing the Royal Navy on a war footing,[3] and any strategy that avoided the vast expenditures of money required for mobilizing the Royal Navy for war had great appeal to the North government.[4] The ministry justified this policy in 1775 and 1776 with the assumption that the rebellion would be put down quickly and the fighting limited to America, with no intervention by a European power. By 1778 all these assumptions would be proved false, for the rebellion in America would not be subdued. The Americans would carry the war to European seas and the French would be on the verge of entering the war as an ally of the Americans. By not augmenting the strength of the Royal Navy in 1775, the government embarked on a great and doomed strategic gamble in order to save money.

The British apparently did not think the Americans would carry the war to European seas. From the beginning of the fighting in Massachusetts, the ability of the Americans to wage war on the high seas was underestimated in London. Lord Sandwich, the first lord of the Admiralty, stated that the more Americans who took up arms against the British, the easier would be the victory for the king's forces.[5] Clearly, Sandwich, who had never been to America, had not thought through the maritime side of the problem, for the ability to wage war at sea was one of the few aspects of American military potential that was susceptible to rational analysis in 1775. In the rush to dispatch the army to America, the government overlooked the fact that British-American colonists had a long history of seafaring and well-developed maritime industries. In 1774, for example, one authority calculated that nearly one-third of all ships in the British merchant marine were American built.[6] Not only did Americans engage in fishing and the carrying trade, they also held a strong tradition of activities like piracy, smuggling, and privateering that would serve them well in waging maritime war. But the government did not make even the most superficial analysis, for such a survey would have revealed that the Americans were well equipped to carry the war to the high seas. The government's blunder was made clear by its failure to increase the strength of the Royal Navy dramatically with the beginning of fighting in America.

To wage a major eighteenth-century war, the Royal Navy required scores of small warships for such duties as escorting convoys and suppressing enemy commerce raiders. It was traditional policy at the beginning of a war for Britain to institute a building program of frigates, sloops of war, and other small warships suitable as cruisers. For example, in the years 1755–57, at the beginning of the Seven Years' War, the Admiralty ordered the construction of forty-two frigates. In the period 1775–78, the first three years of the American war, only nine new frigates were built. Learning from its mistakes, the British government built some sixty frigates during the last three years of the conflict with the Americans.[7] At the beginning of the fighting in America, the London government simply did not believe that the American rebels posed a threat to Britain's maritime interests close to home.

To be sure, the government responded to the fighting in Massachusetts by a substantial reinforcement of the Royal Navy in American waters. At the time of Bunker Hill, the squadron in America consisted of some thirty ships.[8] By the beginning of 1777, the force in American waters had been increased, mostly with small warships suitable for service in American coastal waters, to a strength of sixty-four vessels, while there were an additional nine ships in Newfoundland and twenty-four more in the West Indies supporting the British effort in America. The ships sent to America were mostly drawn from Europe and represented nearly the entire cruiser strength of the Royal Navy. On 1 January 1777 there were only five sloops of war and nine cutters serving in British waters, while a further twenty-four small warships, including 50-gun ships, were fitting in British ports.[9] To fight the war in America, the government took from British waters dozens of the small warships that would have served as cruisers to protect British trade, to interdict American ships carrying warlike materials, and to hunt down American privateers and warships.

The problems and difficulties that the Royal Navy would confront fighting Americans in European seas became quickly apparent when the British attempted to prevent the American rebels from obtaining munitions from Europe. On 15 October 1774 a dispatch arrived in London from the British ambassador at The Hague stating that the Americans were secretly purchasing munitions in the Netherlands.[10] Several days later, an order in council was issued prohibiting the export from Britain of gunpowder, arms, and all other forms of military equipment; at the same time, orders were issued to the Admiralty to seize any ship carrying munitions to America.[11] But the British found it very difficult to prevent the Americans from obtaining munitions from Europe, and by the middle of 1775, according to a secretary of state, "an extensive, illicit, and dangerous commerce is carrying on by vessels belonging to His Majesty's Colonies under Foreign Colours."[12] While Britain was still nominally at peace, however, the Royal Navy could not do much about American ships with false foreign papers. The American colonies had not yet been declared in a state of open rebellion, and a foreign vessel could only be seized when it fell within the prescription of the Hovering Act, that is, when intercepted within two leagues of British territory.[13] Despite these legal obstacles, the ships of the Royal Navy were stationed in the Thames and The Downs to assist customs officials in the search for munitions bound to America.[14] Other ships cruised the English Channel in an attempt to prevent the flow of munitions to the Americans.[15] In the autumn of 1775, HMS *Atalanta*, HMS *Pallas*, and HMS *Weazle* were ordered to "range" along the West African coast and seize any American ships there in an attempt to stop the rebels from obtaining munitions from the Slave Coast.[16] It was not until 22 December 1775 that Parliament passed the Capture Act, which proclaimed the colonies to be in a state of rebellion, prohibiting all trade with America and authorizing the seizure of all American ships.[17]

London quickly saw that stopping the flow of munitions to America was as much a diplomatic problem as a naval one. The British, with varying degrees of success, brought diplomatic pressure to bear on European nations to prohibit the export of munitions to America.[18] But diplomacy was not a very effective means of preventing Americans from obtaining munitions. Even in those countries that were supposed to have prohibited the traffic in arms, the Americans still managed to obtain them; moreover, France—and to a lesser degree Spain—secretly supported the Americans' procurement activities.[19] Lord Stormont, the British ambassador at Paris, thought it would be "natural" for the French to assist the Americans secretly.[20] The British government had good intelligence on the activities of American ships loading munitions in French ports, but could do no more than protest ineffectually.[21] Attempts by the Royal Navy to intercept American ships suspected of carrying munitions outside of French and Spanish ports brought forth violent protests from France and Spain.[22] Even if the British had managed to prevent American ships from leaving European ports with munitions, the problem would not have been solved. There was no way to prevent American agents from sending warlike stores in neutral bottoms to the French, Dutch, or Danish West Indies, where they could then be secretly transshipped to America.[23] The only truly effective way of stopping the flow of arms to the Americans would be to seize all munitions found on the high seas, regardless of the nationality of the ship carrying them. Therein lay the British dilemma: to stop the traffic, they would have to seize neutral ships and run the risk of a European war, while allowing that trade to continue would result in the American rebellion being fed by a flow of munitions from Europe. The British government, however, would not risk a European war in 1775–76 and adopted the ineffectual policy of diplomatic protest and seizure of only those neutral ships carrying arms in clear contravention of the laws and usages of war. As a result, the rebellion in America was sustained by clandestinely exported European munitions.[24]

Neither the best efforts of British diplomacy nor of the Royal Navy could prevent the Americans, aided by neutrals, from shipping munitions across the Atlantic. British warships in European waters had directions from the Admiralty not to seize French vessels *without particular orders,* for as the first lord of the Admiralty knew, "bringing in a French ship upon suspicions that appear not well grounded afterwards may draw us into a war, which our present circumstances ought by all means to be avoided."[25] But even at the risk of precipitating a European war, the British seized French and other neutral ships in European seas on suspicion of carrying munitions to the Americans, and Whitehall was flooded with diplomatic protests.[26] Yet seizing French ships, even if they were loaded with munitions bound for America, was a dangerous practice, for if carried out on a large enough scale to prevent sufficient arms from reaching America, war with France would be unavoidable.

At the end of 1775, when news arrived in London that the Americans were fitting out armed vessels, the government began to take the steps necessary to protect British shipping from attack.[27] An order in council was issued authorizing the arming of British merchant ships,[28] and orders were sent to America calling for the destruction of any American ships being built as armed vessels[29] and the institution of a limited system of convoys. Ships carrying military stores to the king's forces in America were placed under naval escort.[30] Warships were ordered off Ascension Island and St. Helena to intercept the homeward-bound East India trade and to escort these vessels to England.[31] Acting on a petition from the merchants of Poole, the government ordered that the Newfoundland trade be convoyed and that the squadron there be increased to eight warships to protect the fishermen from American attack.[32] Orders were sent to the West Indies directing that the homeward-bound trade in that area be escorted 80 to 120 leagues into the Atlantic to protect it from American cruisers.[33] For the most part, these limited and not very systematic trade protection measures were designed to allay the fears of merchants, but they were the beginning of an effort that would see the strength of the Royal Navy stretched almost to the breaking point before the war was two years old.[34]

The dire consequences of the government's decision not to build large numbers of small warships suitable for trade protection at the beginning of the fighting in America became apparent in the summer of 1776. This season saw the arrival of American cruisers in European seas. Perhaps the first American cruiser to appear in European seas was the privateer *Rover* of Salem. The British consul at Faro which reported on 31 August 1776 that she had captured four British merchant ships off Cape St. Vincent.[35] The *Rover* was quickly followed by a number of other American privateers and warships.[36] The United States had three objectives in sending cruisers to Europe: the capture and destruction of British shipping; the redeployment of units of the Royal Navy away from America by turning European seas into a major theater of maritime war; and most important, but rarely noted, precipitation of conflict between Britain and France by using French ports as sanctuaries from which to stage attacks on British ships on the high seas.[37]

The British soon realized that the French intended to give the American cruisers all possible aid while ostensibly remaining neutral.[38] Commanders of American cruisers found it was generally possible to dispose of prizes, obtain supplies, refit their vessels, and recruit seamen in French ports.[39] The British authorities viewed the opening of French ports to American cruisers as an act of French duplicity that posed a grave threat to British maritime trade and was probably a preliminary step to French intervention in the war. The arrival of American cruisers in European seas thrust a grim choice upon the British: if harsh and decisive measures were not taken, Britain's merchant marine would suffer greatly from American attack; but the only firm action the British could take was denying American cruisers the use of French ports. Accomplishing that would entail naval action likely to precipitate a war with France.

The British attempted to employ diplomatic pressure to deprive American cruisers of the use of French ports. Under the terms of the Treaty of Utrecht, France was not to permit the cruisers or prizes of Britain's enemies to enter her ports. Nor was France to allow her territory to be used to fit out cruisers. Although these articles had been specifically renewed in the Anglo-French Treaty of 1763, the French government's actions artfully violated them. According to the American commissioners in Paris, this policy was one of professing

> to England a resolution to observe all treaties, and prov[ing] it by restoring prizes too openly brought into their ports, imprisoning such persons as are found to be concerned in fitting out armed vessels against England from France, warning frequently those from America to depart, and repeating orders against the exportation of warlike stores. To us [the American commissioners] it privately professes a real friendship, wishes success to our cause, winks at the supplies we obtain here as it can give without giving open grounds of complaint to England, privately affords us very essential aids, and goes on preparing for war.[40]

The spectacular career of Capt. Gustavus Conyngham of the Continental Navy illustrates the obstacles and frustrations the British encountered in attempting to make the French abide by the definitions of neutrality stated in the Treaty of Utrecht. On 1 May 1777, Conyngham sailed from Dunkirk in a cruiser disguised as a smuggler. Outside French territorial waters, Conyngham hoisted American colors and on 2 May captured the Harwich-Helvoetsluis packet *Prince of Orange* and took the British brig *Dove* the following day. On 7 May, Conyngham and his two prizes returned to France. The next morning Lord Stormont, the British ambassador to France, successfully demanded that the two British vessels be restored and that Conyngham and his men be jailed and tried as pirates. In a speech to the House of Commons, Lord North dwelt at length on the apparently satisfactory conclusion of the "Conyngham affair," but several weeks later the British learned that American agents at Dunkirk were fitting out two cutters as cruisers and that Conyngham was to be released from prison. British spies swarmed over Dunkirk in search of the information necessary to force the French government to prevent the cutters' sailing. While the British repeatedly protested this breach of French neutrality, the Americans used various subterfuges to hide the ownership of the cutters and their purpose. On 17 July one of the vessels, the *Revenge* sailed from Dunkirk with a passport stating that her destination was Bergen, Norway. Once outside the French port, Conyngham took command of the vessel and for two months cruised in the North Sea, English Channel, and Irish Sea, capturing or destroying British merchant ships. Insurance rates for English ships shot up and British officials fumed at the French for permitting the *Revenge* to sail from Dunkirk. On learning that most of Conyngham's crew were not American but French, Stormont threatened to break relations with the French unless some action was taken by the Paris government. To placate the British, an American agent was thrown into the Bastille for a short time; the French official supposedly responsible for the escape of the *Revenge* was ordered to attend the court for "punishment"; and directions were issued for Conyngham's arrest should he appear again in a French port. In the meantime, Conyngham shifted the base of his operations to Spain and then to the West Indies, leaving in his wake a series of diplomatic incidents.[41] Conyngham was only one of many American commerce raiders operating from French ports, but he was perhaps the most daring and successful among them. He and other American captains did much to accelerate and ensure the deterioration of Anglo-French relations.

Having failed to close French ports to America by diplomatic means, the British were forced to use the Royal Navy to combat American cruisers in European seas. Lacking the necessary frigates and other small warships, great 64- and 74-gun ships of the line were dispatched to cruise in the Bay of Biscay, the western approaches of the English Channel, and the Irish Sea in search of American commerce raiders. From the autumn of 1776 onward, a succession of ships of the line from the Channel Fleet sailed between such points as Cape Clear, Ushant, and Cape Ortegal, while others were stationed off commonly frequented landfalls, such as Cape Finisterre, and others were dispatched far into the Atlantic to intercept and escort homeward-bound trade safely to

Britain.[42] Month in and month out, the Channel Fleet's ships of the line lumbered across the eastern Atlantic in a vain search for small American armed vessels. One of this effort's few successes occurred on 15 April 1777, when HMS *Terrible* chased and captured the privateer *Rising States* off Belle Isle.[43] For the most part, the ships suffered damage from the natural elements and their cruises were fruitless.[44]

The few small warships, such as sloops of war, frigates, and cutters, that were not serving overseas were deployed by the Admiralty in the seas around Britain to search for American commerce raiders. For example, in July of 1777, HMS *Arethusa* was ordered to cruise in St. George's Channel; HMS *Pelican* and HMS *Cameleon* were stationed off the Shetland Islands; and HMS *Drake,* HMS *Hound,* and HMS *Alderney* were cruising between England and the Dutch coast.[45] Several sloops of war and cutters ranged along the coasts of Britain;[46] others were stationed to protect such ports as Waterford, Dublin, Dartmouth, Penzance, Milford, Shilds, Hull, Liverpool, and Glasgow,[47] while still others searched the coasts of Portugal and Spain.[48] From time to time warships were dispatched off French ports such as Dunkirk[49] and Brest,[50] but from the beginning the situation was hopeless owing to the shortage of war vessels.[51]

The British instituted further measures to protect their shipping from attack in European seas. Restrictions on spending money to build new ships were removed and orders were issued for constructing additional frigates and sloops of war and for chartering armed vessels to be employed in commerce protection.[52] The Navy Board was directed to purchase and arm a number of former East Indiamen to serve as military storeships.[53] Other steps, such as carrying parties of army recruits on transports and storeships were taken to protect military stores.[54] At the request of various groups of merchants, the system of convoys was greatly enlarged. By the end of 1777, nearly every major branch of British seaborne trade was carried on under naval escort. Convoys were organized to protect the West African trade[55] and warships were sent to intercept merchant ships returning from Greenland and Hudson Bay and escort them to British ports.[56] Moreover, on 31 July the Admiralty began planning a comprehensive system of coastal convoys throughout British waters.[57] All military storeships, transports, and victualers were placed under naval escort,[58] as were East Indiamen in the North Atlantic.[59] Naval escort and convoys were also provided for the West Indian,[60] Newfoundland,[61] Canadian,[62] and Baltic trades,[63] and an elaborate system of convoys was instituted between British, Portuguese, and Spanish ports and the Mediterranean.[64] However, despite the dispatch of warships to hunt for American raiders and the institution of convoys, the Admiralty was flooded with complaints about shipping losses sustained at the hands of Yankee cruisers.[65]

Lacking small warships because of their failure to place the Royal Navy on a war footing promptly, the British could not contend with American cruisers in European seas during 1777. From Gibraltar to the North Sea, American raiders appeared to be running wild, capturing British merchant ships at will despite all the convoying and patrols undertaken by the Royal Navy. American cruisers based in French ports freely roamed the seas of Europe. In June of 1777, for example, three Continental Congress warships operating as a squadron captured fourteen British merchant ships in the Firth of Clyde.[66] There was a period during the summer of 1777, when according to Lord George Germain, "We lately had so many privateers upon our coasts and such encouragements given them by the French, that I was apprehensive a few weeks ago that we should have been obliged to have declared war."[67] Scores of British merchant ships were taken by American cruisers in European seas during 1777, while the Royal Navy managed to capture a mere handful of raiders.[68] During 1777 the British were forced to suffer the humiliation of seeing the Royal Navy, the strongest navy in the world and a force with a tradition of victory, unable to defeat a few rebel cruisers.

The dominant concern at the Admiralty during the summer and autumn of 1777 was not American cruisers or the shipment of munitions to America, but the strategic dangers of French entry into the conflict. London saw that the French were moving toward intervention in the war with the Americans. According to Stormont, French policy was "to furnish the Rebellion every assistance we will suffer and to continue in a word to wound us in the dark and stab with stilettoes, till they can venture to draw the sword."[69] The entry of France into the American war would pose huge strategic problems for the British because their navy was not prepared to fight the French—and possibly the Spanish as well. On 25 August 1777 the Royal Navy had some thirty-six ships of the line in varying states of readiness for sea. However, many of these ships were not ready for service because they were being repaired or fitted or lacked seamen. At the same time, it was calculated in London that the French had nineteen ships of the line in commission and that there were another twenty-one Spanish ships of the line in Europe.[70]

The delayed mobilization meant that the Royal Navy did not have the ships of the line ready for service to fight a major European naval war in 1777. In 1775 the Royal Navy had an authorized strength of 18,000 men and seventeen ships of the line in reserve serving as guard ships.[71] In response to the demands of the war in America, the authorized strength of the navy rose to 28,000 men in 1776, while the number of guard ships was increased to nineteen.[72] Vice Adm. Hon. Augustus Keppel, speaking for the opposition in a debate on the naval estimates, was near the truth when he said that the Royal Navy was "inadequate to a war and too large for a peace establishment."[73] The small number of ships of the line ready for service at the beginning of the American war was generally thought to result from peacetime constraints imposed by the cost-conscious North government. It is true that North had said, "Great peace establishments will, if we do not take care, prove our ruin; we shall fail, at the long run, by exhausting in times of tranquillity those resources upon which we are to depend in time of war."[74] But there is more myth than reality in the view that the Royal Navy's strength was seriously weakened by the North government's reduction of expenditures in the years before the American war. Instead, it has been calculated that "the record of peacetime naval upkeep between 1763 and 1775 was only slightly worse than the norm, if that."[75] The Royal Navy's unpreparedness for a major European naval war in 1777–78 arose not so much from underfunding as from a failure to promptly mobilize the navy's ships of the line in response to the French challenge. The North government, ignoring or rationalizing the potential French threat, did not mobilize the 64- and 74-gun ships of the line the Royal Navy required to fight a major European war during 1775–77 to avoid the expense of a general naval mobilization. The war in America was not that popular in Parliament. Huge expenditures and increased taxation could easily have destroyed what parliamentary support there was for the war. The strategy of crushing the rebellion by sending a large army to America was already very expensive. Lord North's government did not want to further increase expenditures in 1775–77 by undertaking what many in the cabinet considered an unnecessary mobilization of the Royal Navy's ships of the line.[76] The North government played down the French threat in order to avoid the expense of making the Royal Navy ready for a European war. For example, on 31 October 1776 North told the House of Commons that the extent of French armaments was "mightily magnified," that French naval preparations "import nothing directly hostile," and that the French government has a "pacific disposition towards us."[77] Clearly, the policy of the North government in 1775–77 was one of holding down expenses by not fully mobilizing British naval power while obfuscating the French threat in the Houses of Parliament.

The role of Lord Sandwich, the first lord of the Admiralty, is key to understanding the naval decision-making process within the British government during 1775–77, as well as later in the conflict. It has been Sandwich's fate to be castigated for presiding over a sea of corruption and neglect during his tenure as first lord of the Admiralty. For example, one historian has declared that Sandwich "probably did more damage to the navy entrusted to his care than any hostile French admiral ever had done."[78] However, the picture of Sandwich as first lord of the Admiralty is much more complex than his detractors would have it. Sandwich was a cultured, music-loving man, a member of the Royal Society, and a supporter of Cook's voyages of exploration. Horace Walpole, that acid-penned chronicler of the times, said of Sandwich: "No man in the Administration was so much a master of the business, so quick, or so shrewd."[79] On the other hand, it is true that Sandwich used Admiralty patronage for political purposes to the hilt, and perhaps beyond acceptable bounds.[80] At the same time, there is no doubt that the earl was a competent, if not great, first lord of the Admiralty. As head of the Admiralty, Sandwich attempted to reform the Royal Dockyards[81] and brought into the Admiralty and the navy's civil bureaucracy such forward-looking and competent administrators as captains Hugh Palliser and Charles Middleton. Perhaps Sandwich would have been a great first lord of the Admiralty under different circumstances.

Sandwich's influence over naval policy and strategy was limited by the very nature of the British government and the limitations of his personal political power. Besides his seat in the House of Lords, Sandwich boasted three additional sources of political strength within the North government: control of three parliamentary constituencies in Huntingtonshire,[82] a connection with

East India House, and the patronage at the command of the first lord of the Admiralty. While this was not an inconsiderable political base, it was a weak one. Lacking a fortune of his own, Sandwich had to remain first lord of the Admiralty in order to maintain his political power and his personal finances. Without the patronage of the Admiralty, Sandwich's political and personal financial position would collapse.[83] Lack of a firm political base independent of the Admiralty greatly weakened Sandwich's power and influence within the North government. His need to remain in office made him a weak first lord of the Admiralty in many respects, for he lacked an independent power base that would have enabled him to impose his views on naval policy and strategy on his colleagues in the cabinet.

All major governmental decisions, including those involving naval policy and strategy, were made jointly by the cabinet members.[84] As Sandwich described the process: "Every expedition, in regard to its destination, object, force and number of ships, planned by the cabinet, is the result of the Collective wisdom of all his Majesty's confidential ministers."[85] Mobilizing the Royal Navy would be a decision for the whole cabinet because it involved questions of diplomacy and a great expenditure of money. As Sandwich posed the question to the House of Lords: "Do my Lords imagine that the First Lord of the Admiralty equips fleets whenever his own fancy leads him to do so? . . . [I]t is the business of the King's administration at large to judge when it shall be advisable to put the nation to the expense of that equipment."[86]

In his capacity as first lord of the Admiralty, Sandwich did not play a major role in formulating strategy for the conduct of the war in America during 1775–77. The navy's role, while substantial, was a subsidiary one of supporting the British army.[87] Sandwich believed that in the long run, France, possibly aided by Spain, and not America was the greatest threat to Britain's security, and that the Royal Navy must prepare for a conflict with these powers by mobilizing a powerful force of ships of the line capable of confronting the enemy's main battle fleet as soon as possible. During 1775–77 there was a running debate within the cabinet over whether to mobilize the Royal Navy, with Sandwich advocating immediate mobilization because of the threat posed by France. This set Sandwich at odds with other members of the cabinet. North opposed a mobilization for reasons of economy and parliamentary politics, while others apparently took the statements of peace, friendship, and neutrality of the French government at face value. As long as the British effort in America appeared to be successful[88] and there was no open French threat to British security, a majority of the cabinet would not agree to a naval mobilization.[89] There is the possibility that if the Royal Navy had been mobilized in 1775, the French might have been deterred from intervening in the war. France and Spain had backed down before when confronted by displays of British naval power.[90]

However, without hard evidence that France was undertaking naval preparations that threatened British security, the cabinet was not willing to undertake a naval mobilization. The French began to prepare for war during the spring of 1776. By the end of May, the British government knew of these preparations from spies and other intelligence sources.[91] In response to such reports, the cabinet met on 20 June and decided to increase the number of guard ships to twenty-four, to enlarge the number of seamen and marines in the Royal Navy, and to prepare, in secret, the required measures to impress additional seamen "suddenly & effectually." At the same time, the cabinet believed that no further actions should be undertaken until receipt of additional intelligence of French naval preparations.[92] Sandwich was not satisfied with these minimal measures and warned North that unless further preparations were authorized, there was a good chance that the French (perhaps joined by the Spanish) could put to sea a fleet superior to the Royal Navy because they could man their ships quickly. Even bearing in mind the diplomatic consequences and the expense of a mobilization, Sandwich believed that the Royal Navy must be prepared to meet not only the French but also the Spanish navy.[93]

In the course of the summer and early autumn of 1776, the government in London continued to receive intelligence of French naval preparations. This so alarmed Sandwich that he wanted a general mobilization. The first lord of the Admiralty insisted that there should be a general press; that the guard ships should be manned to "their war establishment"; that twelve ships of the line should be put into commission while more were made ready to receive men; and that work on ships in the Royal Dockyards should be speeded up.[94] On 28 October, in response to the arrival of American cruisers in European seas and the French naval buildup, the Admiralty ordered a general press. In the next several days orders were issued for thirty-four ships of the line[95] to be fitted, stored, and manned for Channel service.[96] By 1 December 1776 the strength of the Royal Navy stood at 45,591 men.[97] This was a major step toward full mobilization, but Sandwich wanted still more ships, for he thought that "the conduct of France and Spain is so mysterious that it is impossible to say what demands we may have for line of battle ships in the course of the winter."[98] Though the final decision was not made in Paris until July 1777,[99] a number of British officials, including Sandwich, realized that France was moving toward intervention in the American conflict. By the summer of 1777 Britain and France were on the brink of war.[100] During March of 1777 reports of French naval armaments were so alarming that even North concluded that Britain had no choice but "to keep pace" with the French by matching them ship for ship and in August saw no alternative than to prepare for war with France.[101] On 17 September, Stormont wrote from Paris that the French government had secretly informed the Americans that it had decided to intervene in the war.[102]

As Britain slipped toward war with France in the summer of 1777, Sandwich calculated that there were thirty-six ships of the line in commission and fit for sea, of which only thirty would be ready for immediate service because of a shortage of seamen. At the same time, he believed that the French had more than thirty ships of the line based in Atlantic ports with an additional thirteen at Toulon, while the Spanish had at least eleven ships of the line in Europe. Sandwich urged it as "a maxim that England ought for her own security to have superior force in readiness at home to anything that France and Spain united in readiness on their side." Considering the known strength of Britain's potential enemies and the number of British ships of the line available for service, he realized that it would be impossible to protect Britain from attack and possible invasion while simultaneously deploying the naval strength required to protect British positions in North America and the West Indies.[103] This is the strategic dilemma that confronted the British throughout the American war.

The great gambles of 1775 had been lost. To save money at the beginning of the fighting in America, the North government did not place orders in private shipyards for the construction of small warships such as frigates and sloops of war. Wagering that the Americans could not fight at sea, they saw European seas overrun with American cruisers. In a still greater gamble, the North government bet that France would not intervene in the American war and economized again by delaying mobilization of the Channel Fleet's ships of the line. Thus, Britain was left with inadequate naval forces to confront France in 1778 and France and Spain in 1779. Not until the end of the American war did a huge building program involving the expenditure of great amounts of money give the Royal Navy numerical equality with the navies of America's two Bourbon allies.[104]

Chapter 2

KEPPEL AND THE
CHANNEL FLEET, 1778

On 6 December 1777 Paris learned of Burgoyne's defeat at Saratoga. A British army had been trapped, defeated, and forced to surrender to the American rebels. This was a catastrophe for the British and a heaven-sent opportunity for the French. Defeat at Saratoga shattered Britain's hopes for a quick victory over the rebels in America and showed the world that the island kingdom could not win the war in America soon, if ever. To the French, the defeat at Saratoga appeared to be a providential chance to use Britain's misfortunes in America to avenge the defeats of the Seven Years' War by humbling the British and readjusting the European balance of power in France's favor. The British ambassador in Paris, Lord Stormont, quickly learned that the French government was changing its policy from one of ostensible neutrality in the Anglo-American conflict to one of open war with Britain.[1] On 7 January 1778, Stormont informed London that he had intelligence, which proved to be premature, that the French had signed a treaty with the America rebels.[2] This was followed by a stream of other reports from Stormont telling of warlike preparations in France and the negotiation of a Franco-American alliance.[3] Finally, on 6 February, the French and the Americans signed treaties of commerce and alliance, making war between Britain and France inevitable.[4]

George III did not welcome a war with France, but he was "prepared" for it. The king believed he had tried to avoid the conflict, but "France chooses to be the Aggressor," and Britain had taken "all the steps necessary if it should end in war."[5] His Majesty was perhaps "prepared" for armed conflict with the French by remembering British victories over that Bourbon power in the Seven Years' War. During that conflict, French forces had been pinned down in Germany fighting Continental powers while Britain destroyed the French navy and won victory after victory in North America, the West Indies, and India. However, Britain's strategic position at the beginning of 1778 was far different from the one she enjoyed in 1756. Gone was the alliance with Prussia: in 1778 Britain was diplomatically isolated and without European allies. In the first months of that year, Britain attempted, without success, to find a Continental ally to engage the power of France.[6] This failure produced the central strategic fact of the Anglo-French war of 1778: there would be no competing European campaigns to absorb France's strength. Isolation in Europe did not matter in peacetime, but Britain would be at a serious advantage without European allies in war against both the Americans and the French. Unlike previous wars against the French, this one would offer Britain few, if any, strategic options like choosing to fight a Continental war as opposed to one in the Western Hemisphere.[7] The Royal Navy appeared to be unequal to the task of simultaneously defending both the British Isles and Britain's overseas commitments from expected French attack. What was needed was a new strategy to enable Britain to meet the French naval threat.

The recasting of British strategy began on 8 December 1777, when the first lord of the Admiralty, Lord Sandwich, sent a long memorandum to Lord North, first lord of the treasury, stating that the whole conduct of the war must be changed. Sandwich believed that the war in America should be waged mainly by naval forces, with the army's role reduced to defending bases from which the Royal Navy, freed from supporting offensive military operations, would mount a blockade of America while simultaneously conducting raids on American coastal cities to destroy their usefulness as bases for cruisers. Sandwich wanted a defensive war in America because he believed the real danger to Britain at the time was not in America but in Europe. He thought war with France and possible war with Spain posed an "imminent danger," for he believed these two powers had naval forces in Europe equal, and perhaps superior to, the strength of the Royal Navy. Britain would be vulnerable to naval attack not only in the English Channel but also in America, the East and West Indies, and the Mediterranean. Therefore, he argued that fitting out, storing, and manning the ships of the line then in ordinary should be greatly accelerated because as soon as France determines to make war a squadron will be sent to attack us in one of these parts. We shall not know where the storm will fall, therefore the only effective measure of safety will be to have a respectable force in every part, or at least to have a sufficient force in readiness at home to make large and immediate detachments to all our distant possessions. Will our 42 ships supply the necessary detachments to answer this purpose, and to leave us superior at home to anything the House of Bourbon can bring against us in Europe after their detachment is made? Certainly no. Therefore, unless we are sure that France has no hostile intentions, is it prudent for use to remain a moment longer in our present state?[8]

Ten days later at a 1 December cabinet meeting, Adm. Sir Hugh Palliser and Captain Lord Mulgrave, two lords of the Admiralty, repeated Sandwich's assertion that the strength of the Royal Navy would not permit the detachment of a major force from the Channel Fleet for overseas duty.[9] Even though it would take some time for everyone to understand the problem, Sandwich, Palliser, and Mulgrave were pointing out a basic fact that determined British naval policy for the rest of the American war. Britain could survive the loss of America, her West Indian islands, and even her territories in India, but Britain could not survive if the Channel Fleet was overpowered by a superior enemy naval force and the British Isles laid open to invasion. Sandwich was not going to risk the security of the British Isles by hastily making large detachments from the Channel Fleet to reinforce overseas positions. This policy was much more in line with traditional British naval thinking than a number of historians would have us believe. The problem during the American war was not the concept of Sandwich's strategic thinking, but rather the great difficulties in executing it.

The overriding strategic problem confronting Britain at the beginning of 1778 was that her military and naval power was tied up in America while she was on the verge of a European naval war. From the beginning of the fighting in America, Sandwich maintained that the great strategic danger to Britain was posed by the possibility of intervention by the Bourbon powers and that the Royal Navy must maintain a two-power standard to meet this threat. After Saratoga, as London received intelligence of naval preparations in France and Spain and of impending French recognition of the American rebels, Sandwich urged North to mobilize the Royal Navy for war and to ensure that every possible ship be fitted, manned, and commissioned.[10] On 9 February 1778, secret intelligence of the Franco-American alliance reached London, and on 13 March the French ambassador to the Court of St. James's formally notified the British government of the French action.[11] War was now certain, for both London and Paris recognized that the French alliance with the Americans amounted to a declaration of hostilities on Britain. However, fighting did not break out for several months because neither Britain nor France wanted to fire the first shot. France was playing for time to avoid being perceived as the aggressor while Britain did not want to rush into war lest this impede her search for an ally or alienate Spain.[12]

In the days after the declaration of the Franco-American alliance, the entire strategic conduct of the war changed. The earl of Carlisle was named to head a peace commission empowered to concede everything to the Americans except independence—the one thing that would get them to stop fighting.[13] On 14 March the cabinet decided to recall the British ambassador at Paris, mobilize the Royal Navy, prepare a squadron to be sent to the Mediterranean, reinforce British forces in the West Indies, and call out ten thousand militia.[14] Two days later the Admiralty ordered a general press and directed the Navy Board to use all possible speed, including overtime work and the employment of extra men in the dockyards, to fit out ships for service.[15] On 18 March Adm. Hon. Augustus Keppel was ordered to take command of the Channel Fleet.[16] That same day the cabinet met to consider strategy and decided to order the return to Britain of twenty frigates and sloops from North America. No further troops were to be sent to North America from Britain, and Philadelphia was to be evacuated. Five thousand troops, four ships of the line, three 50-gun ships, two bomb vessels, and four frigates were to be sent from America to attack the French island of St. Lucia in the West Indies. Nova Scotia and St. Augustine were also to be reinforced from America, and the commander in chief of the army in America was given discretionary power to evacuate New York and Rhode Island if necessary.[17] Within the next few days the directives required to bring these decisions into effect were issued.[18]

The main British effort was now to maintain naval control of the English Channel and to seize St. Lucia. The decisions that emerged from the cabinet deliberations in March 1778 were at best a compromise designed to meet divergent strategic demands generated by the need to simultaneously achieve three substantial goals with inadequate forces: holding the English Channel, maintaining British positions in America, and taking the offensive in the West Indies. The stark reality of the strategic problem posed by French entry into the American war was that in 1778 maintenance of Britain's commitments abroad were beyond the strength of the Royal Navy. These commitments included Gibraltar and Britain's traditional presence in the Mediterranean and protection of British colonies in the West Indies, India, and the North American continent. It was either politically or strategically impossible to reduce the scope of any of these commitments. Contemporary British observers ignored the possibility that maintaining control of European waters could have prevented Britain's enemies from sailing to India or the Americas, thus easing pressure on British posts there. Spain's entry into the war complicated issues further, and the North ministry remained a prisoner of the policy of trying to maintain worldwide commitments with an inadequate naval force.

In the cold reality of hindsight, it is clear that Britain's best course in 1778 would have been to write off America and withdraw from that troublesome spot as soon as it became apparent the French would intervene. After the debacle of the 1777 campaign, it was clear the conquest of America, if not actually beyond Britain's resources, was a much more difficult undertaking than it appeared in 1775. The beginning of a European naval war in 1778 made the successful military conquest of America a near impossibility. The dispatch of the Carlisle peace commission ordering the evacuation of Philadelphia and the general defensive nature of operations in the northern colonies show that the British realized they would never achieve victory by military conquest in America, at least in the colonies north of the Mason-Dixon line. At the same time, however, the British absolutely refused to grant American independence, the only sure way of ending the war in America. While there was a general recognition of the near impossibility of victory in America, there was also a marked reluctance to cut British commitments in the Western Hemisphere by withdrawing from that theater. The major reason was not the inability to see the strategic risks: On 13 April Sandwich wrote, "We are upon the point of war with France, and perhaps Spain; an American war added thereto is, I fear, more than we are equal to."[19] Instead, the government's inability to withdraw came from political and moral factors that prevented North's often weak government from admitting the failure of its American policy. It would take four more years of fighting and the loss of another army in America to force the British to concede failure and to grant the one point they failed to concede in 1778: American independence. Thus, as British commitments were always larger than the naval force available to fulfill those obligations, British naval strategy was passive, consisting mainly of response to enemy initiatives.

On 24 March, Adm. Hon. Augustus Keppel arrived at Spithead to take command of the twenty ships of the line of the Channel Fleet.[20] Fate and circumstance sometimes conspire to place the wrong man in the wrong position at the wrong time, and one such man was Augustus Keppel in 1778. Said to have been Anson's favorite midshipman during that commander's famous voyage around the world, Keppel openly proclaimed himself to have been "bred" in Anson's school of seamanship.[21] During the Seven Years' War, Keppel commanded a ship at Quiberon Bay, led expeditions to Goree and Belle Isle, and served as second in command to Pocock at Havana in 1762. However, in the ensuing years of peace, Keppel became more a political admiral than a fighting one. At the beginning of the American war, Keppel was a member of the House of Commons, part of the Rockingham faction, and an outspoken critic of the government's American policy. He boasted that "he was ready to do his duty, but *not in the line of America.*"[22] Though deeply involved in opposition politics, Keppel was still very interested in rank, position, and advancement in the Royal Navy. In the spring of 1775 he became enraged when Sandwich refused to honor a request by Adm. Sir Charles Saunders that he be appointed to a position in the Channel Fleet.[23] Like most eighteenth-century officers, Keppel saw failure to obtain a desired promotion or position as at best a slight of his honor. Far worse for a man like Keppel was the spectacle of seeing a person he perceived to be of lesser merit and rank promoted over himself.

On 7 December 1775, Adm. Sir Charles Saunders died. Adm. Sir Hugh Palliser was one of the trustees of his estate and Keppel was bequeathed five thousand pounds and an annuity of twelve hundred pounds.[24] Saunders's death vacated one of the lieutenant generalships of the marines, a sinecure worth fifteen hundred pounds a year. Lord North had promised this post to Adm. Lord Howe, while Keppel, for his part, thought it was his by right.

Sandwich, however, gave the lieutenant generalship to Adm. Sir Hugh Palliser, his right-hand man at the Admiralty and an officer junior in rank to both Howe and Keppel. The two senior officers were enraged at this perceived slight, and Howe, who was closely connected to the royal family, threatened to go to the king and resign his commission in the navy. Howe was pacified by a series of complex negotiations and maneuvers that led to his promotion two ranks from rear admiral of the white to vice admiral of the blue and commander in chief in America.[25] This doubly enraged Keppel, for not only had Palliser, a junior admiral, been given the lieutenant generalship of the marines, but Howe, also his junior, had been promoted two ranks while Keppel was advanced only one rank to vice admiral of the red.[26] In a swirl of correspondence, Keppel protested what he saw as a personal slight on his honor and professional merit. Keppel was especially bitter over Palliser's lieutenant generalship of the marines, and one outburst to Sandwich ended with the menacing phase "what will follow time will discover."[27] Ignoring the politics and disagreements with Sandwich, the government appointed Keppel commander of the Channel Fleet in the event of a European war in November 1776.[28]

Despite his opposition to the government's American policy and his quarrels with the first lord of the Admiralty over promotions, Keppel's appointment was probably all but inevitable. At the beginning of every war a major problem is finding officers fit to take charge of major commands such as the Channel Fleet. In an age before large-scale peacetime maneuvers were common, the government had two pools of candidates: old senior officers from the previous war or young energetic officers without command experience. In 1778 the victorious admirals of the Seven Years' War—Boscawen, Saunders, Pocock, and Hawke—were either dead or retired. This left Howe and Keppel, both of whom had commanded squadrons during the Seven Years' War and had the rank and seniority to command the Channel Fleet. When Howe was given command in America, Keppel was the only remaining officer with the necessary rank and qualifications, and his appointment would be popular with the officers of the Royal Navy.

But if Keppel's appointment to command the Channel Fleet was probably unavoidable, it was not necessarily prudent. Keppel simply did not have the personality for high command in wartime. The picture that emerges from the admiral's letters is one of a sometimes weak man often unwilling to assume the risks and responsibilities of a command of this kind. Further, Keppel was in poor health, described by one observer as plagued by "bad nerves and worse constitution."[29] Keppel was a specialist in amphibious warfare who had never commanded a squadron in a battle, and he had not been to sea nor held an active command since the Seven Years' War.

Keppel's partisan political allegiances made him an even worse choice. In fact, Keppel's cousin, the duke of Richmond, warned the admiral to "suspect" and "not to trust" Sandwich if he became commander of the Channel Fleet because he was certain Sandwich would make Keppel a scapegoat, blaming Keppel if anything went wrong.[30] Conversely, it was possible that Keppel's membership in the political opposition would tempt him to use his position as commander of the Channel Fleet to discredit Sandwich and the government and to push himself forward politically.

Still, despite his disputes with Sandwich over America and promotions, Keppel fully agreed with the first lord of the Admiralty on the strategy to be followed by the Channel Fleet. After arriving at Spithead, Keppel outlined his thoughts on the strategic conduct of the war in a series of letters and conversations with Sandwich and others. Keppel's strategic thinking at this time was remarkably similar to Sandwich's, for the admiral believed that "England and Ireland must be the first object" and that no detachments should be made from the Channel Fleet to chase French ships proceeding overseas until that British force had obtained a strength equal to the enemy's. Even then, the British should send ships to reinforce the object of the enemy's attack only if there was certain intelligence of the destination of the French force. Keppel's thinking was dominated by two fears: the French might draw him out of the Channel by some trick or his force would be so weakened by detachments to defend overseas positions that the French could enter the English Channel and overpower the Royal Navy by sheer weight of numbers.[31]

At a cabinet meeting held on 6 April, Sandwich maintained a strategic position similar to Keppel's when he successfully urged the rejection of a proposal to send a large reinforcement to operate against the French squadron based at Toulon. Proponents of the plan argued that reinforcing the three British warships in the Mediterranean would make it possible either to blockade that squadron in port or to intercept this force before it passed the Strait of Gibraltar.[32] This would prevent the French ships at Toulon from proceeding without warning to India, the West Indies, or America. It would also prevent this squadron from entering Brest or one of Spain's Atlantic ports such as Cadiz, thereby concentrating French and Spanish naval power in the eastern Atlantic. A strong British squadron in the Mediterranean would force the Spanish and French to divide naval forces between the Mediterranean and the Atlantic while preventing the ships at Toulon from making surprise attacks on British positions overseas.

There was strategic merit in maintaining a strong British squadron in the Mediterranean, provided the ships were available to carry it out. Intelligence reports showed that the French had at least twenty-one ships of the line at Brest and twelve at Toulon, while there were an additional thirty-two Spanish ships of the line in Europe, making a total of sixty enemy capital units in European waters against forty-two British ships of the line.[33] On the basis of this information, Sandwich argued successfully to a cabinet meeting of 6 April that there were simply not enough ships available to send a strong squadron into the Mediterranean. Except for Gibraltar, the British position in the Mediterranean had to be abandoned, for Sandwich believed that reinforcing the Mediterranean would risk either naval control of the English Channel or the security of British overseas positions. The Mediterranean could be held only at the cost of withdrawing ships of the line from such services as the Newfoundland squadron or abandoning plans to reinforce places such as India, the West Indies, and North America.[34]

A number of people believed that the failure to send a strong squadron to the Mediterranean at the beginning of April 1778 was one of the great strategic mistakes of the war. On 27 April, Lord George Germain, the secretary of state, whose main responsibility was the conduct of the war in America, stated:

> I never can sufficiently lament the not having sent a fleet to Gibraltar to prevent the Toulon squadron passing the Straits, the risk of that measure was trifling in comparison to what we may suffer by leaving such a fleet at liberty to attack us in North America, the West Indies or Newfoundland.[35]

Whether or not the risks involved in detaching a strong force to the Mediterranean in the first weeks of April 1778 were "trifling" depends largely on whether one views these risks from the perspective of the secretary of state for America or from that of the first lord of the Admiralty. Sandwich's strategic thinking was in many respects similar to that which led to the evacuation of the Mediterranean in 1796. That is, until more ships of the line were available, Britain just did not have the necessary force to maintain a strong Mediterranean presence while simultaneously protecting Britain from possible attack by capital units known to be based in French and Spanish Atlantic ports. To Sandwich, the situation was simple: either risk the security of Britain or temporarily write off the Mediterranean and run the strategic risks that decision would entail. Unlike Germain, whose eyes were always fixed on America, there was not even a choice for Sandwich. Britain could survive any damage wrought by the escape of the French Toulon squadron, but the kingdom might not survive an overpowering enemy action in the English Channel that would open the kingdom to invasion by a French army.[36]

On 13 April, Adm. Comte d'Estaing sailed from Toulon with twelve ships of the line and five frigates. For days London had been alive with rumors about the movements of French naval forces, and on 20 April the Admiralty sent the frigate HMS *Proserpine* to the Strait of Gibraltar with orders to shadow any French squadron leaving the Mediterranean and bring back reports of its destination to England as quickly as possible. Two days later, HMS *Bienfaisant* was ordered to look into Brest to gain information about the French squadron in that port.[37] But before these ships returned, the British government was confronted with a major naval crisis in the form of news that d'Estaing's squadron had sailed from Toulon.

On 23 April, North received unconfirmed reports that d'Estaing had put to sea, information that also suggested his destination was America.[38] Four days later, Germain received "very particular" intelligence from The Hague concerning the lading and equipment of the Toulon squadron that convinced Germain "that the destination of the Fleet must be North America." Germain favored immediate detachment of ships from the Channel Fleet across the Atlantic to reinforce Lord Howe's squadron to "prevent the fatal consequences which may follow from the French having an avowed superiority at sea upon the Coast of North America."[39]

Sandwich basically agreed with Germain's interpretation of the intelligence and was of the opinion that "There is every reason in the world to believe that he is bound to Boston, probably with the intention to attack Nova Scotia and Canada, or perhaps to fall upon Lord Howe's fleet and to cut off our army upon the American Continent." But the first lord of the Admiralty did not agree with Germain that a detachment of ships of the line should be sent to America at once, for "We cannot for certain say where he is going, and therefore our dilemma is very great, particularly as we are not able to make any detachments from home consistent with the security of this island."[40] For more than a month the controversy generated by this "dilemma" tore the government, with Germain demanding the instant dispatch of reinforcements to America and Sandwich, supported by other lords of the Admiralty, doggedly refusing to weaken the defense of Britain until d'Estaing's destination was confirmed.

It was decided that the cabinet should meet on 29 April to formulate Britain's response to d'Estaing's expedition from Toulon.[41] Germain drew up a memorandum for submission to the cabinet calling in the strongest terms for the immediate dispatch of twelve ships of the line to Halifax, Nova Scotia. The thrust of Germain's argument was that

> [t]he fate of this county evidently depends upon the preventing the Toulon squadron from acting with success against our fleet and army and position in North America; and there is every reason to believe it can have no other destination. . . . I must therefore humbly submit my opinion to His Majesty . . . that at least twelve ships should . . . pursue and attack them in whatever station they may have taken, and even to follow them to West Indies. . . . The remainder of the Fleet under Admiral Keppel, with the reinforcements preparing to join him, it is presumed will be sufficient for the protection of this country; but in all military operations of importance some risque must be run, and it is more meritorious to suffer in vigorous and necessary exertion of our force, than to remain inactive and tamely submit to the loss of detached fleets, armies and distant possessions, which must infallibly draw after it the absolute ruin of Great Britain.[42]

At a cabinet meeting the next day, the strength and passion of Germain's arguments prevailed and the cabinet ordered thirteen ships of the line to Halifax "without loss of time." That very day orders were issued to the Admiralty for the immediate dispatch of this force to North America.[43] Germain, however, would find that while it was possible to issue an order to the Admiralty, it was impossible to have that order brought into effect in the face of the united opposition of the lords of the Admiralty and the commander of the Channel Fleet. In fact, there was a series of short delays in the dispatch of the ships to Halifax. Sandwich used this breathing space to gather forces and marshal arguments for reversing the cabinet's decisions of 29 April.

On the morning of 30 April, Sandwich informed North that the quickest way to reinforce America was to dispatch ships from Portsmouth under the command of Rear Adm. Hyde Parker. This squadron was to proceed to Plymouth, where it would be joined by Vice Adm. Hon. John Byron in HMS *Albion*. Byron would take command of the force and sail for America. However, Sandwich asked North for alternative directions if adverse weather prevented Byron from leaving Plymouth. In that case, should Parker proceed to America without the vice admiral or wait off Plymouth for Byron to join him? This question was of some importance because Howe was thought to be returning to England, leaving Rear Adm. James Gambier in command in America. Gambier was senior to Parker, and if both Howe and Byron were absent, Gambier would command the reinforcement when it arrived in America. Gambier was well connected politically but was considered by all to be incompetent, having been dumped at New York to get him out of the commissionership of Portsmouth Dockyard.[44] Thus, North was faced with the dilemma of either delaying the departure of naval reinforcements or risking Gambier's command of those men and ships when they reached America. Unable or unwilling to settle this matter, North wrote to the king for his opinion, and it was decided that Byron should command the reinforcement no matter the resulting delays.[45] What was unmentioned, or perhaps not realized during the exchange of letters, was that Byron was still in London and that his flagship HMS *Albion* was stored and fitted for the East Indian service, with her lower gun deck loaded with provisions that would have to be removed before she would be fit to take part in an engagement.[46]

In the matter of sending the thirteen-ship reinforcement to America, the Admiralty acted with a slowness that must have maddened Germain. Sandwich informed Keppel of the order on 29 April, the day on which the cabinet decided to send the ships to America, but it was not until the morning of 1 May that Byron was directed to attend the Admiralty to be briefed and to receive his orders.[47] The vice admiral lingered in London until the morning of 5 May before setting out for his command at Plymouth.[48] On 2 May, Sandwich informed Germain that a packet ought to be sent to America to inform Howe of d'Estaing's sailing and the impending dispatch of reinforcements.[49] On 3 May the Admiralty issued the official orders directing Parker to sail with eleven ships of the line from Portsmouth to Plymouth, thence to join Byron with two more ships of the line and then sail immediately for America.[50] Thus, five days passed after the cabinet decision to send reinforcements to America before the Admiralty drew up the necessary orders, and two more days elapsed before the squadron's commander left London to take up his command. Whether or not such delays were intentional on the part of the Admiralty bureaucracy is unknown, but one cannot help speculating about the time Byron would need to leave Plymouth with thirteen ships of the line, when the admiral took seven days to get out of London without any ships.

On 2 May the king and a number of dignitaries arrived at Portsmouth Dockyard to inspect the fleet and its fitting out. For the next several days Portsmouth Dockyard and the surrounding waters witnessed all the pomp and pageantry of a royal review of the fleet. His Majesty took an active interest in every detail, investigating the smith's shop, the sheathing of HMS *Centaur*, and the rope works.[51] The king at this time appears to have been thoroughly indoctrinated in the mysteries of naval affairs. In answer to a letter from North telling him of repeated and violent attacks made on the government for failing to send a squadron promptly in pursuit of d'Estaing, His Majesty explained to the first lord of the treasury that the delay in Parker's sailing arose not from neglect but from the need to restore the ships for foreign service, and that

> it is very absurd in Gentlemen unacquainted with the immense detail of Naval Affairs, to trouble the House of Commons with matters totally foreign to truth; if I was now writing from my own ideas only, I should be absurd as them; but Keppel, Palliser, Parker, and Hood are men whose knowledge in that science may be trusted.[52]

But it appears that the naval authorities had told the king less than the whole truth, for on 5 May, Parker received permission from the Admiralty to sail "without additional stores allowed by the establishment (except cordage and sails)."[53]

The king also frequently dined with and probably discussed strategy with such naval officers and officials as Sandwich, Keppel, and various subordinate officers of the Channel Fleet.[54] During his stay at Portsmouth there can be no doubt that Sandwich and Keppel shared with the king their opinions of detaching thirteen ships of the line to chase d'Estaing without knowing the French admiral's destination with any certainty. However, at this time the king did not withdraw his consent to sending the reinforcements to America, but rather made every effort to hasten the departure of Parker's squadron from Spithead.[55]

On 2 May, Sandwich wrote from Portsmouth to Germain in an attempt to prevent Byron's sailing for America until d'Estaing's destination was confirmed, pointing out the dangers to Britain if the French squadron put into a Spanish port.[56] Several days later, the Admiralty read reports from Gibraltar dated 10 April stating that the Spanish had twenty ships of the line fitted and manned at Cadiz and that d'Estaing was expected to join this force.[57] On 7 May, Sandwich wrote to North to urge delay of Byron's departure until d'Estaing's objective was known,

> for a detachment on 13 line of battle ships to America, if the whole fleet of France and Spain remains in Europe, will leave us absolutely at the mercy of the House of Bourbon, whose united force at home, in commission and fit for sea amounts to upwards of 70 sail.[58]

North showed Sandwich's letter to Lords Weymouth, George Germain, Gower, and Dartmouth, all of whom agreed that Sandwich's information did not change things and that Byron should sail at once for America unless word arrived that d'Estaing was destined elsewhere. Informing Sandwich of this on 8 May, North expressed the hope that HMS *Proserpine*'s return might have already resolved any doubts about d'Estaing's destination. He went on to say that he did not think Spain would declare war on Britain at this time, and, even if she did, a Franco-Spanish invasion of Britain was an "enterprise so arduous that they will not for some time be able to carry such a project into execution. The dangers to the army and fleet in North America appear to me more probable and immediate."[59] Thus, North made clear to Sandwich that the cabinet would not change its orders to send the reinforcement to America without delay.

On 9 May the king left Portsmouth and the ships of Parker's command dropped down to St. Helens to await a fair wind before proceeding to Plymouth to join Byron.[60] That day, Keppel wrote a long and pessimistic letter to Sandwich expressing his fears about the weak state of Britain's defenses due to the impending sailing of reinforcements for America. According to Keppel, detaching eleven "of the finest ships" of the Channel Fleet across the Atlantic greatly weakened his force by reducing it far below the intended strength of twenty-one ships of the line fitted and ready for sea. Because of the Channel Fleet's weakness, Keppel greatly feared that the French ships at Brest would either attack and overwhelm Byron's force at Plymouth while staging a coup de main against that dockyard or wait until the reinforcement departed for America and then seize control of the Channel with such numerically overpowering force that Keppel's squadron would be unable to offer any effective resistance.[61] Here Keppel expressed a legitimate fear about the Channel Fleet's weakness coupled with considerable grandiose panic about the intentions and capabilities of the French.

The Channel Fleet was vulnerable because a lack of seamen had slowed making their ships ready for sea. Recruiting landsmen and officers for the Royal Navy was not a problem: it was the procurement of trained seamen that slowed the whole process. In peacetime, most experienced seamen were in the merchant marine, and it was from these crews that the Royal Navy obtained the trained personnel required to man the king's ships at the beginning of a war. Seamen for the ships of the Channel Fleet could only be obtained as fast as they could be pressed from merchant ships entering British ports.[62] On 14 May it was reported to Sandwich that "Keppel's line of battle is composed of 21 fine ships, if they were all manned; but I fear the America, Robust, Cumberland, Elizabeth, Berwick and Victory want many and the Terrible sickly."[63] In order to obtain additional seamen for the Channel Fleet the Admiralty ordered a press from all protections on 23 May. Six days later the government placed a general embargo on the sailing of merchant ships from British ports, a measure requested by the Admiralty to procure additional seamen from the merchant marine.[64] This inability to man the ships of the Channel Fleet quickly made Palliser share Keppel's doubts about the wisdom of detaching Byron's force to America. On 12 May the junior lord of the Admiralty wrote to Sandwich:

Admiral Parker remains at St. Helen's with the wind
fresh at W.S.W. I confess I shall not be sorry to see him
remain there until you are certain whether Monsieur
d'Estaing proceeds to America or Brest, and what use
the Spaniards mean to make of the very formidable fleet
they have ready. No doubt France has already been early
informed of the squadron we have ordered for America;
may they not thereupon order d'Estaing from Cadiz to
Brest although he was originally intended for America?[65]

On 13 May, Sandwich finally succeeded in reversing the decision to dispatch Byron's squadron to America before learning
d'Estaing's destination. The first lord of the Admiralty outflanked
his opponents by appealing directly to the king to countermand
the cabinet's decision of 29 April. It is not known what arguments
Sandwich employed to persuade George III to stop Byron's immediate sailing, but he probably cited Keppel's and Palliser's opinions and reminded the king that HMS *Proserpine* was expected
daily with certain intelligence. The most decisive element for the
king, however, was probably the fact that the first lord of the
Admiralty, the senior professional lord of the Admiralty, and the
commander of the Channel Fleet all opposed the cabinet's strategy. During his visit to Portsmouth Dockyard, George III had come
to the conclusion that naval affairs were too complex to be understood by nonprofessionals. A first lord of the Admiralty with long
experience and two of the most senior professionals, Keppel and
Palliser, had spoken, and the king had little choice but to go along
with their proposed course of action. The result was that the king
acted on the suggestion of Capt. Sir Samuel Hood, commissioner
of the Portsmouth Dockyard, that Byron's objective be changed
from Halifax to New York. The squadron was also ordered to
return from America at the beginning of winter, and an express
directive went to Plymouth ordering Byron not to sail until further notice. The next day the cabinet met at the king's command
and formally approved of His Majesty's decision.[66]

For the next nineteen days rumors about d'Estaing's destination were rife. At one point, Keppel exclaimed that "Exact intelligence at this moment would be worth a treasure."[67] On 17 May,
Keppel received information that d'Estaing was heading toward
America, then a rumor reached the admiral that the French squadron had turned back to Toulon. On 31 May a report arrived at St.
Helens stating that the Toulon and Brest squadrons were to join

each other off Cape Finisterre.[68] At the least, the uncertainty and waiting were extremely vexing and began to test the nerves of some people. This was especially true of Keppel, who thought "The French are most assuredly intent upon invading England and Ireland."[69] The admiral had great fears of having to fight a superior enemy squadron for control of the Channel. As the tensions mounted, Keppel also probably began to wonder if a politically hostile government might cast him as the major bungler in the impending disaster. Keppel had been a member of Byng's court-martial at the beginning of the Seven Years' War and may have had in mind that admiral's fate: conviction and execution for making an error in judgment. Thus, Keppel, while bombarding Sandwich with letters of advice on strategy, also attempted to disassociate himself from any responsibility for making strategic decisions.[70] The government would not, however, permit Keppel to withdraw from this responsibility. On the contrary, it attempted to place the entire burden of the most difficult strategic decisions on the commander of the Channel Fleet. On 26 May, Keppel received by Admiralty messenger two sets of instructions dated 25 April[71] and 25 May.[72]

The earlier instructions had been approved by the cabinet on 21 April and called for Keppel to proceed to sea with the Channel Fleet and to escort a troop convoy carrying reinforcements to Gibraltar to the latitude of Ushant down the Channel. After detaching the convoy, the Channel Fleet was to cruise off Brest to prevent d'Estaing's squadron from entering the port and to bottle up the French squadron based there. If the Brest squadron escaped, Keppel was ordered to pursue it and attack if this action did not result in laying Britain and Ireland open to invasion. If the Brest and Toulon squadrons should join, then Keppel was to attack them unless the French were greatly superior in strength. In that case, Keppel was to return to St. Helens without giving battle to the French. Further, the British admiral was ordered to take or destroy any French ships of the line and East Indiamen he encountered, as well as any French frigates that shadowed the Channel Fleet and any Spanish ships operating in conjunction with the French. The instructions of 25 April were clearly designed primarily to prevent a junction of the Toulon and Brest squadrons and to protect the British Isles from French invasion.

The supplementary instructions of 25 May added a new dimension to Keppel's responsibilities, for they called on him to decide if and when to detach Byron's squadron to reinforce either America or the Mediterranean. Keppel was directed to sail from St. Helens at once with those ships of his command that were ready for sea. While escorting the convoy bound for Gibraltar down the Channel, he was to call at Plymouth to be joined by Byron's squadron. Then, after detaching the convoy for Gibraltar, the combined force was to cruise off Brest in an attempt to prevent a junction of the Brest and Toulon squadrons. If "it should appear by good intelligence" that d'Estaing's squadron had left the Mediterranean and was bound to America or the West Indies, Keppel was to send Byron's thirteen ships of the line in search of the French force. But if the Toulon squadron had not yet left the Mediterranean, Byron was to go to Gibraltar "in quest of it with directions, if it should have passed the Straits bound out of Europe, to follow it." Under the terms of these supplementary instructions, the government gave Keppel the responsibility for making the strategic decision whether or not to detach Byron's squadron. Further, Keppel was also to decide when that detachment should be made and whether Byron should go to America or the Mediterranean. This was a vast responsibility, one which might have been willingly embraced by a great admiral who was prepared to run risks. Keppel was not a great admiral, but rather a political creature who had begun to see himself as a potential scapegoat serving under a hostile government.

Keppel found the supplementary instructions of 24 May intolerable and, officially, he merely acknowledged their receipt.[73] However, the admiral lost no time in registering his protest to Sandwich in a private letter. Keppel wrote that "both in case of detaching Vice-Admiral Byron's squadron or detaining him a time may be thought too long in the event, the blame must fall upon myself." He went on to ask what he was to do if he learned that d'Estaing had left the Mediterranean for America and received equally reliable information that the Brest squadron was about to sail in a strength that would outnumber the Channel Fleet "in nearly three ships to two." Should Byron then be sent after d'Estaing, even if this left the Channel Fleet to face a greatly superior force from Brest? According to Keppel, the instructions of 25 May did not cover this contingency, and the admiral himself was not prepared to make a strategic decision of this magnitude.[74]

In order to blunt some of Keppel's objections, the government issued him additional instructions on 27 May. These supplementary instructions, like those of 25 May, called for detaching Byron's squadron to chase d'Estaing, but if the Channel Fleet encountered a superior French squadron from Brest after Byron's departure, Keppel was to return to St. Helens for reinforcements without engaging the French.[75] In many respects, the supplementary instructions of 27 May were nothing more than a reworking of a section of the original instructions of 25 April to allay Keppel's fears by clearly authorizing him to withdraw in the face of a superior French squadron without giving battle. But by this time quibbles over the clauses in Keppel's instructions dealing with detaching Byron's force were becoming academic. The wind had turned fair for proceeding to Plymouth and Parker had already joined Byron there on 24 May with eleven ships of the line from the Channel Fleet.[76] On 28 May the first ships of the Channel Fleet began to drop down to St. Helens ready to put to sea. On 1 June, Keppel informed the Admiralty that he would sail from St. Helens with the first favorable wind.[77]

The next day, HMS *Proserpine* arrived at Falmouth after shadowing d'Estaing's squadron as it left the Mediterranean and headed into the Atlantic. The British frigate's captain, Evelyn Sutton, had sent a dispatch by express to the Admiralty before going to St. Helens to join Keppel, informing their lordships that d'Estaing "From the regular course of the fleet steered and the great press of sail they carried, I cannot help supposing it was for the West Indies." On 3 June, HMS *Enterprize* of the Mediterranean squadron arrived at Plymouth with intelligence similar to the *Proserpine*'s. At about the same time, Sutton reached St. Helens and immediately went to London to report to the Admiralty. The information brought to England by the two frigates made it a certainty that d'Estaing was not going to join the Brest squadron but was bound to either the West Indies or America. The French squadron's cargoes made many discount the West Indies as its destination. It was believed that d'Estaing was going to America by the southern great circle route, probably headed for either the Chesapeake or Delaware Bay.[78] On 5 June the cabinet concluded that d'Estaing was in fact sailing to America, whereupon Byron was ordered to sail for New York at once with thirteen ships of the line and a frigate. Warnings went to the British army in America and to Lord Howe of the impending arrival of the French squadron on the American coast.[79]

Byron received his orders to proceed to New York at 3:00

A.M. on 7 June, but owing to contrary winds, the squadron did not leave England until 9 June.[80] Forty-three days had elapsed from the time that Germain first received reports that d'Estaing had left Toulon and was going to America until the actual sailing of the British reinforcements for America. Keppel, Palliser, and especially Sandwich have been criticized for arguing successfully against detaching ships from the Channel Fleet before the destination of the Toulon squadron was clear. It has been contended that the "proper and traditional" strategy of clamping a close blockade on Brest while intercepting d'Estaing before his force left Europe should have been followed. In some respects, this line of reasoning reads the strategic lessons of the French Revolutionary and Napoleonic Wars into the situation confronting the Royal Navy in May 1778. Furthermore, this argument does not take into account the potential odds Britain faced in the spring of 1778.

Contrary winds delayed Keppel's departure with the Channel Fleet from St. Helens until 13 June.[81] When the wind was fair that day, the Channel Fleet, consisting of twenty ships of the line, three frigates, two cutters, and a fire ship, proceeded down the Channel.[82] At Keppel's request, the convoy carrying troops to Gibraltar was not closely escorted by the Channel Fleet, but rather proceeded independently after Keppel's force had sailed from St. Helens. Keppel's second in command was Vice Adm. Sir Robert Harland and his third in command was Palliser. It was not unusual for a lord of the Admiralty to have a seagoing command, and Capt. John Jervis, commander of HMS *Foudroyant,* thought that Harland and Palliser were "tough fellows and will do well."[83] In hindsight, though, it probably was unwise to give Palliser a Channel Fleet command. Considering the personalities involved and Keppel's known opinion of Palliser, there was always the possibility that any minor misunderstanding or mishap might be blown up into a major dispute between the two admirals.

On 17 June, twenty-three miles south of The Lizard, the British sighted two French frigates accompanied by two smaller vessels. Keppel concluded that the French were "reconnoitring" the Channel Fleet and ordered that the frigates be chased and brought to his flagship by force if necessary. In the late afternoon, HMS *Milford,* supported by HMS *Hector,* overhauled the French frigate *Licorne.* The captain of HMS *Milford* requested that the *Licorne* stand toward the Channel Fleet, and *Licorne* complied after HMS *Hector* fired a shot across her bow. The French frigate

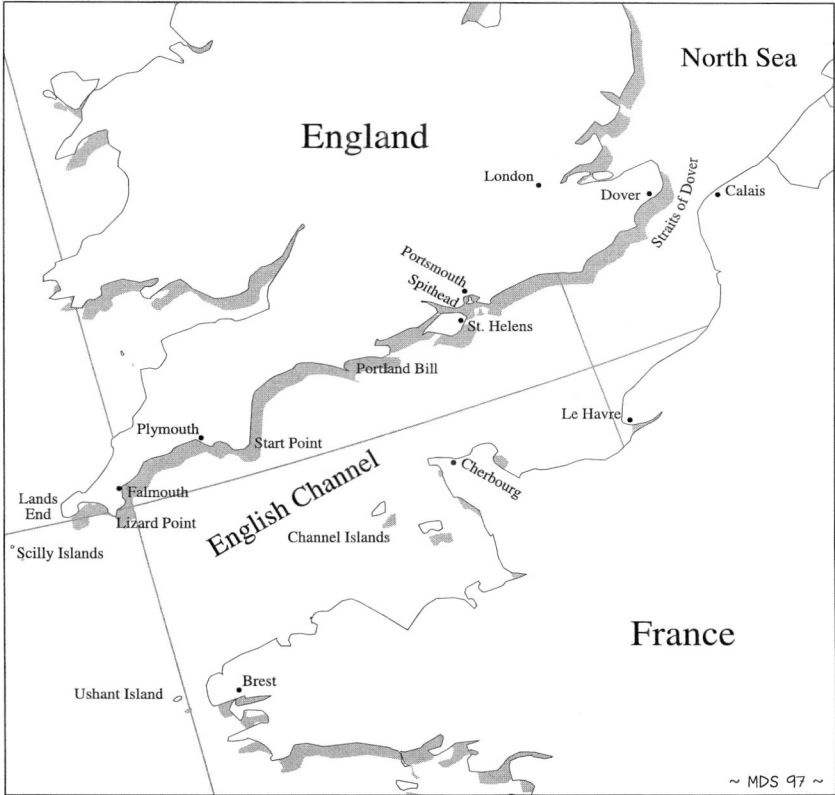

The English Channel

Map labels:

North Sea

England

London
Dover
Straits of Dover
Calais

Portsmouth
Spithead
St. Helens

Portland Bill

Plymouth
Start Point

Le Havre

Lands End
Falmouth
Lizard Point
Cherbourg

Scilly Islands

English Channel

Channel Islands

France

Ushant Island
Brest

~ MDS 97 ~

remained with the Channel Fleet throughout the night, but at about 9 A.M. the next morning the *Licorne* suddenly went on the opposite tack, apparently attempting to escape from the British. A shot was fired across the French frigate's bow and the *Licorne* thereupon fired a whole broadside into HMS *America* and then struck her colors.[84]

In the meantime, HMS *Arethusa* and HM cutter *Alert* pursued the other French frigate, the *Belle Poule* and her consort, the 10-gun cutter *Le Courier*. At sunset the British ships overtook their chases and the captain of HMS *Arethusa* informed the *Belle Poule* that he had orders to escort the French frigate to his admiral's flagship. When the French captain refused to comply, the *Arethusa* fired across the bow of the *Belle Poule,* which answered with a broadside of her own. There ensued a battle between the two frigates that lasted for two hours until the *Belle Poule* managed to escape from HMS *Arethusa*. At the same time, HM cutter *Alert* engaged the *Le Courier* in an hour-long action that ended in the French vessel's surrender. On 19 June, HMS *Milford* and HMS *Proserpine,* supported by three ships of the line, chased and brought back another French frigate, the *Pallas,* without firing a shot. Because of the hostile actions of the *Licorne, Belle Poule,* and *Le Courier,* Keppel decided to "detain" the *Pallas* and removed the French crew from the vessel and put British men into the frigate.[85]

The Channel Fleet's seizure of the three French ships signaled the advent of open hostilities between Britain and France even though war was not officially declared by France until 10 July.[86] Keppel was astonished by the actions of the French captains. The admiral had intended to release the *Licorne* after speaking to her, and on 17 June he permitted a number of French merchant ships to pass through the Channel Fleet. However, after the *Licorne*'s broadside and battles with the *Belle Poule* and *Le Courier,* Keppel decided to seize any other French frigates the Channel Fleet encountered, for he had believed that the captains of the French frigates had orders to provoke the British into "what they may pretend to construe into an insult or act of hostility."[87] Palliser also concluded that the French frigates had orders to "provoke" the British into beginning hostilities.[88]

On the morning of 20 June the outward-bound convoy to Gibraltar passed the Channel Fleet. Keppel hoped "that what has happened among the French frigates will allow of its getting clear of the Channel."[89] Later in the day Keppel sent, without comment, a number of documents found on the French frigates plus reports of intelligence gained from prisoners on the state of the French squadron at Brest.[90] The next day a prisoner changed his story and Keppel began to consider the implications of one item in the captain's cabin of the *Pallas*: a copy of *Ordre de Mouillage de L'Armee de Rois dans La Rode de Barest, en 1778* showing the anchorages for twenty-seven ships of the line. From this information Keppel concluded that the French squadron at Brest numbered at least twenty-seven ships of the line and an "extraordinary" number of frigates. He reasoned further that his squadron, consisting of twenty ships of the line and two or three frigates, was "manifestly inferior to the French fleet." Now that the convoy was safely clear of the Channel and unwilling "to risk the fate of England," the admiral decided the only prudent action was to invoke the terms of the supplementary orders of 27 May and to return forthwith to Spithead for reinforcements.[91] Palliser agreed with Keppel that the Channel Fleet was inferior in force to the French squadron at Brest and agreed with the admiral's decision to return.[92] Both feared that the security of Britain would be jeopardized if the Channel Fleet was overpowered by a superior French fleet in the English Channel.[93]

On 25 June the Channel Fleet arrived back at St. Helens.[94] The king was "hurt" by Keppel's decision to return, fearing that "this step will greatly discourage the ardour of the country."[95] Keppel, however, would not remain at sea with a force he believed to be weaker than the French squadron at Brest. Indeed, Keppel was determined to sail only when the Channel Fleet consisted of exactly the number of ships of the line called for in his instructions. On 2 July, Keppel informed Sandwich that "the Kings Councils have determined twenty-four ships' force sufficient; I will sail when I am joined by that addition of ships."[96] Several days later the admiral informed the first lord of the Admiralty that "I cannot take upon myself sailing with less force then my instructions determine to be sufficient."[97] It is not known to what degree Keppel's actions were based on political considerations. While it is clear that the admiral feared being made a political scapegoat in the event of a disaster, Keppel was also on strong tactical grounds, for it was widely believed that a numerically inferior squadron of ships of the line could not defeat a superior one in battle. Keppel's refusal to put to sea until the Channel Fleet was reinforced to twenty-four ships of the line was unpopular with some members of the government who thought that the admiral should be at sea.[98] Keppel probably wanted to protect himself politically by holding the government to the exact force required by his instructions, but he also felt genuine reluctance to put to sea with a force he honestly believed to be inferior to the French.

On 9 July the Channel Fleet, consisting of twenty-four ships of the line and five frigates, sailed from St. Helens.[99] Keppel's orders called for him to call off Plymouth, then take station off Brest and cover mercantile convoys entering the Channel bound to Britain. On 4 July the admiral informed the Admiralty that he intended to take station from five to twenty leagues south of The Lizard because he thought this was the best position to protect British trade. The future movements of the Channel Fleet would depend on the condition of the ships and the intelligence received by the admiral. Keppel on 8 July told the Admiralty that if he left the station south of The Lizard, the Channel Fleet would then be eight to twenty leagues west of Ushant. However, if the wind turned to the west, Keppel would "stretch" northward toward the Isles of Scilly, returning to the Ushant station when the wind returned to an easterly direction. Keppel considered this to be the best deployment for the protection of British trade entering the English Channel.[100]

On 14 July the Channel Fleet was off Plymouth and in the next two days was reinforced to twenty-six ships of the line. On 16 July, Keppel's strength was brought to twenty-nine ships of the line and the fleet proceeded toward its station south of The Lizard. The next day, Keppel decided to take station off Ushant where the fleet arrived on the evening of 19 July and was joined by HMS *Terrible*. At 10 A.M. on 20 July, as the Channel Fleet stood in toward Brest, a northeast gale began to blow and Keppel was forced to stand out to sea. During the storm, HMS *Victory* lost her main mast and several other ships were also damaged. For the next several days the British encountered fog and heavy seas as they worked their way northward to regain the latitude of Brest.[101] Keppel at this time "wondered" where the French were and thought that perhaps if the French ships were not in Brest, they "may be to the westward."[102]

Shortly after noon on 23 July the British were some sixty miles west of Ushant when the fog lifted and they sighted the French squadron from Brest. This force consisted of thirty-two ships of the line, nine frigates, five corvettes, and two luggers commanded by Adm. Comte Louis Guillouet d'Orvilliers.[103] The weather was hazy, and upon sighting the French ships, Keppel formed the Channel Fleet's thirty ships into a line of battle and stood to the northeast in pursuit of the French, who were sailing on the same course.[104] At 7 P.M., with the wind west northwest, the French squadron tacked and stood toward the Channel Fleet. Not wishing a night action, Keppel "brought the Fleet to, with the larboard tack, leaving the option to the French." The British ships lay to during the night, riding out a gale of wind blowing out of the west.[105]

At daylight on 24 July the British discovered that most of the French squadron had moved to windward during the night and were now northwest of the Channel Fleet. Two of the French ships, the *Duc de Bourgogne* and the *Alexandre,* were leeward of the British. Keppel attempted to use these two ships as bait to draw d'Orvilliers into a battle. The French admiral ignored the ruse and the *Duc de Bourgogne* and *Alexandre* escaped to Brest, reducing the French squadron to thirty ships of the line. The Channel Fleet was between the French squadron and its base at Brest. The wind being out of the west and d'Orvilliers being to windward, British could not force the French to do battle.[106] For the next three days Keppel tried to bring the French to action, but d'Orvilliers frustrated the British admiral's endeavors by retreating further out into the Atlantic.

On the morning of 27 July the Channel Fleet was proceeding northwest in a loose line-abreast formation and Keppel's flagship flew the signal for a general chase. At 6 A.M. Keppel ordered several ships of the British rear division to chase to windward. This order caused some of the rear division ships commanded by Palliser to draw ahead of the main body and break up the formation of the British rear. The French squadron was about six to ten miles to windward and in line-ahead formation on a course perpendicular to that of the British. At 9 A.M. d'Orvilliers, wishing to observe the British more closely, ordered his ships to tack in succession. As the lead French ships began to execute this order, turning around and sailing in the direction opposite to their former course, the French squadron placed itself slightly closer to the British. Just as the French van was committed to this maneuver, the wind changed from southwest to south southwest, throwing the bows of the French ships to a course heading roughly south. The change in wind direction, coupled with the French tacking in succession, gave Keppel the opportunity to attempt to close with the enemy and engage them. The Channel Fleet thus continued on a westward course in line-abreast formation until the British were astern of the French fleet and only slightly to their leeward. At 10:15 A.M. the British ships tacked together, forming a line-ahead formation on the same course as the French and almost in the wake of the rearmost enemy ship. Shortly thereafter, a rain squall came up, temporarily obscuring visibility.

With the onset of the rain, the wind returned to the southwest, giving the advantage to the British. If the wind held and both fleets remained on their courses, the British van would overhaul the rear of the French column and possibly overpower it. When the weather cleared at 11 A.M., d'Orvilliers ordered the French ships to go about simultaneously on to the port tack, reversing the order and the course of the French line. Now d'Orvilliers would meet the British line head on and pass slightly to its windward, thus bringing the entire French force into action.

The different sailing qualities of the various ships and the general lack of practice among the officers of both nations in executing fleet maneuvers left both the British and French formations in loose order. As the vans of the British and French lines passed each other, Keppel ordered the signal for battle to be made. The British ships were close hauled and the French were several points off the wind. Just before the engagement began, d'Orvilliers signaled the French ships to form a close hauled line of battle. As the three ships at the head of the French squadron began to carry out this order, the French line began to steer slightly away from the British. The battle began at about 11:20 A.M., when the fourth ship in the French line opened fire on the leading British ships.

The action became general as British and French ships drew abreast of each other and great masses of powder smoke blanketed both squadrons. As Keppel passed the van of the French squadron in HMS *Victory,* his ship received the broadsides of six enemy ships without firing a shot, as Keppel wished first to engage the enemy flagship. When HMS *Victory* drew abreast of the *Bretagne,* d'Orvilliers's flagship, Keppel fired a whole broadside into the vessel and then engaged, in succession, six more enemy ships as he passed down the French line to the rear of the enemy column. On passing the rear of the French line, Harland signaled the ten ships he commanded in the van to go about and follow the rear of the French column. Meanwhile, the British rear division of ten ships commanded by Palliser was not formed into a proper line, but rather passed down the French line in a scattered and irregular formation. This confusion among the ships of the British rear division arose in part from that morning's earlier order for some of this division's ships to chase to windward, an order that had broken up the formation of the British rear before the battle. Because of their poor formation, individual ships of the British rear division engaged the enemy piecemeal and sometimes found themselves under the fire of several enemy ships at the same time, suffering greater damage than the ships of the British van or center.

At 1 P.M., Keppel, in HMS *Victory*, cleared the last ship in the French line and emerged from the battle. The admiral saw the ships of Harland's division tacking in pursuit of the rear of the French line while there were a number of British ships to leeward in various states of disorder and confusion, disabled by battle damage after following Harland's maneuver. The French, as Keppel quickly perceived, had not fired at the hulls of the British ships, but rather directed their fire toward "disabling the King's ships in their masts & sails." Keppel attempted to follow Harland, but the *Victory*'s rigging and masts were so damaged that she could not tack and the admiral was forced to wear the ship. It was about 2 P.M. before the *Victory*, followed by several ships of the British center division, was on the opposite tack. At about 2 P.M., Palliser, in the badly shot-up HMS *Formidable*, cleared the rear of the French line and passed to Keppel's leeward. After traversing the length of the French line, the ships of the Channel Fleet had been heavily damaged aloft by gunfire and the fleet was disorganized and divided into four separate groups of ships.

Shortly after 1 P.M., seeing the disorder and confusion in the Channel Fleet, Admiral d'Orvilliers ordered the French squadron to wear in succession and form a line of battle on the starboard tack (the line of French ships turned south to pass the Channel Fleet to leeward). Thanks to confusion and misunderstanding among the French commanders, the maneuver was not begun until 2 P.M. About half an hour later, Keppel saw the French line turning toward the Channel Fleet. Flying the signal for forming a line of battle, Keppel's HMS *Victory* wore on the starboard tack and stood down toward the crippled British ships. On seeing Keppel's signal, Harland also wore his ship, followed by the rest of his division. By 4 P.M. they had formed a line of battle with Keppel. Palliser's rear division did not attempt to form a line of battle with the rest of the Channel Fleet. Instead, the ships of the rear division joined Palliser to form a line of battle on HMS *Formidable* some two or three miles to windward of the main body of the fleet. The captains of the ships of the rear division later stated that they understood that the fighting instructions directed them to form a line of battle not with the commander in chief, but rather with the commander of their division. In any event, as the French line of battle approached the British ships in the late afternoon, the Channel Fleet was divided into three separate groups. If d'Orvilliers had pressed home an attack at this time, he might have been able to defeat the Channel Fleet by attacking its units piecemeal. Apparently, the French admiral was thinking defensively, not offensively. The French did not attack the British but instead stationed themselves leeward of the fleet, while Keppel repeatedly signaled Palliser to join him and form a line of battle. At 5 P.M. the British admiral sent the frigate *Fox* to Palliser with orders to join the main body of the Channel Fleet. Two hours later, Keppel bypassed Palliser, signaling orders with each ship's individual pennant for the rest of the fleet to join him. It was not until after dark that all the ships of Palliser's division joined Keppel and formed a line of battle. During the night the French withdrew, and at first daylight on 28 May the French ships were fifteen to twenty miles southeast of the Channel Fleet.[107] There was now no possibility of the British continuing the battle, and Keppel decided to return to England to repair his damaged ships. At noon on 31 July the Channel Fleet entered Cawsand Bay near Plymouth and anchored.[108]

The action off Ushant on 27 July was indecisive. No ships were sunk or captured, although the masts and rigging of Keppel's ships were badly damaged by the French tactic of aiming their guns high. The Channel Fleet lost 133 seamen killed and 373 seamen wounded.[109] One reason for the indecisive outcome was the French reluctance to fight a pitched battle. As Jervis observed on 31 July, "two fleets of equal force never can produce decisive events, unless they are equally determined to fight it out; or the commander-in-chief of one of them misconducts his line."[110] Perhaps of greater importance was the fact that a number of ships were newly commissioned, manned by green crews, with a general lack of experience among the British and French officers in carrying out large-scale fleet maneuvers. No officer in either fleet had taken part in a major action since the Seven Years' War and, as a result, a number of maneuvers were conducted ineptly. The French lost

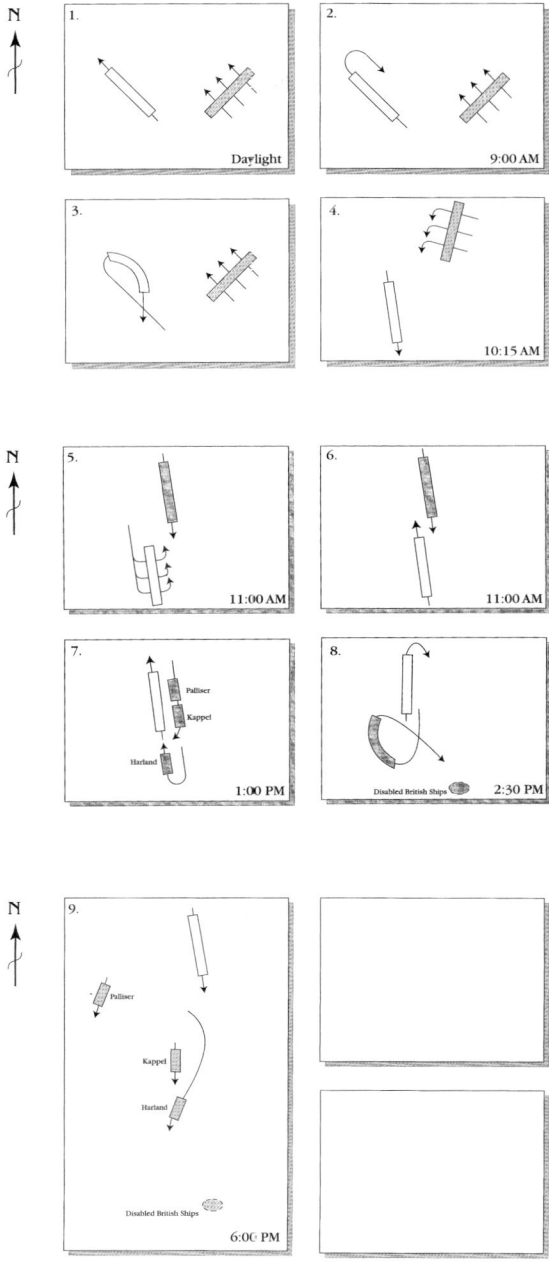

N

1.	2.
Daylight	9:00 AM

3.	4.
	10:15 AM

N

5.	6.
11:00 AM	11:00 AM

7.	8.
Palliser	
Kappel	
Harland	
1:00 PM	Disabled British Ships 2:30 PM

N

9.	
Palliser	
Kappel	
Harland	
Disabled British Ships	
6:00 PM	

☐ French Fleet (30 Ships)
▦ British Fleet (27 Ships)

BATTLE of USHANT
July 27, 1778

Movement of ships in the Battle of Ushant from 9:00 A.M. to 6:00 P.M.

the opportunity to win decisively when d'Orvilliers failed to attack the disabled and disorganized ships of the Channel Fleet during the afternoon of 27 July. Keppel pointlessly allowed the ships of the Channel Fleet to be badly damaged when they passed along the French line without engaging the enemy at close quarters. Further, Keppel did not realize the extent of the damage to the ships of the rear division. Palliser's ships suffered more casualties than Keppel's and Harland's ships combined. On the other hand, Palliser brought the ships of his division into battle in a disorganized formation and never informed Keppel of the extent of the damage his ships had suffered. Despite the indecisive outcome of the battle, Keppel proclaimed himself the victor because the French had broken off the action.[111] His official dispatch, published in an extraordinary edition of the *London Gazette,* praised the "spirited Conduct" of Harland and Palliser, as well as the officers and men of the Channel Fleet.[112]

For over three weeks the ships of the Channel Fleet lay in Cawsand Bay and Plymouth Sound being repaired. The damage sustained in the battle off Ushant was greater than first thought. In addition to extensive losses in all the ships' masts and rigging, four ships had been holed below the waterline and would have to be either docked or heeled for repairs.[113] The Admiralty dispatched Edward Hunt, one of the surveyors of the navy, to Plymouth to expedite the repair of the ships. The Admiralty also dispatched a commissioner of the sick and hurt to oversee the care of the fleet's wounded and ailing seamen. At the same time, the Victualling Board was directed to send fresh provisions to the Channel Fleet.[114]

There was much apprehension that while the Channel Fleet was immobilized at Cawsand Bay, the French squadron from Brest would put to sea and attack British trade convoys entering the English Channel. Germain, for example, thought that "whoever is first at sea may fairly claim the advantage in the late engagement."[115] The fear that the French might intercept a major trade convoy was reduced when an East India convoy passed up the Channel on 5 August, followed nine days later by a convoy from the Leeward Islands.[116] On 7 August the Admiralty told Keppel that when he sailed with the Channel Fleet again, he was to follow the orders issued before the battle off Ushant.[117] However, in a private letter Sandwich informed the admiral that "The principle object is watching and defeating the Brest fleet."[118] When the Channel Fleet sailed from Cawsand Bay to resume its station off Ushant, intelligence was received onboard the *Victory* that twenty-seven French ships of the line had sailed from Brest on 16 August. This was followed immediately by news from a neutral ship that she had sighted thirty-nine French ships twelve leagues west of Ushant the day before.[119] Upon receiving this intelligence, Keppel wrote to Sandwich, "The *happy* issue of a decisive battle with them this country looks for, and no one of it more desirous than myself."[120]

For the sixty-one days after sailing from Cawsund Bay, the Channel Fleet crisscrossed the western end of the English Channel between the Isles of Scilly and Ushant in search of the Brest squadron.[121] In the third week of September, Keppel proceeded as far south as 46°42' N in the Bay of Biscay after receiving intelligence that the French were off Cape Finisterre.[122] When he sailed from Cawsund Bay, Keppel wanted and expected a decisive battle. However, during September the weather began to turn bad and, as the chances of intercepting the Brest squadron receded, the admiral became more and more pessimistic. On 9 September, Keppel wrote: "My patience is worn out, I despair except by chance of seeing the French fleet."[123] Keppel's pessimism in September must have turned to resignation in October, when any chance of intercepting the French and fighting a decisive battle disappeared. Frustration, rage, and occasional terror must have gripped the officers and men of the Channel Fleet as day after day they searched vainly for the Brest squadron through autumn gales and fogs in the western approaches of the English Channel. The weather damaged most of the ships' masts and rigging and forced others to part from the Channel Fleet.[124] In the last weeks of the cruise, seamen fell sick by the score. Keppel himself became ill on 16 September, while Palliser suffered greatly from an old wound in his leg.[125] Finally, a series of gales and fogs drove the sickly and damaged ships up the Channel, and on 26 October the ships of Keppel's command anchored at Spithead.[126]

When the Channel Fleet arrived back in port, both Keppel and Palliser were tired, ill, and frustrated by their inability to bring the French fleet to a decisive action. Relations between the two admirals appeared to be, if not close, at least correct. The resentment over the lieutenant generalship of the marines seemed to have been pushed aside, and Keppel had not publicly taken Palliser to task for disobeying the signal to form a line of battle during the 27 July action off Ushant. Keppel and Palliser were known to have quarreled in August at Plymouth when the fleet was refitting, but this was thought to have passed quickly.[127] Palliser was probably appointed to the Channel Fleet to act as a liaison between the Admiralty and Keppel, and Sandwich had made a great effort to stay on Keppel's good side and to keep politics out of his relations with the Channel Fleet's commander. In this effort the first lord was apparently successful, for there was no hint of conflict in the letters written before the two commanders brought their ships in on 26 October.

As the Channel Fleet warped its way into Spithead, both Keppel and Palliser wrote the Admiralty for permission to come to London, and both requests were granted.[128] In a private letter to Sandwich on 26 October, Keppel said the fleet had been greatly damaged by storms, that fourteen hundred sick men had been sent ashore to the hospital, and that he was "much fatigued both in body and mind."[129] In a letter of the same date, Palliser informed Sandwich that a lack of "luck" kept the Channel Fleet from an encounter with the French fleet during its last cruise and that "everything else has been unpleasing," owing to the "boisterous and bad" weather that damaged a number of ships. Palliser's letter ended by saying that he suffered "more fatigue and pain from the disorder in my foot," which might require surgery.[130] All of Keppel's and Palliser's letters of 26 October convey a sense of tiredness and resignation.

Keppel remained onboard HMS *Victory* during the evening of 26 October while Palliser went ashore to get "a little rest and quiet."[131] In Spithead, Palliser saw the 15 October issue of the *General Advertiser and Morning Intelligencer,* an opposition London newspaper that carried an anonymous account of the action on 27 July off Ushant between the British and French fleets. This article accused Palliser of causing the British to lose the opportunity for a victory by not supporting Keppel properly with his division and hinted that politics or cowardice was the motive.[132] The article's authorship remains uncertain. Modern scholars,[133] as well as Palliser's nineteenth-century biographer,[134] point to Lt. Hon. George Berkeley, Keppel's nephew who served as a fifth lieutenant on his uncle's flagship. However, Capt. Hon. Robert Boyle Walsingham, of HMS *Sandwich* and a Keppel supporter, stated in Parliament that a lieutenant in Palliser's own ship was the author.[135] No matter who wrote the piece, Palliser probably believed that it had been instigated by Keppel and reflected his opinion. It was an open and public attack on Palliser's honor and professional integrity as a navy officer. No gentleman could let such an insult pass without redress. This was especially true of Palliser. While Keppel was the son of an earl, Palliser was a self-made man of humble origins who had made his way to a seat on the Board of Admiralty and the top of his profession through hard work.[136] To Palliser, an attack of this type, with its hint of cowardice, had to be answered, for his life was his honor and career as a navy officer.

On reading the article, Palliser was outraged and "determined" that the country "shall be rightly informed whither I or anyone else are blamable for what passed on that day." However, he would not do anything "rashly" and would "speak" to Keppel in "very serious terms."[137] What Palliser wanted was Keppel's public repudiation of the offending article.

When Palliser arrived in London at the beginning of November, he quickly discovered that a number of Keppel's officers, especially Berkeley, had spread the news that the anonymous newspaper account of the action was the truth. Learning that Keppel had also arrived in London, Palliser on 3 November asked Keppel to "contradict" the newspaper article by signing an account of the action prepared by Palliser. This account would then be published. If Keppel could not agree to this, Palliser suggested they might be able to issue a new account of the battle prepared jointly.[138] Keppel did not answer this letter.[139] According to Palliser's biographer, Palliser called on Keppel at his London house the next day with the objective of meeting "every objection" to gain the admiral's signature. When the signature was not forthcoming, Palliser offered to forgo Keppel's "signature to the paper," stating that he would accept any statement to which both could agree that cleared Palliser's name of the "aspersions cast upon him by the published slander." However, Keppel refused to deny or confirm the truth of the article.[140] It was a heated meeting and Keppel afterward told Jervis that he, Keppel, "was quite rude" and that he would have nothing to do with Palliser in the future.[141]

With Keppel's refusal to repudiate the newspaper article, Palliser saw no alternative but to publish his own account of the action off Ushant. On 5 November, Palliser's narrative appeared in five London newspapers.[142] In a covering letter printed at the same time, Palliser said that he was publishing his account of the action to disprove "many gross falsehoods" in the account in the

General Advertiser and Morning Intelligencer so that the "public" would "be fully informed of the truth" as well as "to vindicate my own conduct." Palliser added that he was prepared for any type of public inquiry into his conduct during the battle.[143]

The newspaper publication of Palliser's letter and account of the action off Ushant set off a huge controversy. The king thought that Palliser had no choice but to offer his account of the battle, Walsingham wrote Sandwich to say that everybody, including Keppel, "laments" the dispute.[144] The Duke of Richmond, one of Keppel's political cronies, told the admiral that he did not "understand" Palliser's account of the battle, but that it showed the author to be "perhaps one of the most artful men living."[145] Viewing the conflict between the two admirals from HMS *Foudroyant* at Spithead, Jervis thought it "will terminate in Parliamentary inquiry and ultimately in a Court Martial."[146]

Jervis was not alone in believing that the dispute would find its way to Parliament. Many observers thought that the opening day of the next session would be marked by "disputes between Generals, Admirals, Ministers and Commissioners."[147] In the general election of 1774, seventy army and navy officers won seats in the House of Commons. Their presence meant that military, naval, and political business were closely interconnected now.

It was not unusual for disgruntled officers to voice their opinions at Westminster,[148] but in normal times these outbursts were usually personality clashes or disputes over patronage. The year 1778 was not a normal political time. The ideological nature of the American war deeply divided the ruling classes of Britain from which the officers of the Royal Navy were drawn. Since the beginning of the fighting in America, a number of navy officers had opposed the government's American policy. For example, Walsingham, who sat in the House of Commons for Knaresborough, voted against the government on three divisions concerning the American war in 1775–78.[149] The first years of that conflict had been frustrating ones for the officers of the navy. There was little in the way of glory or prize money, and the Royal Navy, with its tradition of victory, appeared to be publicly humiliated by its inability to deal effectively with a handful of rebel cruisers and blockade runners.[150] This discontent was aggravated among senior officers by the fact that before the French joined the war in 1778 there were very few good commands available to flag officers. Sandwich had compounded the problem by tending to surround himself at the Admiralty with comparatively junior officers like Palliser and Mulgrave. This produced a sense of neglect and unease among senior officers, who suspected him of trying to create his own political following among the officer corps.[151] Political differences, personality conflicts, and professional frustrations ran high within the officer corps of the Royal Navy in the autumn of 1778.

This simmering discontent was exploited by a number of discredited and defeated admirals and generals who arrived in London during 1778 determined to salvage reputations lost on the field of battle through campaigns in the House of Commons. At first, Burgoyne and the two Howe brothers—Adm. Lord Richard Howe and Gen. Sir William Howe—intended to fix the blame for their failures on anyone but themselves, but they quickly discovered that they could not expect the assistance and support of the parliamentary opposition if they defended themselves on narrow military grounds. Instead, they had to join the opposition in a broad-based political attack designed not simply to save their reputations but rather to overthrow the government by placing the entire blame for the failure of the war on the ministry.[152] Throughout the summer of 1778, the government's conduct of the war was subjected to vociferous but ineffective attacks by the opposition aided by dissident service officers. At the beginning of December the political opposition—discredited general and flag officers as well as dissident elements in the officer corps of the Royal Navy—seized upon the dispute between Keppel and Palliser as a means to attack Sandwich and perhaps bring down the government.

This was all the easier because both principals were members of Commons. Keppel had sat in Parliament since 1755, first as the member for Chichester and then as member for New Windsor. As the son of a leading family in the region, he became de facto naval spokesman for the opposition in the House. Palliser was a comparative newcomer to Parliament. In 1774, North arranged for Palliser's election as the member for Scarborough to ensure that the government would have a spokesman on naval affairs in the lower House, serving the same function that Sandwich did in Lords.

During the debate on the Navy Estimates on 2 December, the dispute between Keppel and Palliser burst forth on the floor of Commons. Keppel attacked Palliser for publishing his account of the action off Ushant in the newspapers and declared that "he was so shocked, that he resolved never to set his foot aboard ship again, because he thought there was an end to all obedience and command." Palliser replied that he had resorted to publishing his account of the battle to protect his reputation only after Keppel refused to repudiate the scurrilous anonymous account of the battle. Palliser ended by saying that "he was neither guilty of neglect of duty nor of inactivity and, in fact, was by no means instrumental in preventing a re-action with the fleet of Mons. d'Orvilliers." Keppel angrily retorted that Palliser had

> alluded to signals, and said that it was no fault of his, that the fleet of France was not re-attacked. As to that, he could only say, that he presumed every inferior officer was to obey the signals of his commander; and now, when called upon to speak out, he would inform the House and the public, that the signal for coming into the Victory's wake, was flying from three o'clock in the afternoon till eight in the evening unobeyed; at the same time he did not charge the vice admiral with actual disobedience.

The exchange ended when a motion calling for Palliser to be court-martialed was gaveled out of order.[153]

Palliser, who was overly sensitive to criticism, reacted irrationally and rashly to Keppel's accusation that he had not complied with the signal for "coming into the Victory's wake." On 9 December, Palliser, apparently without consulting anyone, formally asked the Admiralty to court-martial Keppel for misconduct and neglect of duty during the battle off Ushant. Palliser specifically charged Keppel with attacking in disorder, not properly supporting the rear division of the fleet, hauling down the signal for battle too soon, sailing away from the enemy which "had the appearance of flight," and not pursuing "the flying enemy."[154] It was most unusual to request the court-martial of a superior officer. It would have been more traditional for Palliser to demand his own court-martial to clear his name.

Palliser's request for Keppel's court-martial placed the Admiralty and Sandwich in a difficult position. If the Admiralty suppressed the charges, Sandwich would be accused of using his power and office to protect Palliser; but if Keppel was tried, Sandwich would be attacked for using a court-martial to destroy Keppel. Sandwich quickly concluded that court-martialing Keppel was the better course. Keppel was officially informed that he would be tried on Palliser's charge of "misconduct and neglect of duty" that same day.[155]

The Admiralty's decision to charge Keppel created a political storm. To many people, especially officers of the Royal Navy, Keppel's court-martial seemed a plot that, if successful, would result in the judicial murder of the admiral. The charges under which Keppel would be tried were worded identically to those for which Byng had been executed. From the time of his appointment to the command of the Channel Fleet, Keppel had maintained that if anything went wrong he would be sacrificed by a politically hostile Admiralty. Now Palliser, a protégé of Sandwich, was vindicating his honor by having Keppel tried for his life.[156] As Jervis put it, "every military man literally serves with a halter about his neck."[157]

The Admiralty's acceptance of Palliser's request that Keppel be court-martialed meant that the affair would again be debated in the House of Commons. On 11 December, Hon. Temple Luttrell, notorious for his attacks on the Admiralty and his opposition to the American war, introduced a motion asking the king to order Keppel's court-martial. During the debate, Keppel and Palliser again exchanged angry words, with Keppel closing his speech by declaring:

> Thank God, he was not the accuser, but the accused! He was called out to serve his country at a very critical period; he had performed his duty to the best of his abilities; and whatever the issue might be, he had one consolation, that he had acted strictly to the best of his judgement. He should decline to say a syllable to the question, as he could not think of voting, and should quit the House. [There was an almost general plaudit at the end of each sentence.] He then went away.

After Keppel left the House, opposition speaker after opposition speaker heaped abuse on Palliser, Sandwich, and the administration of the navy before the motion passed without a division.[158] Five days later, on 14 December, the controversy again came before Parliament when Vice Adm. Hugh Pigot, an enemy of Sandwich and a supporter of Keppel, introduced a bill in Commons to hold Keppel's court-martial ashore rather than on a ship as required by law because of the admiral's ill health. This passed without extended debate.[159] The government at first opposed moving the court-martial ashore,[160] probably feeling that the proceedings would be packed by Keppel's supporters.[161] However, in the end, the government dropped their opposition, not wanting to appear to endanger Keppel's health.

As the Keppel-Palliser affair was debated in the House of Commons, the king suggested ending the crisis by replacing Sandwich as first lord of the Admiralty with Vice Admiral Lord Howe. This appointment would prevent Lord Howe and his brother from pressing further their demands for a parliamentary inquiry into the conduct of the war in America, while simultaneously blunting the attacks by navy officers on the government's management of the Admiralty. Howe was a capable officer, and the appointment would be popular among the officer corps of the Royal Navy. There were, however, several disadvantages to this scheme. It would be viewed both as a condemnation of Sandwich's and Germain's conduct of the war and as a bribe to the Howes. Further, if Howe became first lord, Sandwich would have to be made a secretary of state. Germain would then surely resign and need to be pacified with a peerage or some other reward. This, in turn, would enrage those like the attorney general who thought they deserved peerages more than the secretary of state for America. All in all, the king's plan seemed to carry too high a price tag for buying off attacks on the government's handling of naval affairs. North thought it unnecessary, for he believed that the government could survive the Keppel-Palliser affair.[162]

Still, the negotiations with Howe began at the end of 1778. The effort was abortive because of Howe's conditions for becoming first lord of the Admiralty: the removal of both Germain and Sandwich from office, an official government statement approving the Howe brothers' conduct of the war in America, and rewards for both Howes in the form of sinecures or peerages. This seemed too much to pay for ending the criticism of government naval policy generated by the Keppel-Palliser dispute. With the breakdown of negotiations with Howe, it became government policy to ride out the controversy.[163]

On 7 January 1779 the Keppel court-martial met onboard HMS *Britannia* and the proceedings were immediately removed ashore to the house of the governor of Portsmouth. Holding the court-martial here permitted opposition politicians and peers, navy officers, and the general public to attend the trial.[164] To add authority to the proceedings, the government asked Admiral of the Fleet Lord Hawke to be the presiding officer of the proceedings, but Hawke declined, citing poor health.[165] In the end, after several other senior admirals had been deemed unsuitable, the unwilling Adm. Sir Thomas Pye, the commander at Portsmouth, was ordered to be president of the court.[166] From beginning to end, the trial was a political event with many aspects of a popularity contest. Capt. Sir Samuel Hood, the commissioner of Portsmouth Dockyard, thought the quickest way for the court to reach a decision would be "for each captain to be called to declare at once whether the Commander-in-Chief did right or not, and let the most voices carry it."[167] A furor erupted when it was discovered that there were alterations in the log of HMS *Robust*. Even though there appeared to be alterations in other logbooks presented as evidence, this almost ruined the career of Capt. Alexander Hood, *Robust*'s captain and a supporter of the government. Throughout the proceedings, Palliser and witnesses giving evidence on his behalf were jeered and abused by the opposition peers, politicians, and navy officers in the audience, while Keppel and his witnesses were cheered and applauded. In this manner, the court-martial proceeded until it reached the conclusion that the charges were "malicious and unfounded," and Keppel was "unanimously and honourably" acquitted.[168] Though the court was obviously prejudiced in Keppel's favor, Palliser failed to prove the charges. The court had no choice but to acquit, for Keppel was not guilty of anything except poor judgment. To have found otherwise would have repeated the Byng verdict, an act of judicial murder. On 21 February, Keppel was directed to resume command of the Channel Fleet.[169]

With the acquittal, Keppel's supporters went wild with joy. His well-wishers formed a procession around the admiral. Preceded by a band playing "See the Conquering Hero Come," the parade made its way through the streets of Portsmouth to the cheers of the populace. In London, most houses were illuminated, and Tower Hill was the site of a huge bonfire where an effigy of Palliser was burned. A mob attacked and gutted Palliser's house in St. James's Park and burned his furniture. Only the reading of the Riot Act and the intervention of troops saved North's residence at Number 10 Downing Street from the same fate. The windows of the houses of other members of the government were smashed by Keppel's riotous supporters. The next day, Keppel was voted the thanks of both houses of Parliament. This honor was quickly followed by others, such as the freedom of the cities of London, Norwich, York, Londonderry, and Dublin.[170]

A political disaster of this magnitude required that the government make a sacrifice in atonement. The obvious victim was Palliser. To prevent the opposition from instituting a hostile inquiry into Palliser's conduct, Sandwich decided on 5 February that the admiral should be court-martialed. Palliser agreed that this was "necessary," and on 10 February he wrote to the Admiralty requesting a trial.[171] At Portsmouth a memorial to the king was circulated among navy officers calling for Palliser's dismissal from all his offices. To draw the teeth from this memorial and to head off the expected parliamentary demands for Palliser's removal, Sandwich recommended to the cabinet on 13 February that the admiral be dismissed "instantly" from the lieutenant generalship of the marines and the governorship of Scarborough Castle and that notice of this action be published at once in the *London Gazette*.[172] While convinced that a court-martial was unavoidable, the cabinet did not want to send the admiral to trial under the cloud of censure by dismissal from office. But political pressure generated by Parliament's vote of thanks to Keppel and the naval officer's Portsmouth petition was so great that the government was forced to dump Palliser. On 17 February, Sandwich and John Robinson, the secretary to the treasury and North's chief political agent, met Palliser in secret outside of London "to persuade" him to resign his offices. Palliser complied, resigning from all his posts and vacating his seat in the House of Commons. The resignations were accepted the next day by the king, who thought that the action was "a mean subterfuge."[173] In the House of Commons on 19 February, Charles Fox moved for Palliser's dismissal from the Royal Navy, but the motion was withdrawn when it was learned that Palliser was to be court-martialed and had resigned his offices.[174]

The Admiralty decided that Palliser's court-martial should begin on 12 April 1779. The opposition did an about-face. Instead of demanding Palliser's court-martial, they now attempted to prevent the trial, or at least discredit the proceedings. Keppel refused to act as a prosecutor or to prefer any charges against Palliser "for his disobedience of my orders on 27th July last,— however clear it may have appeared by the evidence of my trial."[175] Because of Keppel's refusal to bring any charges against Palliser, the court was directed "to enquire into the conduct and behavior of the said Vice-Admiral," and the inquiry was to be conducted by George Jackson, second secretary to the Admiralty Board and judge advocate of the Fleet. The lord chancellor considered this the best and most legal mode of proceeding under the existing circumstances.[176] The opposition disagreed. On 31 March, Richmond declared in a speech in the House of Lords that Palliser's court-martial was legally improper in the absence of specific charges made by Keppel and that the trial would be nothing more than a whitewash of Palliser that impugned Keppel. George Jackson was then brought before the bar of the House and cross-examined by a number of opposition peers. After Jackson left Lords, the debate continued. When the law lords took the opposition to task for ignorance of the law, and Richmond admitted "that the object he wished to obtain would be the consequence of his agitating the question."[177]

Palliser's court-martial began on 12 April onboard HMS *Sandwich* in Portsmouth Harbor. The trial lasted until 5 May, when the court acquitted Palliser, declaring that his "conduct and behavior on those days were in many respects highly exemplary and meritorious; at the same time [the court] cannot help thinking it incumbent on him to have made known to his Commander-in-Chief the disabled state of the Formidable."[178] One officer called the court's decision a "censoriously acquitting sentence."[179] To Palliser, the acquittal was at best a pyrrhic victory. His career was destroyed; he had lost all his offices and spent on his defense three thousand pounds that he could ill afford. He was now deeply hated by many of his follow officers and would never again be employed in active service.

While Palliser's court-martial was in progress, the opposition in both houses of Parliament mounted a major attack on Sandwich's administration of the Admiralty. On 19 April, Fox made a motion in the House of Commons calling for Sandwich's removal as first lord of the Admiralty. The main thrust of Fox's argument, which was supported by Keppel, Howe, and other dissident navy officers, was that in 1777 Sandwich misrepresented to the House of Lords the number of ships of the line fit for service; that he had permitted the Toulon squadron to escape by not sending a force to the Mediterranean; and that he had sent Keppel to sea with a force inferior to that of the enemy. Further, Sandwich was charged with trying to cover his own mistakes at the Admiralty by blaming them on Keppel and Howe.[180] In the House of Lords, the attack was opened by Lord Bristol, a vice admiral and vehement critic of the first lord. Bristol's arguments were in many respects similar to those made by Fox.[181] When all the speeches had been made and the votes counted, the opposition was crushed. Fox's motion lost in Commons by 118 to 221 votes, and the government defeated Bristol's motion in Lords 78 to 39. This was the end of direct attacks on the Admiralty over the Keppel-Palliser affair, but not the end of attacks on the government over the war in general. The Howes and their supporters in the House of Commons instigated an inquiry into the conduct of the war in America that dragged on into the summer.[182]

The opposition failed to bring down the government or remove Sandwich from the Admiralty over the Keppel-Palliser affair for a number of reasons. Most significantly was the makeup of the membership of the Parliament and the composition of the opposition party. The backbone of parliamentary opposition in 1778 and 1779 consisted of three small and interconnected groups. First there were members of Parliament like Burke, Fox, Grafton, Barre, Shelburne, Richmond, and Rockingham, who opposed the government on political and ideological grounds. Another faction included disgruntled admirals and generals like the Howes, Burgoyne, and Keppel, who were trying to protect their reputations on the floors of the Houses of Parliament. A third group comprised navy officers, within and without Parliament, who opposed the government, and especially Sandwich, on the Keppel-Palliser affair and other naval matters.

Combined, these three groups and their personal allies lacked the strength to overthrow the government or force Sandwich from office without the support of those members in Parliament who were independent country gentlemen. These men owed their seats neither to political patronage nor the Crown. They were independent in their political judgments and, except in times of extreme political crisis, tended to support the king's government.[183] In a speech in the House of Commons on 3 March, North declared that the whole cabinet accepted responsibility for the decisions and policies of the Admiralty and that a vote of censure against Sandwich would be considered a censure of the government as a whole.[184] Therefore, a vote for Sandwich's removal from the Admiralty would be a vote for the overthrow of the whole North government. North understood that this was a step most country gentlemen in the House of Commons were not prepared to take in 1779.

North's political judgment was correct, for the government withstood the political pressures generated by the Keppel-Palliser affair without having to place Lord Howe in Admiralty. While the government had weathered the crisis without sustaining any lasting political damage, the resulting bitterness and ill feeling within the officer corps split the naval service into two warring factions. Keppel's and Palliser's flagships had to be berthed at Portsmouth at a distance from each other because it was feared that the two crews would fight a pitched battle.[185] The officers of the Royal Navy, especially those serving in the Channel Fleet, were deeply divided. A number of officers imitated Lord Howe and Keppel by refusing to serve as long as Sandwich was first lord of the Admiralty. There was also a marked reluctance among some navy officers to believe in the good faith of those with whom they differed politically. In 1780 Adm. Sir George Rodney noted:

> The unhappy difference between Mr Keppel and Sir H. Palliser has almost ruined the Navy. Discipline in a very great measure is lost, and that eager willingness of executing orders given by the Board of Admiralty, or by those acting under their authority, is turned to neglect; and officers presume to find fault and think, when their duty is implicit obedience.[186]

It would be years before the schisms produced by the Keppel-Palliser affair disappeared from the Royal Navy. As late as 1785, Capt. Hon. John Levenson-Gower abused one of his midshipmen just because the young man's father had been Palliser's flag captain.[187]

The bitterness generated by the Keppel-Palliser affair was augmented by the ghost of the Seven Years' War. In 1778 everybody longed for, and even expected, a decisive battle like Quiberon Bay that would sweep the French navy from the seas. A clear victory over the Brest Squadron in 1778 would have permitted Britain to break out of the strategic trap created by French entry into the war, but the Channel Fleet's operations in 1778 failed to produce any clear-cut victory.

Keppel did not repeat Hawke's feat at Quiberon Bay, because the strategic situation of 1778 was closer to that at the beginning of the Seven Years' War in 1757 than to the one existing in 1759, the year of victories. In 1757, the threat of French invasion discouraged the cautious British government from detaching ships from the Channel Fleet for service in the Mediterranean, and Minorca was lost. In the end, the problem came down to how far a government was prepared to risk the security of the British Isles in the face of a threatened invasion. Churchill took such a risk in 1940 when he sent reinforcements to the Middle East, but Sandwich was unwilling to run such risks in 1778. Thus, Byron's squadron was held in England until the intended line of French action became absolutely clear. Only when Byron's squadron sailed to America did Keppel take the Channel Fleet to sea in search of a decisive battle with the Brest squadron. The resulting action off Ushant was indecisive, and Keppel had no better luck afterward. The Channel Fleet's extended cruise in the western approaches of the English Channel in the late summer of 1778 was plagued by bad luck and faulty intelligence. The ships were damaged by the elements and scores of seamen became sick. Although Sandwich has been taken to task for ordering that cruise as well as for not imitating the 1759 close blockade of Brest, such autumn cruises were not unprecedented and there were strategic advantages to be gained from a cruise in that season.

Keppel's strategy may not have brought a brilliant victory, but it was not a failure. The French squadron at Brest was rendered strategically ineffective and Britain's trade was protected. Even without a decisive battle, the Channel Fleet held the western approaches of the English Channel, the possibility of a French invasion was thwarted, and no British military or trade convoys had been intercepted and captured.

Chapter 3

THE ATTEMPTED FRANCO-SPANISH INVASION AND THE FIRST RELIEF OF GIBRALTAR, 1779–80

In March 1779 the Admiralty began to repair the damage done to the navy by the Keppel-Palliser affair and to prepare the Channel Fleet for the next campaign. The first task was replacing Keppel as commander in chief of the Channel Fleet, but Keppel refused to surrender that command, even while refusing to serve while Sandwich remained at the Admiralty. Here Keppel hoped to force the king to take sides in the Keppel-Palliser dispute, but Keppel had misread the situation.[1] After an exchange of correspondence with the Admiralty, Keppel was summarily ordered "to strike his flag and come on shore" on 18 March.[2]

With Keppel's removal, a new commander in chief for the Channel Fleet had to be found. The challenge confronting Sandwich and the Admiralty was finding a man who was competent as well as politically acceptable. The ramifications of this problem can be judged by the fact that Sandwich felt it was necessary to draw up a secret list of navy officers that showed whether or not these men were pro- or anti-government.[3] Sandwich was looking for a fighting admiral with the right political allegiances.

It proved impossible to find such a man. The choice fell to Adm. Sir Charles Hardy, the governor of Greenwich Hospital, who was appointed on 19 March.[4] Hardy had served as a governor of New York and had been Hawke's second in command in the Channel Fleet when Keppel and Howe were mere post captains. The sixty-four-year-old Hardy was in poor health and had not been to sea in years. He appears to have been chosen because his great seniority placed him above such matters as the Keppel-Palliser affair.[5] Even so, Adm. Sir Robert Harland, second in command to Keppel, refused to serve under Hardy.[6] Vice Adm. George Darby replaced Harland as second in command of the Channel Fleet, while captains Sir John Lockhart Ross and Robert Digby were promoted to the rank of rear admiral to serve as subordinate admirals in the fleet.[7] Thus, the need to smooth over the conflicts generated by the Keppel-Palliser affair resulted in giving command of the Channel Fleet to a man whose only claim was seniority and backing him up with three untried subordinates.

Hardy's appointment was made in the hope that the senior and good-natured admiral would be able to heal the wounds suffered by the navy's officer corps during the Keppel-Palliser dispute. In a further effort to end ill feeling among the officers of the Channel Fleet and to give them an officer of high intellectual caliber and drive, the king suggested that Capt. Richard Kempenfelt be made Hardy's captain of the Fleet, a position similar to a modern chief of staff.[8] Of Swedish decent and only two years younger than Hardy, Kempenfelt was considered one of the most brilliant officers in the Royal Navy.[9] A keen student of naval affairs and a specialist in tactics and signals, Kempenfelt was a member of a small group of reform-minded officers who fought to break through tradition in order to revamp British tactics and methods of signaling by studying and applying French methods.[10] The comptroller of the navy, Charles Middleton, wanted Kempenfelt to serve at the Navy Board so that this organization could profit from his skills. It was expected that his appointment as Hardy's captain of the Fleet would enrage some captains who were his senior,[11] but these considerations were pushed aside. Kempenfelt was appointed captain of the Fleet on 24 March[12] because of his great ability and, in the words of the king, because he was "much respected by all parties and one well qualified to heel all the little breaches."[13]

At the very time the command structure of the Channel Fleet was being refurbished, the British began to institute a number of technological innovations to improve the performance of their ships. The most important was the decision in 1779 to sheathe the bottoms of the ships of the Royal Navy with copper plates. Marine growths such as weeds and what is generally known as the "worm"—a boring mollusk called *Teredo navalis*—had attacked ships' bottoms ever since the introduction of wood as a building material. As the weeds grew thicker on the bottom of a vessel, they slowed its speed, while the *Teredo navalis* literally ate the bottoms out of wood ships. At various times experts had tried unsuccessfully to deal with these problems by applying different substances to the bottoms of wooden ships: tar, resin, pitch, quick lime, lead sheathing, and varnish among them.[14] From the end of the Seven Years' War, when the frigate HMS *Alarm* was sheathed with copper plates, the Royal Navy had experimented with this technique in desultory fashion. These experiments showed copper plating not only greatly increased the speed of a ship by keeping the hull clean of weeds, but also appeared to prevent the entry of *Teredo navalis*. The efforts were unsuccessful, however, because ships with copper-covered bottoms literally fell apart due to "corrosion by galvanic action of the copper on iron bolts which secured the main frame and planking," which could not be prevented.[15] At the beginning of the American war there was renewed interest in coppering the bottoms of ships. A number of small warships had copper sheathing put on their bottoms. Experiments were carried out using bolts of various alloys and painting the hulls of ships to be coppered with white lead and linseed oil. Although none of these measures solved the problem of corroding iron bolts, the performance of ships with coppered bottoms greatly impressed a number of navy officers and pressure grew to copper the whole fleet. Still the Admiralty and the Navy Board hesitated. At the beginning of 1779 the Navy Board did an about-face and recommended that ships of the line be sheathed with copper. The Navy Board believed that it had found a method to prevent the iron-corrosion problem by placing thick sheets of paper between the hull of the ship and the copper sheathing to keep water away from the iron bolts. Later, layers of tar and white lead mixed with linseed oil would also be used in conjunction with paper to form a watertight barrier between the ship's hull and her copper sheathing. When this method appeared to be successful, orders were given to sheathe the hulls of the whole fleet.[16] Unfortunately, the Navy Board did not appreciate the fact that the hulls of wooden ships are not rigid. Instead, when a vessel encounters a sea, the planking moves or "works," breaking the watertight seal formed by the paper and permitting water to come into contact with the iron fastenings, causing corrosion by galvanic action.[17]

Ignoring this, the Royal Navy undertook a prodigious campaign. By the end of the war most of the ships of the Royal Navy had been sheathed with copper. This gained the navy several advantages. Copper sheathing greatly reduced the need for docking ships so that their bottoms could be cleaned. Without copper sheathing, a ship of the line would have spent an average of one year and three months of the American war in a dockyard being refitted and having its bottom cleaned. Copper sheathing greatly reduced the frequency with which a ship had to be docked.[18] Further, copper sheathing increased the speed of British ships compared to that of French and Spanish warships. By 1781, when most of the ships of the Royal Navy had been sheathed with copper, British squadrons enjoyed a marked advance in performance over those of their enemies who still employed uncoppered ships.[19] Sandwich looked upon sheathing the fleet with copper as one of his great achievements, believing that "Copper bottoms need fear nothing."[20] Copper sheathing has been cited as an "English technological victory," for it did greatly multiply combat effectiveness of the Royal Navy.[21] It was also a huge gamble based on misinformation, and the corrosion problem would not be truly solved until 1786 and the introduction of a mechanically hardened copper and zinc bolt for use in a ship's fastenings.[22]

The year 1779 also saw changes in the ammunition used by the Royal Navy. While sitting as a member of the Palliser court-martial, Kempenfelt realized that the French could have won a crushing victory in the action off Ushant if they had attacked Palliser's ships after they were immobilized by heavy damage in their masts and rigging. According to Kempenfelt:

> There is no strength and force without motion and direction. Deprive a giant of one of his legs and a stripling shall master him. 'Tis plain to me that our fleet, after that action, for all the first part of the afternoon, was at the mercy of the French. Unconnected to succor and support each other, what defence could they have made against a close well-formed line of ships? (NRS, *Barham*, 1:291)

Kempenfelt felt that a British fleet should be able to immobilize an enemy force by shooting up a ship's rigging and masts. Because grapeshot consisted of musket balls, it made only small holes in a ship's sails. Keppel argued that langridge, a case shot consisting of irregular bits of iron, should be issued to all British warships for destroying the sails and standing rigging of enemy ships.[23] This suggestion was adopted in an Admiralty order of 5 August 1779 directing the issuance of langridge for the use of guns mounted on the upper decks, quarterdecks, and forecastles of all British warships.[24]

By issuing langridge, the Royal Navy was not, however, abandoning the doctrine of close engagement of the enemy in favor of one of crippling a vessel's rigging at long range. It was an article of faith in the Royal Navy that the way to defeat an enemy was to fight a gun port to gun port battle and beat an opponent down by a superior rate and weight of gunfire. In pursuance of the doctrine of close engagement, 1779 saw the adoption of the carronade by the Royal Navy. Called the "smasher" by contemporaries, carronades were developed by Gen. Robert Melville and were initially produced by the Carron Iron Works in Scotland. Carronades were short-barreled guns with a chamber for powder similar to those in mortars that fired hollow or cored shot. Carronades were capable of firing a very heavy shot at close range, and they were much lighter than ordinary naval guns. For example, a 32-pound carronade is the same weight as a 6-pound long gun. Because of their light weight, carronades could be mounted on the forecastles and poop decks of ships where ordinary heavy guns could not be placed.[25] In addition to the their usual armament, ships of the line could mount up to ten carronades on their poop decks and forecastles.[26] Test firing of carronades was conducted, and on 28 July 1779 the Admiralty officially adopted them for use on British warships.[27] The adoption of carronades was pushed through by Middleton, perhaps the most innovative comptroller the navy ever had, over the opposition of the Ordnance Board[28] and a number of navy officers.[29] Carronades would give increased fire power at close range to the ships of the Royal Navy.[30]

Copper sheathing and carronades, perhaps the industrial revolution's first effects on the Royal Navy, gave British warships a technological advantage; but at the beginning of 1779 a more immediate need was mobilizing ships and men for the forthcoming campaign in the Channel. At the beginning of 1779, the Admiralty calculated that there were 80 ships of the line in commission, of which 39 were detailed for service with the Channel Fleet. There were also 108 smaller warships, ranging in strength from 50-gun ships down to naval storeships, stationed in British waters.[31] It was expected that a further 36 warships of which 10 were 74-gun ships of the line would be ready for commissioning in the course of 1779.[32]

The real problem in readying the Channel Fleet in 1779 was not ships but the shortage of seamen to man the vessels. On 17 March it was calculated that thirty-nine ships of the line in Britain required 5,668 men to bring their complements up to full strength.[33] In 1779, as in 1778, the manpower problem was closely related to sick rates among the seamen. Figures amassed by Dr. Gilbert Blane show the impact of disease on the navy's manpower problem. In 1779, Parliament voted that the Royal Navy should be manned by 70,000 seamen and marines. According to Blane, 28,592 men out of this force were sent sick, 24,626 were discharged, 1,658 died, and 997 ran. Thus, out of 70,000 men authorized in 1779, the Royal Navy lost 55,906 men for varying periods. The sick rate throughout the whole navy was 1 man sick out of every 2.45 men. The Channel Fleet was hardest hit, for out of the 28,592 men sent sick from the whole navy, 21,940 came from that fleet's ships at Portsmouth and Plymouth.[34] This problem was created by the practices of press gangs who seized sick men (mostly Londoners) and placed them in the ships of the Channel Fleet, thus guaranteeing that the force would be repeatedly swept by infectious disease.[35] Sickness among seamen meant that 2 or more men had to be raised for every 1 the Channel Fleet required.

In the spring of 1779, the Channel Fleet was mobilized and made ready for sea as quickly as press gangs could sweep up the necessary number of seamen. On 14 April the Admiralty began the process by ordering a general press of all seamen from protection except those serving on privateers, ships under charter to the government, or those exempted by act of Parliament.[36] This measure did not produce the required number of seamen, and officials toyed with ideas like requiring every parish in England to produce one landsman for service in the Royal Navy.[37] On 21 June the Admiralty ordered that seamen be impressed "from all protection whatsoever," exempting only those who served on shipping under charter to the government.[38] Two days later, the East India Company offered bounties for men who would enter the Royal Navy.[39] Next, orders were issued to press five hundred watermen, and warrants were issued to the constables in the City of London, the Home counties, and coastal counties to press "all seamen and seafaring men." On 19 July the secretary at war was requested to order the military to assist the Impress Service in its quest for seamen.[40] Still, no matter what action the Admiralty took, seamen could be obtained only at the rate at which they became available in British ports from returning merchant ships. Not until then could press gangs sweep them up for service in the Royal Navy.

In the spring of 1779, as the Channel Fleet prepared for the next campaign against the French, the strategic situation was unclear. Intelligence reports reaching Whitehall indicated that the Spanish might ally themselves with the French, and as early as 19 February, information arrived in London that the Spanish were moving cannon and munitions into the region around Gibraltar.[41] On 27 March intelligence arrived that the Spanish at Corunna had eleven ships of the line and several lesser ships of war, all being fitted out for service.[42] It was also thought that the French had thirty-three ships of the line at Brest.[43] At first, British officials did not know what these and other intelligence reports meant, and at various times during the spring they offered conflicting interpretations of the intentions of the French and Spanish. The king, for example, on 30 March "began to credit the supposition that the court of Spain will not take part in the war."[44] Several days later, however, Germain concluded that if Spain did not enter the conflict, France would make peace.[45] Speculation of this type was false optimism. Sandwich had long held that Spain would enter the war, and the British government had concluded that it was just a matter of time before the Spanish entered the conflict as France's ally.[46] Since the beginning of the war with France, it had been British government policy to delay Spanish belligerency as long as possible.[47] In the late spring of 1779 it was clear to most observers that Spain was on the verge of entering the American war.

The 1779 campaign in the English Channel began off The Needles on 2 May, when a privateer from Jersey encountered Vice Adm. Mariot Arbuthnot as he escorted a military convoy bound for New York. The privateer informed Arbuthnot that a French force had attacked Jersey in the Channel Islands the day before. The admiral left the convoy and took the bulk of its escort and some troops to succor the Channel Islands.[48] Arriving off Jersey on 4 May and finding that the French had left after attempting a landing, Arbuthnot promptly returned to his convoy anchored in Torbay.[49] As Arbuthnot proceeded to Torbay, intelligence reached London that there were twenty-five French ships of the line ready to sail in Brest.[50] The threat posed by these French vessels perled the Admiralty to order Arbuthnot's convoy to remain at bay until reinforced by ten ships of the line under Darby. This joint party would then escort the convoy out into the Atlantic as far as the longitude of Cape Clear.[51] On 22 May, Darby's squadron sailed from St. Helens[52] and returned on 10 June after Arbuthnot's convoy had been seen safely on its way.[53]

On the same day Darby sailed out from St. Helens, the cabinet considered and approved a draft of instructions for Hardy, and the king approved them the next day.[54] As issued on 29 May, Hardy's instructions called for him to sail from Spithead on the return of Darby's detachment. Twenty-seven ships of the line would then be ready for service. Hardy was to proceed down the Channel, take station off Brest, and blockade the French fleet in that port. If Hardy found that the French fleet had sailed from Brest before his arrival, the Channel Fleet was to pursue the enemy. If Hardy could not ascertain the whereabouts of the French ships, he was to take station off The Lizard until further orders came from the Admiralty. Hardy was also directed to take any Spanish ships of war found attempting to enter French ports or operating with the French fleet. Above all, Hardy was reminded that the security of Britain and Ireland "must always be the principle object of your care and attention."[55]

On 12 June the English government learned that the French fleet from Brest was at sea, and Hardy was directed to sail without "a moments loss of time."[56] Hardy immediately sailed from Spithead with twenty-eight ships of the line and a number of frigates.[57] That same day, the Spanish ambassador to the Court of St. James presented the British government with an ultimatum that amounted "to a declaration of War" and left England four days later.[58] The day after the Spanish ultimatum, the Admiralty ordered Hardy "to seize and destroy all ships and vessels belonging to Spain or Spanish subjects which he may meet with."[59] War with Spain was considered unavoidable. Capt. John Jervis was only expressing a common British belief when he wrote his sister on 10 June that "the war with Spain cannot be much more averted."[60]

Spanish entry into the American war greatly altered French naval strategy in European seas and increased the strength of the naval forces arrayed against Britain. In May of 1778 intelligence showed twenty-eight Spanish ships of the line based at Cadiz,[61] and by 1 April 1779 this figure had grown to thirty-four and were "said to be completely manned and victualled."[62] In 1778 French strategy focused on operations in America. The task of the fleet at Brest was to provoke war with the British and divert the Royal Navy's attention away from America with operations in the English Channel.[63] Spanish entry into the war made the invasion of England the center of French strategy during 1779.

The French had intervened in the war in 1778 to redress the balance of power in Europe by reducing the strength of Great Britain. The French intended to achieve this by supporting the American rebels while drawing the Spanish into the conflict so that the combined French and Spanish fleets could confront Britain with an overpowering naval superiority. French diplomacy skillfully obtained Spanish entrance into the war. France paid a price for Spain's alliance against Britain: a promise to continue the war until Spain regained Gibraltar. Further, France had to agree that the invasion of England would be the major objective of the 1779 campaign.

Since Britain's 1701 seizure of Gibraltar, foreign control of the fortress had been a national affront to the Spanish—*un pundonor.* How could a great and honorable kingdom permit the greatest fortress in the land to be held by the soldiers of a foreign king? At the end of previous wars, Spain had vainly attempted to regain Gibraltar by diplomacy.[64] Spain was determined not to fail again. Spanish strategy in 1779 was two-sided: to win Gibraltar by besieging the place and reducing it by force of arms while simultaneously invading England and capturing territory that the island kingdom would be forced to trade for the fortress. At Spain's insistence, the Convention of Aranjuez, the agreement between France and Spain calling for Spanish belligerency, contained a clause requiring an invasion of England in 1779.[65] Spain believed that only occupation of a part of England would persuade England to return Gibraltar. This clause thrust Gibraltar into the very center of French, Spanish, and British naval strategy. "That pile of stone" at the entrance to the Mediterranean would twist and distort naval strategy to the very end of the American war.

The French and Spanish plan for invading England in the summer of 1779 called for gaining naval superiority in the English Channel before landing a French army in southern England. They intended to concentrate the French and Spanish fleets in Europe into a force large enough either to destroy the British Channel Fleet or to drive the British out of the Channel. The scheme called for a French squadron at Brest, some thirty-five ships of the line, to join with a squadron of twenty Spanish ships off Corunna not later than 15 May. Then, the combined Franco-Spanish fleet would proceed to the English Channel and gain control of those waters. Once the Franco-Spanish fleet controlled the English Channel, a twenty-thousand-man French army would cross the Channel to capture the Isle of Wight by "*coup de main*" and then seize mainland Gosport in order to bombard or destroy the dockyard at Portsmouth. If this operation succeeded, other attacks, like capturing the army provision depot at Cork or the ports of Liverpool or Bristol, could be undertaken. If the attack on the Isle of Wight proved impractical, there were alternative plans for attacking the Channel Islands or Plymouth.[66] The success of all these plans depended absolutely on the ability of the combined fleet of the Bourbon allies to gain control of the English Channel.

On 20 June, Hardy and the Channel Fleet arrived off The Lizard with several convoys under escort. Three days later, off Ushant, Hardy received additional instructions from the Admiralty.[67] If he received intelligence that the French and Spanish fleets had joined forces, he was authorized to fall back to either Torbay or Spithead.[68] At this time, the admiral also obtained intelligence from captured French and American vessels confirming that both the French fleet at Brest and the Spanish fleet were at sea. However, neither vessel had information as to the positions or movements of the enemy fleets. These reports persuaded Hardy that he should proceed to The Lizard and, if the wind came out of the west, to go on to Torbay "for the better security of the Channel."[69]

On 2 July the Channel Fleet was off The Lizard, where Hardy learned that a fleet of forty-seven sail had been sighted off Cape Finisterre. He also learned that gossip in Bordeaux of early June indicated there was a fleet of forty-seven ships off Ushant. The wind came up strongly from the west, forcing Hardy and his fleet to the eastward. At 5 P.M. on 5 July, the Channel Fleet came to anchor in Torbay. Hardy then informed the Admiralty that he had received intelligence that the French fleet, consisting of thirty ships of the line, not in company with any Spanish ships, was off Ferrel. He also reported that the Channel Fleet would remain in Torbay awaiting further orders.[70]

Hardy and the Channel Fleet did escort several convoys down the Channel and off shore, but no enemy fleet was sighted, nor was there any clear intelligence on the location of the French and Spanish ships. Nevertheless, an invasion was feared and the government began to undertake defensive measures. In June 1779 there were only 52,602 troops, including 28,998 militia, in Britain, plus another 10,529 in Ireland.[71] That month, a bill to increase the strength of the militia was pushed through Parliament.[72] On 19 June a battalion of infantry was ordered to Plymouth to reinforce defenses there. At the end of June, orders in council called for the removal of aids to navigation from the Thames River and the removal of all horses from coastal areas in case of invasion.[73] As word reached London of preparations in France for the invasion of England and the buildup of French troops along the Channel coast,[74] many recognized that Britain was unprepared militarily to beat off an invasion by a French army. The king only expressed a widely held belief when he wrote: "[T]here is no doubt 20,000 men landed in England and 10,000 in Ireland would cause great fear," and that the Channel Fleet formed Britain's first, and perhaps only, line of defense against a French invasion.[75]

To many navy officers, the combined Franco-Spanish fleet did not appear as formidable as the expected size of this force warranted. Both Admiral Lord Mulgrave and Adm. Sir Thomas Pye, the commander in chief at Portsmouth, argued in letters to Sandwich that a squadron of thirty ships of the line was about as many ships as a single commander could control in a battle. If the Channel Fleet encountered more than thirty or so French and Spanish ships operating as a tactical unit, the result would be, in Pye's words, "anarchy and confusion" in the enemy's ranks. Further, French and Spanish officers were not used to working together and the Spaniards' ability to conduct a major fleet action seemed doubtful. In light of these considerations, Pye thought the size of the Channel Fleet should be limited to about thirty ships of the line, with any additional ships to be kept in harbor to act as "*a coupes de reserve.*" Mulgrave thought that the Channel Fleet was "sufficient at least to fight any force of the enemy's they may meet" and that Hardy should be ordered to put to sea and seek out the enemy. Middleton, on the other hand, saw nothing to be gained by ordering Hardy to sea immediately and suggested that the Channel Fleet remain in Torbay for the time being to prevent the ships from being damaged and to give more time for additional ships to be manned and fitted for service.[76]

Any thoughts of following a strategy of caution were swept

aside by a general feeling that the Channel Fleet ought to be at sea. On 8 July the Admiralty sent Hardy orders to put out to sea. If positive intelligence was obtained that the French and Spanish fleets had joined, the Channel Fleet was to take station off The Lizard far enough west so that it could not be blown into and up the Channel by westerly winds.[77] At the same time, Sandwich sent Hardy a private letter, at the king's request, informing the admiral that His Majesty wished the fleet to sail at once, for "the sooner things come to a decision the better it will be."[78] After taking on supplies and waiting for a favorable wind, the Channel Fleet sailed from Torbay on 14 July.[79]

A week later the fleet was some fourteen leagues north of Ushant, attempting to make its way southward in the face of southerly winds. Off Ushant several days later, Hardy obtained intelligence that it was "very probable that a junction of the French & Spanish fleet was made." On the basis of this information, the admiral decided to take station to the westward of The Lizard. However, owing to westerly winds, the Channel Fleet was forced eastward and northward, and on 25 July the force was off Plymouth. Hardy thereupon informed the Admiralty that he intended to remain off Plymouth unless forced eastward by the weather. In that case, he would take station in Torbay until he received further orders from London.[80]

When the Channel Fleet appeared off Plymouth, the government was "concerned." The prospect that Hardy might enter a port would "occasion very extraordinary sensations in this country." Both the king and Sandwich thought that Hardy and the Channel Fleet ought to take station west of The Lizard. The objective of the combined enemy fleets was unknown. It was thought that if the Channel Fleet took up a station west of The Lizard, it could protect both England and Ireland as well as cover East and West India convoys returning to Britain.[81] The next day, after a meeting of the cabinet, orders were issued to Hardy to take station west of The Lizard and remain there until his ships ran out of provisions and water. Hardy could abandon the position only if "some other Event should happen which from your professional knowledge and experience, may lead you to think it *absolutely necessary* to return into port."[82]

On 30 July, Hardy intercepted a trade convoy homeward bound from the Leeward Islands and sent it up the Channel. This convoy's safe arrival was a great relief to the West India merchants, for it was said to be worth four million pounds.[83] On 1 August, Hardy, still off Plymouth, received the Admiralty's instructions for the Channel Fleet to take station west of The Lizard. Hardy thereupon informed the Admiralty that, as soon as permitted, he planned to take the Channel Fleet to station ten to twenty leagues west southwest of the Isles of Scilly. In his opinion, this was "the most proper Station for the security of the trade from the East and West Indies, & for meeting the Fleets of enemy should they attempt to come into the Channel."[84] On receipt of this dispatch, the Admiralty issued a directive approving of Hardy's intentions,[85] and Sandwich wrote the admiral a letter saying:

> I dread the thought of your coming in to port; for believe me the public will not be satisfied if you return for want of provisions or even if you are driven in by contrary winds. Your enemies and mine are watching to take every advantage against us, and nothing can give them fairer ground than your coming home without having seen the enemy's fleet.[86]

Hardy was thus put on notice that he had to remain at sea until he encountered the enemy fleet. However, the wind remained contrary, and on 6 August the Channel Fleet was still off Plymouth when it encountered the homeward-bound Jamaica convoy. Because of adverse winds, the Channel Fleet, consisting of some thirty-six ships of the line, could not reach its assigned station to the west of the Isles of Scilly until 12 August.[87] By this time provisions and water were running short and sickness had broken out among the crews of some ships.[88] In a letter to Sandwich, Mulgrave stated that the Channel Fleet could probably maintain its station until the end of the month but not much longer before being forced to return to port.[89] The Franco-Spanish fleet's impending arrival in the Channel held Britain in a state of strategic suspense. Rumors concerning the enemy's intentions flew back and forth between various government officials and politicians. The marquis of Rockingham wondered "how or *how soon* it is to end."[90] Capt. Sir Samuel Hood, the commissioner of Portsmouth Dockyard, spoke with the master of a Portuguese merchant ship who claimed to have sighted "upward" of sixty French and Spanish warships twelve to fourteen leagues southwest of Ushant.[91] Lord North had information that the combined Fleet numbered seventy sail, while the king tended to view the situation in terms of Elizabeth I and the Spanish Armada and saw the threatened invasion as a religious as well as a naval test of strength between Britain and the Houses of Bourbon. His letters are laced with statements such as, "I trust in Divine Providence, the Justice of Our cause, the Bravery and Activity of my Navy."[92]

At the direction of the cabinet, the Admiralty issued further orders to Hardy on 19 August. If he had reason to believe that the Franco-Spanish fleet was avoiding battle by attempting to enter Brest, he was to attack the enemy formation. Further, Hardy was authorized to leave his station west of Scilly if remaining there meant that he could not give the "Enemy battle and prevent them going into Port." These instructions were issued after London received news that sickness and damage plagued a number of French ships and that the enemy would avoid battle by entering Brest.[93]

When the French and Spanish conceived the plan for the invasion of England, they apparently did not take into account what Clausewitz called "friction" in war: a series of unforeseen and unavoidable errors, delays, and accidents that can fatally affect operations. Admiral Rodney, for instance, accurately predicted that the Spanish fleet would be delayed by adverse winds off the coast of Portugal in the voyage north from Cadiz to rendezvous with the French fleet from Brest.[94] The meeting between the French and Spanish fleets was originally to take place between 20 and 25 May. This was postponed until 15–20 June. The Spanish fleet did not even sail from Cadiz until 22 June and did not join with the French fleet off Corunna until 22–23 July. While the French fleet was standing off the northwest corner of Spain waiting for the Spanish fleet to appear, an epidemic disease broke out among the French crews. By the first week of August there were some fifteen hundred ill among the French. After spending a week exchanging signals and conducting maneuvers, the Franco-Spanish fleet headed north toward the English Channel. Again, contrary winds were encountered and it was mid-August before the forty-five[95] ships of the combined Franco-Spanish fleet arrived in the western approaches of the English Channel.[96]

Forty-two miles southeast of Scilly, HMS *Marlborough*, HMS *Ramillies*, HMS *Isis*, and HM sloop *Cormorant* fell in with the Franco-Spanish fleet on their way to join Hardy. At first, the British did not realize that this huge force "like a wood on the water" was the enemy, and HMS *Marlborough* was almost captured before discovering the identity of the fleet. Chased by enemy units, the British ship managed to escape, and the captain of HMS

Marlborough sent his first lieutenant, Sir Jacob Wheate, into Plymouth on HM sloop *Cormorant* to carry the news of the enemy fleet's arrival in the Channel to the Admiralty in London. Wheat arrived at Plymouth in the early hours of 16 August, and the lieutenant mounted the first of a succession of horses to carry the news to London.[97]

Pandemonium burst forth at Plymouth. Admiral Lord Shuldham, the navy commander at Plymouth, immediately ordered two fast vessels to be sent with this news and ordered HM sloop *Cormorant* to proceed to Portsmouth to warn any British ships that might be sailing down the Channel that the enemy was off the Cornish coast. At 1 P.M., the panic at Plymouth increased when the lookout on Marker Heights reported that the Franco-Spanish fleet was in sight. Troops of the Plymouth garrison, which consisted of the two battalions, were moved into position to oppose an enemy landing, and the militia from the surrounding countryside began to arrive in the city. Some five hundred seaman and dockyard workers were mobilized to serve as gunners while arms were issued to other workers.[98] But after the initial alarm had passed, the British command structure at Plymouth began to fall apart. The only high official who appears to have kept his head was Shuldham, who sent a lieutenant to Marker Heights to keep him informed of the movements of the enemy and at the same time ordered Capt. Hon. George Berkeley of HMS *Firebrand* to reconnoiter the enemy fleet in a fast-sailing boat.[99] Capt. Paul Ourry, the commissioner of Plymouth Dockyard, appears to have panicked and informed Sandwich that "For some days past I have put the question to myself, Shall I, Paul Ourry, or Jack Dovilliers, set fire to the dockyard?" Ourry demanded that he be made a colonel because he had formed the dockyard workers into a battalion of infantry. Ourry also wanted to block the entrance of Plymouth harbor with a system of booms "so that no ship in may opinion can force its way through the narrows."[100] When Sandwich learned of these schemes, he concluded that "Ourry's head is turned."[101] The army commander at Plymouth, Gen. Sir David Lindsay, was so afraid of being made a scapegoat for the forthcoming disaster that he asked to be relieved of command, complaining of poor health.[102]

On 17 August the Franco-Spanish fleet, having made no hostile move toward the British, was still within sight of Plymouth. The enemy was not close enough to the port to prevent a convoy from Cork entering Plymouth.[103] HMS *Ardent,* however, was not so lucky. This ship of the line blundered into the enemy fleet and was captured as it proceeded down the Channel to join the Channel Fleet.[104] On 18 June the Franco-Spanish fleet was still about four or five leagues southwest of Plymouth, but the enemy did not undertake any action against the British other than sending a cutter to reconnoiter the entrance to Plymouth harbor. Then, on the morning of 19 August the enemy ships vanished.[105]

In the early hours of 17 August, Lieutenant Wheate arrived from Plymouth at Sandwich's house in Blackheath to inform the first lord of the Admiralty that the combined Franco-Spanish fleet was "in the Chops of the Channel" and that it "consisted of 63 sail and that they had no transports with them."[106] When this news arrived in London, it became British strategy to take every possible measure to counter the threat of invasion while at the same time attempting to trap the enemy fleet in the Channel. The French had no naval base on the Channel coast east of Brest, and the Channel Fleet was cruising to the west of the Isles of Scilly. As Sandwich explained the situation: "Sir Charles Hardy is off Scilly, & while the Wind is easterly cannot get back into the Channel, but the first shift of wind must bring him back, & a battle seems inevitable."[107] If the Franco-Spanish fleet could be driven or drawn up the English Channel, the enemy might suffer the same fate as the Spanish Armada.

In an attempt to block the eastern end of the Channel, the Admiralty issued orders on 18 and 19 August that every possible ship at the Nore and Spithead proceed to The Downs. At the same time, directions were issued for assembling pilots, press gangs with their tenders, and other armed vessels at The Downs. The commander in chief at The Downs, Rear Adm. Francis William Drake, was ordered to recall all his cruisers and collect his whole squadron. Simultaneously, all navigation aids along the south coast of England were ordered removed.[108] On 21 August two squadrons of frigates and cutters were ordered to range along the French coast to intercept invasion craft and obtain intelligence.[109] The next day, all post office packets and revenue cutters were placed under the orders of the Admiralty. On 28 August all French prisoners of war began to be moved to places of confinement inland.[110] In the end, none of these measures was necessary, for the Franco-Spanish fleet never came up the English Channel and there was no attempt to invade England.

On 17 August, some twenty leagues southwest of the Isles of Scilly, HMS *Southampton* joined the Channel Fleet and informed Hardy that the Franco-Spanish fleet was off Cornwall.[111] With the *Southampton*'s arrival, Hardy's force consisted of thirty-eight ships of the line, three 50-gun ships, and seventeen smaller warships.[112] Upon receipt of the *Southampton*'s intelligence, Hardy, though outnumbered, attempted to work eastward toward the enemy. However, almost continual contrary winds meant that it took several days for the Channel Fleet to beat its way eastward, and it was 29 August before Land's End was sighted. At about 4 P.M. on 29 August, HMS *Cumberland* made the signal for seeing many ships to the south. At first the British thought these ships, a convoy of French victuallers sent to resupply the enemy warships, were the Franco-Spanish fleet itself. With the wind out of the east southeast, Hardy ordered the Channel Fleet to form a line of battle and to steer south. This course was held until after midnight, when the wind altered to the south. By the morning of 31 August, the enemy had disappeared, fog greatly reduced visibility, and the Channel Fleet stood to the south "under easy sail." The Channel Fleet was now eight or nine leagues southwest of Land's End and the Franco-Spanish fleet was sighted to the westward. With the enemy in sight and the wind now out of the northwest, Hardy ordered the Channel Fleet to stand toward The Lizard in the hope of drawing the French and Spanish ships into the English Channel. Some enemy frigates appeared to be attempting to close with the Channel Fleet, but the main body of the Franco-Spanish fleet seemed to be avoiding an engagement. However, the British ships, outsailing the French and Spanish vessels, drew away from the enemy. At 4 P.M., only six enemy ships could be seen from the masthead of HMS *Terrible*. The wind changed to the eastward as darkness fell. The next morning, 1 September, the weather was hazy and the Franco-Spanish fleet was not to be seen. With the wind out of the west, the Channel Fleet came to anchor off Plymouth to prevent being forced to leeward up the Channel.[113]

While the Channel Fleet was at anchor off Plymouth, Hardy wrote a dispatch to the Admiralty stating that the Franco-Spanish fleet was thought to be to the southeast and that he would do his "utmost to draw them up the Channel." However, as soon as the wind and tide permitted, he would proceed to St. Helens with the Channel Fleet in the hope of being further reinforced and resupplied with beer and water. He also wanted to put "a great number of sick" ashore at Portsmouth. When the wind shifted to the north and the tide turned to flood on the evening of 1 September, the Channel Fleet proceeded eastward up the Channel toward Portsmouth. In the evening of 2 September, the Channel Fleet was off the Bill of Portland. At 4 P.M. on 3 September, fifty-one days after sailing from Torbay, the Channel Fleet came to anchor at Spithead without having fired a shot at the enemy.[114] The question on everybody's mind when the Channel Fleet arrived at Spithead was what had happened to the combined Franco-Spanish fleet? Nobody in Britain knew the enemy's location or intentions. What the British did not realize was that the enemy fleet sighted on 31 August was already crippled as a fighting force, with provisions running short and the crews of the ships increasingly sickly. Further, the Franco-Spanish fleet had no pilots with any knowledge of the south coast of England. Several days after losing contact with the Channel Fleet, the commander of the Franco-Spanish fleet, Admiral d'Orvilliers, decided to end the operation and proceed to Brest. On 10 September the Franco-Spanish fleet entered Brest Harbor. The French ships alone sent several thousand men ashore sick.[115] The attempt to invade England in the summer of 1779 failed without any assistance from the British, collapsing under the weight of poor planning, lack of coordination, and ill luck.

Hardy's arrival at Spithead with the Channel Fleet caused consternation. The Franco-Spanish fleet was still thought to be off the southern coast of England, and it was feared in some quarters that the Channel Fleet would be blockaded in Spithead.[116] Even though Sandwich thought that anchoring the Channel Fleet at Spithead rather than St. Helens made little difference "with regard to their getting to sea," both the first lord of the Admiralty and the king thought it best for Sandwich to go to Portsmouth to ensure that the Channel Fleet was resupplied and quickly made ready for sea.[117] Aside from speeding the Channel Fleet back to sea, Sandwich probably wanted to inspect the force personally in order to see if the disputes generated by the Keppel-Palliser affair had subsided. He may also have wished to verify reports that Hardy was an ineffectual commander.[118]

Sandwich arrived at Portsmouth on the morning of 5 September and first met with Mulgrave. In the course of this meeting, Mulgrave expressed his general approval of Hardy's conduct and informed Sandwich "it is absolutely necessary" to support Hardy "against the remains of Admiral Keppel's party." Sandwich next went onboard HMS *Victory* and held a long meeting with Hardy and informed the admiral that it was absolutely imperative that the Channel Fleet put to sea as soon as possible. While onboard, Sandwich also consulted with Kempenfelt and the first lord of the Admiralty, then left the flagship and proceeded to other ships of the fleet to consult with their officers. That night, Portsmouth was thrown into a panic when a convoy of victuallers was mistaken for the enemy battle fleet.[119]

The next day, Sandwich inspected the Victualling Office at Portsmouth and continued his consultations with officers of the Channel Fleet. Fears of a renewed outbreak of the Keppel-Palliser affair were heightened by the arrival of a number of opposition politicians in Portsmouth.[120] According to Sandwich, one of these, Benjamin Keene, began "fishing everywhere" for information to discredit Hardy and to promote Lord Howe to the command of the Channel Fleet. However, nothing came of his efforts and Sandwich concluded that, while "the remains of Admiral Keppel's party still exists," everything in the Channel Fleet was "in perfect good humour, as much as it can be." After visiting the Portsmouth Victualling Office again on 7 September "to see that everything went as right about sending off the water and provisions," Sandwich concluded that his presence at Portsmouth was no longer required and decided to return to London the next day.[121]

While Sandwich was at Portsmouth, intelligence began to arrive in England indicating that the Franco-Spanish crews were sickly and that the force was proceeding to Ushant.[122] Although the threat from the enemy fleet appeared to be receding, Britain was still subjected to a continuing series of panics and alarms. On 6 September, London learned of unusual activity along the French coast.[123] It appeared the French were assembling shipping at St. Malo and Cancale Bay to invade the Channel Islands.[124] To counter this threat, Hardy was ordered to remain at Spithead with the bulk of the Channel Fleet, while Rear Adm. Sir John Lockhart Ross cruised off the French coast with a force of twenty-one warships to protect the Channel Islands.[125] After cruising off St. Malo without result, Ross's squadron returned to Spithead on 25 September.[126]

While Ross's detachment from the Channel Fleet was off the French coast, London heard the first reports of Commodore John Paul Jones's "mad cruise."[127] Jones, a Scottish-born American navy officer, was perhaps the best known of a number of American naval raiders who operated out of French ports during the war. On 14 August, Jones sailed from Groix Roadstead in Brittany in command of a small squadron of warships and privateers.[128] Nine days later, Jones's squadron appeared off the south coast of Ireland. Heading north through the Irish Sea, Jones captured the British military storeship *Union* off the west coast of Scotland and then sailed around the northern end of Britain. On 17 September, Jones's squadron could be seen from the walls of Edinburgh Castle. After leaving the Firth of Forth, Jones proceeded south along the east coast of Britain, spreading alarm and panic among the population who deluged the Admiralty with letters.[129] On 23 September, Jones's squadron intercepted a homeward-bound Baltic convoy off the coast of Yorkshire. The merchant ships escaped, but the convoy's escort, the frigate HMS *Serapis,* was taken by Jones after a celebrated single-ship action. Then, eluding the numerous British warships that had been dispatched to hunt him down, Jones arrived in the Texel on 3 October.[130]

The appearance of the Franco-Spanish fleet in the Channel, Hardy's seeming retreat to Spithead without giving battle, and Jones's cruise around Britain all gave the impression that the Royal Navy was incapable of countering the king's enemies in British seas. The situation demanded action, and on 7 October the government directed the Channel Fleet to sea.[131] Hardy's instructions were to sail from Spithead and cruise between The Lizard and Ushant "or on any such station as from any intelligence you may receive of the motions of the enemy's Fleets" to protect the coasts of Britain and Ireland as well as the trade proceeding to England. The admiral was further ordered to stay at sea for as long as the Channel Fleet's provisions and water permitted and only then return to Spithead.[132]

Because of westerly winds, it was 22 October before Hardy sailed from Spithead with thirty-seven ships of the line. Six days later, the weather forced the Channel Fleet into Torbay, where Hardy received intelligence that widespread sickness meant that the Franco-Spanish fleet was in no condition to put to sea.[133] The Channel Fleet remained in Torbay until 16 November, when Hardy again put to sea to attempt to take station at the western entrance of the English Channel. Six days later, Hardy received Admiralty orders directing the Channel Fleet to return to harbor to avoid the risk of ship damage from autumn weather. It was now "highly probable that the Combined fleet will not put to sea to invade

Great Britain and Ireland," these orders explained.[134] Accordingly, Hardy returned to Spithead and the Channel Fleet came to anchor in that port on 24 November.[135] The fleet's short autumn cruise did not accomplish much, if anything, for Hardy had gotten to sea too late to protect the homeward-bound trade, most of which had already reached England before the fleet left Spithead. There was, in fact, no enemy threat to Britain and Ireland, for the Franco-Spanish fleet was not at sea. After Hardy's autumn cruise, a number of officers like Kempenfelt concluded that perhaps the best future policy would be to keep the Channel Fleet in port in late autumn to avoid exposing the ships to damage from the stormy weather.[136]

To many, the Channel Fleet's performance in 1779 had been less than stellar. There had been no engagement with the Franco-Spanish fleet even though the enemy had entered the English Channel and appeared off Plymouth. The enemy allies' attempt to invade Britain had not collapsed because the enemy was decisively defeated in a pitched battle. The British learned later that the invasion attempt had collapsed because of disease among the enemy crews, bad planning, faulty coordination, and poor execution. To many observers, the Channel Fleet seemed to have contributed nothing, sailing aimlessly to the west of Scilly without fighting while the Franco-Spanish fleet entered the Channel, appeared off Plymouth, and then inexplicably disappeared.

None of this inspired confidence in Hardy as a commander. Even before the end of the 1779 campaign, many dismissed him as aimless and indecisive. The gossip Horace Walpole thought the admiral a "dotard."[137] More to the point, his captain of the fleet, Kempenfelt, thought that while there was "a fund of good nature in the man," there was also "not one grain of commander-in-chief."[138] In fairness to Hardy, it should be noted that in the summer of 1779 he was the only person on the British side who could have lost the war in an afternoon by seeking out the enemy, fighting a decisive battle, and losing it. Hardy was cautious and fought no battles. In the end, the enemy invasion never occurred.

Nevertheless, what Britain and, above all, the government wanted in the autumn of 1779 was an admiral with the skill, drive, and luck to fight and win battles. The search for a fighting admiral lead to Number 4 Cleveland Row, London, the residence of Vice Adm. Sir George Bridges Rodney. Unemployed since 1774 and living in the verge of St. James's palace to escape his creditors,

Rodney was a political supporter of the government's American policy, as well as an officer who would not permit any kind of insubordination and an admiral who could win battles. Overbearing, carrying himself with aristocratic hauteur, displaying his Tory principles like a flag, at loggerheads with everybody, and always just one step ahead of his creditors, Rodney crashes across the pages of history, alternately grasping for and squandering money. He had made a fortune in prize money but was said to have spent thirty thousand pounds on one parliamentary election and gambled away great sums at White's. When commander at Jamaica, Rodney became embroiled in an almost endless fight with the Navy Board over his handling of official monies and finally had to flee to Paris to escape his creditors. The last king's letter boy to enter the Royal Navy, Rodney was feared and disliked by his subordinates, of whom he had a low opinion. Rodney used and abused the patronage opportunities of high command to the fullest possible extent and even went so far as to promote his fifteen-and-a-half-year-old son, a junior lieutenant, to the rank of post captain in a period of ten days. Though Rodney was overbearing, avaricious, difficult, and uncongenial, he was, nevertheless, a great admiral and an original thinker in naval matters.[139]

During the negotiations, which resulted in the admiral being appointed commander in chief in the Leeward Islands, Sandwich and Rodney must have approached each other like two wary old dogs. Rodney knew by looking at the navy list and reading the newspapers that Sandwich needed an admiral who could fight and win battles. Sandwich, from an endless succession of petitions and begging letters knew that Rodney desperately wanted employment. The trick would be to get the admiral's creditors to stop hounding him and to figure out a way to put Rodney in command of a fleet without giving him opportunities to misuse public money. These problems were overcome when Rodney negotiated a separate truce with his creditors by convincing them that the only way they would ever recover their money was to allow him to leave his home so that he could return to active service.[140] Sandwich, knowing Rodney's lack of restraint with public funds, surrounded the admiral with agents of the controller of the navy, the chief guardian of the service's finances. As the first lord explained to the king, Rodney would not "have any temptation to make advantage of purchasing stores or anything else of that sort, he will have no means of doing it at present, as there will be a Commissioner on the Spot thro' whose hands all that business must be transacted."[141] The commissioner was Capt. John Laforey, a friend and confidant of Middleton, appointed on 26 November 1779 with exceptional powers.[142] As a further precaution, another of Middleton's men, Lt. Walter Young, was made a member of Rodney's official family. An agent for transports at Deptford, Young was yanked out of the Deptford Dockyard and promoted to captain to serve as Rodney's captain in HMS *Sandwich*.[143] Surrounded by Middleton's agents, Rodney's troubles at the Navy Office over his accounts from the Jamaica command miraculously disappeared, and on 1 October 1779 he was appointed to be commander in chief in the Leeward Islands.[144]

While the threat of invasion was receding in the autumn of 1779, the government undertook a strategic reassessment of the war.[145] On 16 September the cabinet decided to send five thousand troops and nine or ten ships of the line (five or six from the Channel Fleet) to the West Indies. The decision to reassign ships to the Indies from the Channel and Rodney's appointment to command in the Leeward Islands were steps toward making the West Indies the major seat of the naval war. This reversed the traditional British strategy of controlling the western approaches of the Channel in great strength, and later critics claimed that failure to maintain naval superiority in European seas gave the French and Spanish the strategic initiative in the American war. Simultaneously, the government decided to resupply the garrisons of Gibraltar and Minorca.[146] At the end of October, the cabinet ordered the reinforcements for the West Indies and the ships carrying the supplies to Gibraltar and Minorca to sail together escorted by a squadron under Rodney's command. At this time, Sandwich was directed to draw up all the necessary plans, lists of ships, and orders required for the operation. On 4 November, Sandwich proposed to the cabinet that Rodney sail from Spithead as soon as possible. The naval escort would consist of five ships of the line: a 44-gun ship, three frigates, and a sloop. When the force was well out into the Atlantic, the ships bound to the West Indies, escorted by three small warships, would be detached while Rodney proceeded to Gibraltar with the ships of the line and the transports, storeships, and victuallers for the resupply of the Mediterranean bases. After Gibraltar and Minorca had been resupplied, Rodney was to sail to the West Indies with four ships of the line, while the fifth ship of the line returned to England. Sandwich's suggestion that Rodney's force for the resupply of Gibraltar and Minorca be reinforced by a detachment from the Channel Fleet was rejected.[147]

The decision to support the resupplying of the Mediterranean bases with only five ships of the line was overturned. Many besides Sandwich thought it dangerous to cover this operation with so few ships. For example, John Robinson, North's right-hand man at the treasury, estimated that a squadron of at least ten capital ships would be required.[148] In the end, the advocates of a strong force won out and it was decided to detach ships from the Channel Fleet to form a squadron of twenty ships of the line under Rodney to resupply Gibraltar and Minorca.[149]

Eighteenth-century military machines were, even at the best of times, incapable of leaping into instant action. Rodney arrived at Portsmouth to take up his new command on 16 November and informed the Admiralty that he would use "all possible dispatch" in getting his flagship HMS *Sandwich* ready for sea.[150] Nevertheless, well over a month passed before Rodney's force was ready for sea. Not only would the warships have to be made ready for sea, but the ships also had to be loaded with troops, stores, and provisions. The first order for transports to carry the troops was issued on 23 October. It was not until 10 December that all the necessary troops, stores, and provisions had been embarked at Spithead and Plymouth.[151] This was no small task, for Rodney's force at Spithead consisted of fifteen ships of the line, one 44-gun ship, six frigates, and nineteen transports carrying the 88th and 89th regiments and recruits for both Gibraltar and the West Indies, twenty-five victuallers, and eleven naval and military storeships. At Plymouth, a further seven ships of the line, a frigate, and nine transports carrying the 2/73rd foot waited to join Rodney off that port.[152] That a force of this size could be assembled, fitted out, and equipped in just two months was no small achievement in an era not noted for rapid governmental action.

As the ships, supplies, and men were being assembled, Rodney passed the time writing letters when not actually supervising the preparations. To the Admiralty, he sent letters about technical matters such as signal flags, the embarkation of flat-bottomed boats, and the fitting of locks on the guns of the ships of his squadron.[153] These locks were mechanisms similar to those used to fire muskets and, according to Rodney, they would allow the guns to be fired faster than those fired by matches. In 1779 the Admiralty refused to fit locks on ships' guns because there was no "establishment for it," but Rodney persisted and by 1782 the Royal Navy was fitting locks to ships' guns. The use of locks not only increased the rate of fire of guns but also reduced the number of casualties from accidental gunpowder explosions.[154] To Sandwich, the admiral wrote encouraging letters, at the same time complaining of the actions of other navy officers such as Adm. Sir Thomas Pye, the commander at Portsmouth.[155] Rodney also sent a number of letters to leading politicians on matters of patronage.[156] Then, on 9 December the Admiralty issued a complete list of ships under Rodney's command and the secret orders calling for him to escort the West India convoy out into the Atlantic and resupply Gibraltar and Minorca before proceeding to the West Indies.[157]

On 11 December, Rodney wrote to thank Sandwich for giving him such an important command and to say that he would put to sea as soon as the wind came around to the east.[158] With an eastern wind on Christmas Day, Rodney's squadron and the two convoys sailed from St. Helens.[159] Rodney's departure was so precipitous that some of the West India trade was left behind in The Downs. After being joined by the ships from Plymouth, Rodney proceeded out of the Channel into the Bay of Biscay. On 4 January 1780 at 46°2' N, 13°12' W, Capt. Sir Hyde Parker Jr. was detached with HMS *Phoenix*, HMS *Hector*, HMS *Greyhound*, and HM cutter *Tapageur* to escort the West Indies convoy and the transports carrying the 88th and 89th regiments and recruits.[160]

Far out in the Atlantic to the westward of Portugal, Rodney's squadron sighted twenty-two strange sails on the northeastern horizon at daylight on the morning of 8 January. With the wind blowing from the southeast, Rodney ordered the convoy to lay to under the escort of HMS *Pearle* and hoisted the signal for a general chase. The copper-bottomed British ships quickly overhauled the strange sails, which proved to be a Spanish convoy of fifteen merchant ships escorted by a ship of the line, four frigates, and two smaller warships.[161] At 11 A.M. the leading British ship, HMS *Bienfaisant*, entered the main body of the enemy convoy. As the Spanish flags were being hauled down, the *Bienfaisant* drew alongside and began to engage the single Spanish ship of the line, the 64-gun *Guipuzcoana*, which quickly struck after filling the requirements of military honor. By noon the British victory was complete, for every one of the Spanish ships had been captured after only token resistance.[162]

The British had captured a convoy belonging to the Royal

Company of Caracas carrying naval stores, provisions, and bale goods from San Sebastian to Cadiz. Rodney took the newly built *Guipuzcoana* into British service commissioning her as HMS *Prince William* in honor of the king's son who was serving in his squadron.[163] HMS *America* and HMS *Pearle* were ordered to escort back to England all the prizes except for several Spanish warships and those vessels loaded with provisions for the Gibraltar garrison.[164]

As Rodney's squadron proceeded, intelligence was received that a Spanish squadron of fourteen ships of the line was cruising off Cape St. Vincent to intercept British ships proceeding to Gibraltar. Rodney could have attempted to avoid this Spanish squadron by not making a landfall at Cape St. Vincent and swinging farther out into the Atlantic to approach the Strait of Gibraltar from the west or southwest. Instead, though encumbered with a convoy, Rodney decided to fight the Spanish with his eighteen ships of the line and the undermanned HMS *Prince William*.[165] Before reaching Cape St. Vincent, the British admiral issued orders to his captains to prepare for a fleet action.[166]

On the morning of 16 January, Rodney's squadron and convoy sighted the northern shore of Cape St. Vincent. By noon most of the British ships had passed around the cape ten or fifteen miles from the Portuguese coast. At 1 P.M., HMS *Bedford* sighted "a fleet of 15 sail to the SE," and a little later, eleven enemy ships could been seen from Rodney's flagship HMS *Sandwich*.[167] With nineteen ships of the line, Rodney had intercepted a Spanish squadron of eleven ships of the line and two frigates commanded by Adm. Don Juan de Langara.[168]

At this point, the tactical situation was far from clear. The wind was blowing fresh out of the west, there was a heavy swell, the sky was overcast, and it was hazy with occasional squalls. The meteorological conditions were very similar to those twenty-five years later at Trafalgar. The Spanish were obviously taken by surprise, for they would not have remained off Cape St. Vincent had they known the strength of the British force. De Langara must have been taken aback when the whole of Rodney's squadron hove into sight. Several months after the event, Young wrote to Middleton that when the Spanish were first sighted, he urged Rodney, who was ill and in bed, to order a general chase. Had the admiral followed his advice, Young claimed, the whole Spanish squadron would have been captured by nightfall. The picture that

Young paints of Rodney is one of a weak, indecisive, and ailing admiral who was dragged into battle by a captain.[169] Things were not this simple. For one thing, it was contrary to Rodney's character, whether in good or bad health, to have fleet tactics dictated to him by a newly minted captain. Secondly, Rodney had to consider the protection of the convoy and the lee shore. Finally, Rodney had to weigh the question of whether de Langara was alone or whether the Spanish squadron was part of a larger force hidden from the British by haze and squalls. Rodney had to exercise caution until the enemy's strength was known.

Rodney quickly discovered that de Langara's force was not the vanguard of a superior enemy fleet. The admiral began to issue a series of orders that resulted in the destruction of the Spanish squadron. Shortly after 2 P.M., Rodney ordered the signal for a general chase. This was quickly followed by orders to engage the enemy in rotation: as the Spanish ships were overhauled, the leading British ships attacked the first unengaged Spanish ship they encountered. Next came the signal to engage the enemy from the leeward, for the heavy swells prevented the enemy from opening the leeward lower-deck gun ports. At 3 P.M. the Spanish ships of the line were fleeing to the southward in disorder, while eighteen British copper-bottomed ships quickly overhauled de Langara's squadron.

At about 4 P.M. the leading British ships began to engage the rearmost enemy ships. Outnumbered and attacked from the rear by a succession of British ships, the Spanish squadron would be destroyed piecemeal. Each minute the engagement lasted, more and more British ships went into action. Rodney's tactics in the Moonlight Battle were the naval equivalent of Liddel Hart's concept of the "expanding torrent." The battle began when HMS *Edgar* passed the sternmost Spanish ship, the *Santo Domingo,* giving her a broadside. Within minutes the *Santo Domingo* received another broadside from HMS *Marlborough* and then another from HMS *Ajax.* At 5 P.M., as HMS *Bienfaisant* approached the stern of the Spanish ship, the *Santo Domingo* exploded in a sheet of flame and completely disappeared. After being raked by HMS *Marlborough* and HMS *Ajax,* the next Spanish ship, the *Princesa,* was engaged for more than an hour by HMS *Bedford* before surrendering. At 5:30 P.M., the shot-riddled *Princesa* was taken by a boarding party from HMS *Resolution.* Two hours later, HMS *Defence* overtook the 80-gun *Fenix,* approaching de

Langara's flagship on the port quarter and engaging her for an hour and a half. HMS *Montagu* then passed along the windward side of the *Fenix*, firing two broadsides into the Spaniard. Next, HMS *Prince George* appeared on the *Fenix*'s starboard quarter and shot down her mizzenmast. By now the *Fenix* was helpless, with her lower deck awash, de Langara wounded, and her mizzenmast gone. About 8:30, HMS *Bienfaisant* drew near and with a few rounds shot away the *Fenix*'s main-topmast, bringing the Spanish flagship's surrender.

Relentlessly, the British pursued the hapless Spanish squadron through heavy seas illuminated by flashes of gunfire and the watery light of the winter moon. After passing the hard-pressed *Fenix*, HMS *Montagu* chased the *Diligente* and at about 9:15 P.M. overtook that Spanish ship of the line. The British fired a broadside into the *Diligente* that brought down her main-topmast and the Spanish ship struck to HMS *Montagu*, which put a prize crew onboard the enemy ship. The next Spanish ship to be overtaken was the 70-gun *San Eugenio*, which surrendered about 11 P.M., when HMS *Cumberland* shot away all her masts. Because of heavy seas and the floating wreckage surrounding the Spanish ship, it was daylight before a prize crew from HMS *Terrible* could board the *San Eugenio*. HMS *Culloden* and HMS *Prince George* passed the mastless *San Eugenio* and overhauled and engaged the *San Julian*, which surrendered at 1:05 A.M. Despite the heavy seas, HMS *Prince George* managed to place a thirty-five-man prize crew onboard the enemy vessel. The last Spanish ship to be engaged and captured was the 70-gun *Monarca*. About 1 P.M., after escaping from one British ship of the line, the *Monarca* prevented HMS *Alcide* from pursuing her by shooting down the British ship's main-topmast. The *Monarca* might have escaped but for the frigate HMS *Apollo*, commanded by Capt. Philemon Pownell. Pownell fought an unequal running battle with the Spanish ship for about an hour and had actually forced the enemy to pull down the Spanish flag. Still, the *Monarca* might not have actually surrendered to HMS *Apollo* without the timely arrival of HMS *Sandwich*. At 2 A.M., twelve hours after first ordering a general chase, Rodney approached in HMS *Sandwich* to within musket range of the *Monarca*. Unaware that the Spanish ship had already lowered her flag, Rodney fired a broadside into her, bringing an end to the Moonlight Battle. The British victory was nearly total: only five Spanish ships of the line escaped, while one was destroyed and five others captured.

The situation confronting Rodney at the end of the Moon-light Battle was similar to what Collingwood faced after Trafalgar. At daylight on the morning of 17 January, Rodney's ships and their prizes were scattered along the coast of Algarve with a heavy sea and an onshore wind. There was a great danger that the British ships and their prizes would be forced to leeward and wrecked on the Portuguese coast. Closest to shore was HMS *Sandwich*, Rodney's flagship, attended by several other British ships and the prizes *Monarca* and *San Julian*. The British ships and the *Monarca* were able to work their way offshore and rejoin the convoy, which had plodded along all night toward Gibraltar. Nothing, however, could save the partially dismasted *San Julian*, and that ship was driven ashore shortly after 10 A.M. Meanwhile, HMS *Terrible* was standing by the dismasted *San Eugenio*, but the situation was helpless and this ship was also driven into the breakers just before noon. All the British ships with the remaining prizes—*Fenix, Diligente*, and *Princesa*—managed to work offshore. Rodney then sent two frigates to Tangier to inform the British consul "that Great Britain was again Mistress of the Straits," and on 18 January Rodney's squadron and the convoy were sighted from Europa Point on Gibraltar. With the arrival of Rodney's powerful force, the small Spanish squadron that had blockaded Gibraltar fled to the protection of the batteries at Algeciras.[170] Contrary winds and currents forced Rodney's ships past Gibraltar into the Mediterranean, and it took several days for all the British ships to beat their way into Gibraltar Harbor. Rodney himself, after first paying a visit to Tangier, did not arrive at Gibraltar until 27 January.[171]

Gibraltar was relieved, and a great victory had been won. On the voyage from England, Rodney's squadron had captured a Spanish convoy, destroyed one Spanish ship of the line, and captured seven others.[172] In his public dispatch to the Admiralty, Rodney wrote: "The Gallant Behaviour of the Admirals, Captains, Officers and Men, I had the Honor to Command, was Remarkably conspicuous. They seem'd actuated with the same Spirit and anxiously eager to exert themselves with the utmost Zeal to serve His Majesty and humble the Pride of His Enemies."[173] Privately, Rodney held a far different opinion of the conduct of his officers. In a private letter to George Jackson, the second secretary to the Admiralty and judge advocate of the Fleet, Rodney stated:

Providence has allowed me to be the happy instrument of restoring in some measure the honour of the British flag, to restore the old, good, necessary discipline, of the British navy will be of much more consequence, tis lost, it shall, it must be restored, I avoid all complaints, many, many. I had the greatest reason to make, and if the fleet I am going to command, should be as negligent and disobedient as part of that which sailed from England with me, you will hear of dismission, upon dismission, I must, I shall be obey'd. I will not tell you particular men, many brave excellent, active good officers. Others negligent, slow, inactive, disobedient, and fit for nothing.[174]

This outburst was no doubt brought about by the failure of a number of captains to obey Rodney's signal to engage the enemy from the leeward position,[175] and Rodney ascribed this breakdown of discipline to the Keppel-Palliser affair.[176]

Even before he sailed from Spithead, Rodney began the process of systematically imposing higher standards of order and discipline on the officers under his command. By issuing a constant stream of directives, complaints, threats, and orders, Rodney made it absolutely clear from the moment he took command that he would stand for nothing less than immediate obedience. For example, on 13 December 1779, Rodney issued a memorandum setting forth the duties and responsibilities of each lieutenant on every deck of a ship of the line.[177] The failure of his squadron's ships to maintain proper stations on several occasions prompted Rodney to direct that the lieutenant of the watch sign the ship's log at the end of each watch so that he would know which officer or officers to punish for permitting a ship to be out of station.[178] On 30 January 1780, Rodney ordered the captains of the ships of his command to follow "the old established customs" of the Royal Navy by forbidding the unauthorized discharge of muskets and cannon at sunset. Seventeen days later, Rodney issued a memorandum outlining the duties and responsibilities of each lieutenant onboard his flagship.[179] Rodney's memorandums and directives ranged across the whole spectrum of naval affairs. Quickly and forcibly, he made it clear to the officers of his command that he wanted things done according to established navy regulations.

Rodney sent three ships of the line and a frigate to escort victuallers and storeships to Minorca as well as to carry money to that island. However, by order of the governor of Gibraltar, Gen.

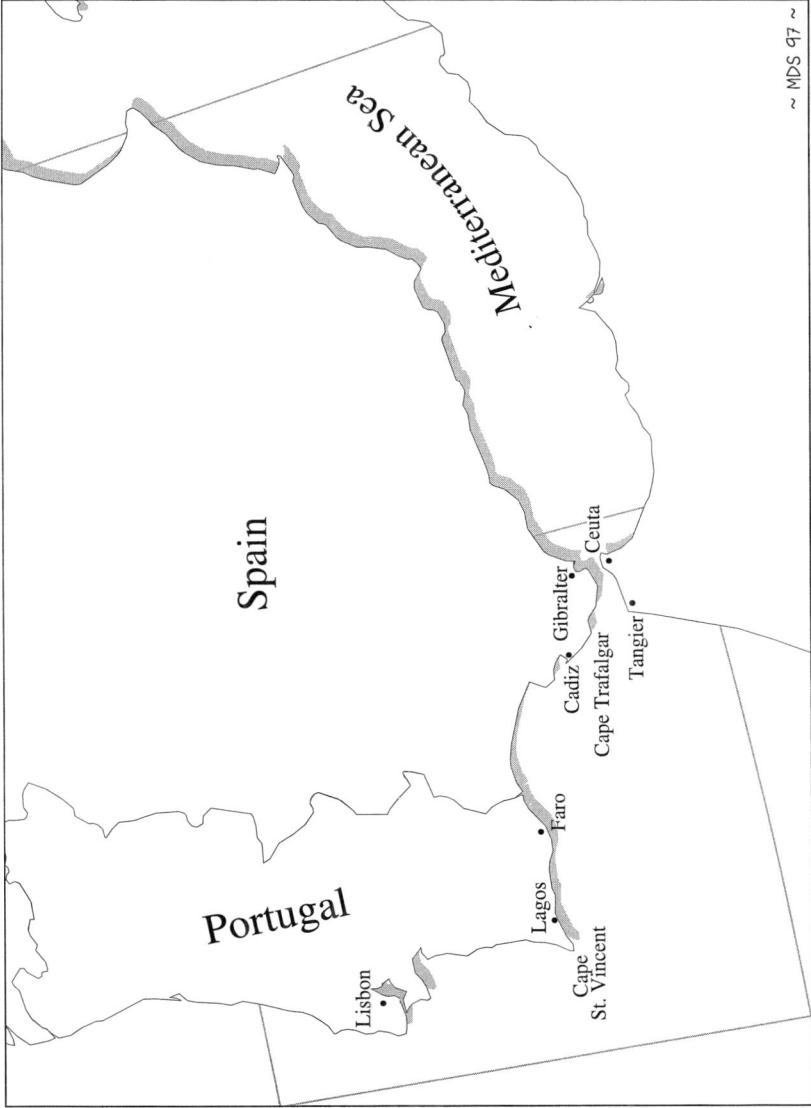

The Mediterranean Sea

~ MDS 97 ~

Spain

Portugal

Mediterranean Sea

Lisbon

Lagos

Cape
St. Vincent

Faro

Cadiz

Gibralter

Cape Trafalgar

Ceuta

Tangier

George Elliott, the 2/73rd foot was not sent on to Minorca as originally intended but instead was made part of the garrison of Gibraltar.[180] While the troops were disembarking and storeships and victuallers were being unloaded, Rodney exercised his prerogative as senior officer present to transfer and promote a number of officers into the positions created by the addition of the Spanish prizes to the Royal Navy. For example, Rodney made Capt. Sir Chaloner Ogle of HMS *Resolution* a commodore. When Sandwich made the request for political reasons, Lt. Lord Robert Manners was jumped over the rank of master and commander to replace Ogle as the captain of HMS *Resolution*.[181] Rodney became carried away with his largesse when he made Capt. John Elliot a commodore, appointed him to the navy command at Gibraltar, and then, against instructions, permitted Elliot to keep the ship of the line HMS *Edgar* at Gibraltar to fly his broad pendant. This action later produced a rebuke from Sandwich, who had to send a frigate to Gibraltar with orders for the *Edgar* to return to England.[182] The most important appointment made by Rodney while at Gibraltar was making Gilbert Blane, M.D., physician of the Fleet under his command.[183] Rodney invented this position and gave Blane authority to deal with all the medical problems of the ships under his command. In the words of one authority, this was "an act of high-handed patronage which had the most beneficial results," for Blane took his duties seriously and became one of the greatest medical reformers in the history of the Royal Navy.[184]

The four warships that had been sent to Minorca having returned, Rodney's squadron sailed from Gibraltar on 13 February, with the wind out of the east.[185] In the Atlantic Ocean on 18 February, Rodney separated from the main body of the squadron with four ships of the line and two smaller warships[186] and steered for the West Indies as his instructions directed.[187] Digby proceeded to England with fifteen ships of the line,[188] escorting empty storeships, transports, and victuallers.[189] To the westward of Brittany on 23 March, Digby's squadron intercepted a French convoy of thirteen merchant ships escorted by two 64-gun ships of the line and a frigate bound to the Indian Ocean with military stores. Digby immediately gave the order for a general chase, but as soon as he sighted the mastheads of the British ships, the French convoy's commander ordered his ships to scatter while the French ship of the line *Protee* attempted to shield the other vessels as they escaped. HMS *Resolution,* supported by HMS *Bedford,* overhauled and engaged the *Protee,* which was quickly overpowered and surrendered. When the British boarded the *Protee,* they found she was carrying about sixty thousand pounds worth of silver and base coin. However, the French commander had ordered the convoy to scatter so quickly that the British were able to capture only three French snows, while the other ten French merchant ships, the ship of the line *Ajax,* and the frigate *Charmant* were able to escape. Digby sent HMS *Bienfaisant* and HMS *Royal George* into Plymouth with the *Protee* and the prizes, while the rest of his squadron proceeded to Spithead, where he arrived on 26 March.[190]

The relief of Gibraltar and Minorca was successful beyond the wildest dreams of the British. The reasons for British victory were many. The Mediterranean expedition had been mounted quickly and carried out with adequate force. It was luck that led Rodney to intercept a Spanish convoy and then a Spanish squadron of inferior strength. Copper bottoms on the British ships enabled Rodney to chase, overhaul, and engage the Spanish squadron, and Rodney's skill as a tactician resulted in every Spanish ship being engaged by more than one British ship. As well, the British outfought the Spanish during the Moonlight Battle man for man and ship for ship. After the battle ended, British seamanship saved more than two prizes from being driven on to the lee shore and destroyed. On the return voyage, luck returned to help Digby intercept and scatter a French convoy, capturing three merchant ships and a ship of the line. The British successes during the first relief of Gibraltar resulted from planning, copper bottoms, superior skills in tactics, and superb ship handling topped off by luck.

Rodney's relief of Gibraltar was the first great British naval victory during the American war. This victory was not a petty one like the capture of an American cruiser, nor a meaningless encounter like Keppel's engagement off Ushant in 1778. The first relief of Gibraltar bore no resemblance to the Channel Fleet's aimless 1779 cruises under Hardy. Gibraltar and Minorca had been resupplied and a Spanish convoy of fifteen merchant ships escorted by a ship of the line and seven smaller warships had been captured. A battle had been fought during which the British had suffered only minor casualties and one Spanish ship of the line had been destroyed, four others brought into Spithead, and two others driven on to the Portuguese coast after capture. Digby's return voyage to England scattered a French convoy and captured a

French ship of the line and three merchant ships. Booty valued at more than a million pounds sterling and about four thousand prisoners had been taken by the ships of the Royal Navy during the first relief of Gibraltar.[191] By any reckoning, this was a triumph in the best tradition of the British Navy.

Chapter 4

NEUTRALS, NAVAL STORES, AND THE ROYAL NAVY, 1778–82

Blockades have always been employed as a strategy in naval wars. In simplest terms, a blockade is the use of naval forces to deny an enemy the ability to move ships and goods across bodies of water. Though the general concept of a naval blockade is easy to understand, the conduct of a blockade not only involves the deployment of warships but also generates a complex set of diplomatic and legal problems. Whenever a naval blockade is instituted, admiralty courts and foreign offices in both belligerent and neutral nations must consider many non-naval questions. What kinds of goods are contraband? What constitutes a legal blockade? And what will be the rights and duties of neutral vessels on the high seas?

From the beginning of the American war in 1775, the Royal Navy used the weapon of blockade against the American rebels with varying degrees of success. While this policy inspired a string of protests from neutrals over the violation of their rights on the high seas, it was generally agreed in principle that international law and the laws of war gave Britain the right to seize the ships and goods of the American rebels as well as warlike materials such as arms and gunpowder onboard neutral vessels en route to America. However, with the beginning of the naval war with France in 1778, the British instituted blockades and related policies that produced diplomatic crises with neutral European powers and a war with the Netherlands.

The sinews of naval power in the age of wooden ships were naval stores. Masts, timbers, planking, tar, pitch, canvas, hemp, and ironware such as nails were required to build and maintain eighteenth-century warships. The primary European sources for most of these articles were the Baltic and Scandinavian nations. The British Isles lay like a barrier reef between the major ports and naval bases of France and Spain and the maritime approaches to those sources of naval raw materials. As a result, naval stores bound for France and Spain had to run a gauntlet of British naval bases and cruisers. During a war with France or Spain, British policy was to use blockades to keep naval stores and certain other materials from Scandinavia and the Baltic from reaching French ports. This policy produced an endless series of incidents and crises over neutral rights on the high seas, as the French, finding it impossible to use their own merchant ships to import naval stores, employed the cover of neutral flag merchantmen to accomplish that end. At the same time, it was British policy to intercept all vessels on the high seas and to seize warlike goods or naval stores bound for France.

On 29 July 1778, even before war had been officially declared, the Royal Navy was directed by an order in council to capture or destroy all French goods and ships encountered on the high seas.[1] Twenty-five days later, the Admiralty was directed to order the navy to intercept, seize, and bring into British ports any neutral vessels found to be carrying "Naval or Warlike Stores" to French ports.[2] This directive's intent was to prevent France from using the protection of a neutral flag to import naval stores for her navy. This policy embraced the doctrine that "free ships do not make free goods" and defined both contraband and blockade in terms not only unacceptable to a number of European nations but even contrary to some treaties Britain had signed.[3] In the narrowest legal definition of the term, contraband of war embraced only those items that were clearly warlike materials, such as arms and munitions. In 1778, however, the British government, as it had done before and would do again, followed a flexible definition of contraband formulated by authorities like Grotius, who divided all goods into three types. The first was arms and munitions that are clearly contraband in time of war; the second, articles of no use whatsoever in military operations that can be freely carried to an enemy; the third, goods that are not in themselves warlike materials but can be of military assistance to the enemy under certain circumstances, and, therefore, are subject to seizure as contraband on the high seas if transported by a neutral to an enemy port if owned by enemy citizens.[4]

On 22 October 1778, George Harris, the Admiralty's advocate, clearly stated Britain's legal justification for seizing naval stores and other goods found on neutral ships:

> And I further apprehend, that under particular circumstances, (of which I take the Govt. to be at liberty to admit proof if occasion should require it) even those goods, which are enumerated in the Spanish and Dutch treaties as not contraband, may also be stopped and sold in England, if they are merchandise of promiscuous use, [of which France] is either publicly known to be in great want of such merchandize for the purpose of war, or proved by the affidavits of indifferent and credible persons so to be.[5]

Depending on military and strategic circumstances, then, any object could become contraband and subject to seizure. This doctrine led the British to follow what many observers thought to be at best a contradictory policy with regard to defending contraband. For example, on 5 April 1780, the Admiralty's proctor, George Gostling, advised the Admiralty not to seize the Danish ship *Maria,* loaded with foodstuffs bound to a French port, while on 9 February 1782 the high count of Admiralty ordered that a cargo of flour onboard the Imperial ship *Saint Paul* be sold to the Royal Navy in order to prevent the flour from reaching the enemy.[6] In a legal opinion about staves written from Doctors' Commons, George Harris clearly stated the British definition of contraband:

> Stave of no sort have been as yet in my remembrance, regarded as naval stores not withstanding the quantity, in many instances have been much larger than at present. On the whole, unless it could be made to appear, or was a known fact, that the French at Brest were, at this time, in very particular want of casks for carriage of their ship provisions, I think the vessel ought not be detained, under the general order for stopping naval stores going to the enemy.[7]

This doctrine of military necessity, when carried to its logical conclusion, did not protect even goods specifically defined as non-contraband in treaties between Britain and other nations. To British admiralty courts, treaties were international agreements similar to civil contracts in that if an enemy used an article of a treaty to subvert that treaty's intent, that article of the treaty became void. For example, article four of the Anglo-Dutch Treaty of 1674 stated that naval stores were not contraband. Thus, if the French conspired with citizens of the Netherlands to use this clause to obtain naval stores under cover of the Dutch flag to wage war against the British, the treaty's intent would be clearly subverted and naval stores on Dutch ships belonging to French subjects or bound to France would be subject to seizure.[8]

Even if the Royal Navy intercepted a neutral ship carrying material that was not enemy property or bound to the enemy, the entire burden of proof still fell on the ship's master and owners. According to Harris:

> I do not apprehend it to be the meaning of any treaty, between England and Russia that the Russians shall be at liberty to carry the goods of the enemies of Gt. Britain and if I am right in this assertion, the captain of the Russian ship will be in fault, if the papers on board do not express that the cargo is for the account and risque of Russians—for, if ye cargo should in reality be Russian property, that the papers on board do not declare it so to be, the Russians have no just cause of complaint either on the foundation of general law or of treaties.[9]

To British admiralty courts, the legal definition of contraband changed according to strategic requirements and the neutral ship's master and owner were responsible for showing that a cargo was not contraband.

In addition to this constantly changing mosaic of legal opinions on the nature of contraband, the British government also employed a strategy of blockade many considered illegal. To some nations—Russia, for example—the only legal naval blockade was a "close" or "effective" blockade[10] in which warships were stationed so that they could always prevent any ship or vessel from leaving or entering a besieged port or place. If these conditions were not met, the protesting nations argued, the blockade was illegal. However, for strategic reasons, it was British policy during the American war not to blockade "closely," particularly in enemy European ports. Instead, they conducted a "distant" blockade, which called for the seizure of enemy and neutral merchant shipping on the high seas. In order to intercept all east-west movements of merchant ships along the northwest coast of Europe, British squadrons were stationed at focal points or choke points of maritime trade, like the eastern approaches of the English Channel. This strategy was considered by some a "paper" blockade and thus illegal because it was not a blockade of a particular place or port. It resulted in a general Royal Navy searching of all merchant ships passing through the English Channel.

Because of the confusion caused by disagreements over what constituted contraband and legal blockades, many neutrals, as well as belligerents, did not understand that the British government based its right to stop, search, and seize merchant ships on the high seas on the principle of national self-defense and ultimately the survival of Great Britain as a nation state. The British government believed and acted on the assumption that the unwritten law of national self-defense overrode articles in treaties and legal definitions of legal blockades and the nature of contraband. On 27 October 1778, Lord Suffolk, a secretary of state, stated Britain's position bluntly and clearly in a dispatch to the British ambassador at St. Petersburg: "The great & unanswerable principle of Self-Defense indispensably obliges His Majesty to prevent, as far as possible, his enemies from being supplied with naval or warlike stores."[11]

This failure to understand that Britain would go to almost any lengths to prevent naval stores from reaching her enemies led many neutrals and belligerents to political and strategic miscalculations. From the beginning of the fighting with France in 1778 until the end of the war, it was the unchanging policy of the British government to seize all naval stores found onboard neutral ships if they belonged to enemy subjects or were bound to enemy ports "what ever may be the consequences."[12] British diplomats stationed in Baltic and Scandinavian ports and capitals were instructed to supply detailed intelligence on all ships carrying naval stores to France. Through the use of spies, money, and all the other means at a diplomat's command to obtain information, the British Admiralty received a steady flow of intelligence from such places as Helsingör, Göteborg, Gdansk, Riga, and St. Petersburg, indicating that French agents were secretly procuring and shipping naval stores to France in neutral ships, most of them Dutch.[13] On 29 August 1778, Vice Adm. Matthew Buckle, commander in chief in The Downs, reported to the Admiralty that he had seized and brought into British ports Dutch, German, and Scandinavian ships loaded with French-bound naval stores.[14]

The Royal Navy used the squadron stationed in The Downs

as its primary instrument to prevent naval stores from reaching France. The squadron usually consisted of one ship of the line, a few frigates and sloops of war, and a score or more of small armed cutters. These were stationed in The Downs, in the Strait of Dover, and off the English and French coasts. At times, British ships even ranged along the coasts of the Netherlands.[15] It was the task of these armed cutters to intercept and inspect every merchant ship they encountered. If a merchantman, no matter what flag it flew, carried naval or warlike stores to France and Spain, the ship was to be seized and brought into an English port, by force of arms if necessary. Day after day, the warships of The Downs squadron cruised in the narrow seas between England and the Continent, seizing neutral merchant ships.

Legally, neutral merchant vessels did not have to submit to search on the high seas. British admiralty courts considered the detention, searching, and seizure of neutral merchant ships by the Royal Navy on the high seas to be "an act of superior force."[16] Using the threat or actual force of arms, the British government seized neutral merchant ships carrying naval stores on the high seas to enemy ports and imposing its own interpretation of "contraband" and legal "blockades" on various neutrals. Almost as soon as fighting began between Britain and France in 1778, the British government instituted a number of measures intended to moderate, if not prevent, the protests of neutral nations whose ships were being seized by the Royal Navy. For example, on 29 September 1778 the Admiralty was ordered to release all Dutch ships held in British ports unless they had cargoes of naval or warlike stores bound to French ports or to the American rebels. Orders were also issued to all British privateers and warships not to seize any such ships in the future.[17] At the same time, Parliament passed an act that set aside various parts of the Navigation Acts and authorized the commissioners of the navy to buy for the king's use all naval stores and other contraband found on neutral merchant ships brought into British ports.[18] On 19 October 1778 the Admiralty was directed to order the Navy Board to purchase at fair market value all naval stores that were either condemned as enemy property or "restored to the claimant upon the condition that the same shall be sold for the King's use." Further, the commissioners of the navy were ordered to pay all the neutral merchant ships' legal fees, freight, demurrage, and similar expenses.[19]

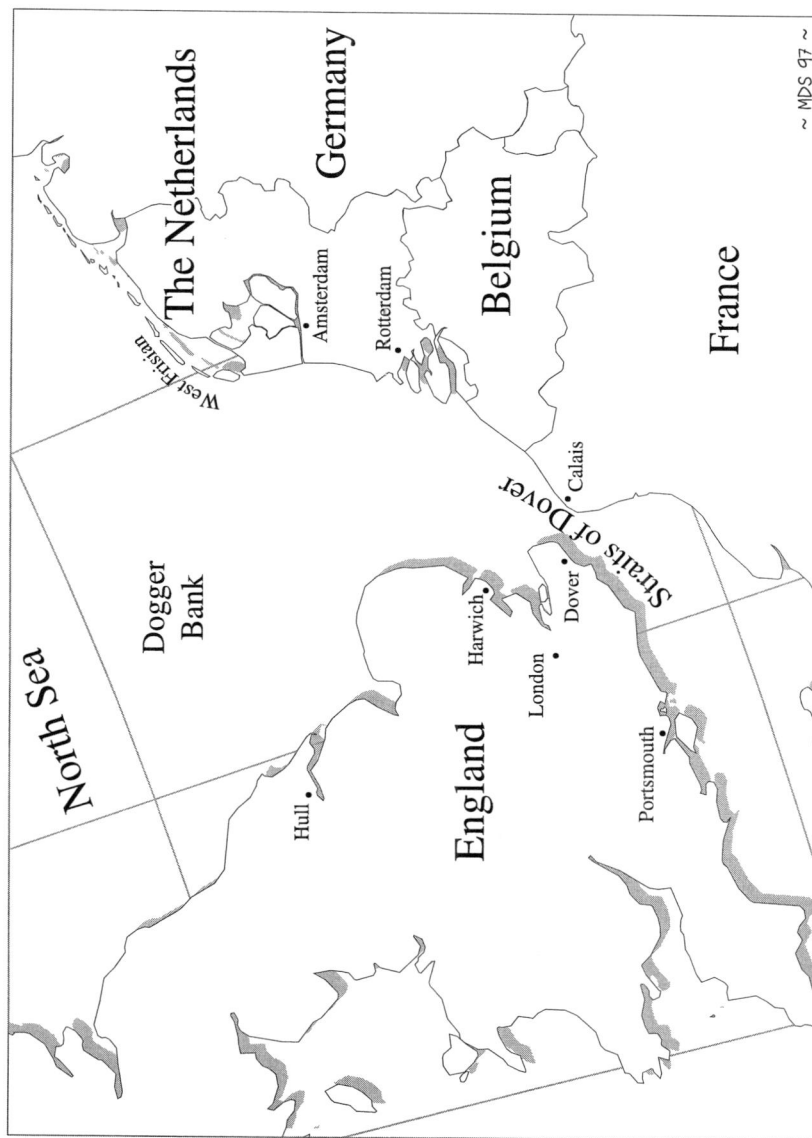

The Strait of Dover

~ MDS 97 ~

Preemptive buying of naval stores by the British government was intended to obtain additional naval stores for the Royal Navy while simultaneously preventing naval stores from reaching the French and, later, the Spanish. Further, by not condemning neutral merchant ships, by buying all naval stores not condemned as enemy property, and by paying expenses such as freight, insurance, etc., the British minimized the financial loss to the owners of the merchant ships seized by the Royal Navy. Economically, it should matter little to the owners of a Dutch merchant ship carrying a cargo of French-owned naval stores if the British seized their ships, for the cargo did not belong to the shipowners and their vessel would, in due course, be released with all expenses paid by the British government. While the preemptive buying of naval stores was very costly to the British government,[20] it was designed to show that British policy was not one of simply seizing neutral property without compensation, but rather a legitimate effort to prevent naval stores from reaching Britain's enemies.

Nevertheless, a huge diplomatic crisis erupted in various European capitals when it became known that the Royal Navy had seized merchant ships in the English Channel and carried them all, regardless of nationality, into British ports if their cargoes included naval stores bound for France. To some neutrals, the outbreak of fighting between Britain and France in 1778 was a chance for economic gain. The Dutch, for example, had earlier profited handsomely by running guns and other munitions to the American rebels through the free port on the Dutch West Indian island of St. Eustatius.[21] These profits, however, were insignificant compared to what could be made by supplying naval stores to the French by running or breaking the British blockade under cover of a neutral flag.

Other neutrals, however, saw hostilities between Britain and the French as a chance to settle noneconomic scores. For some, the issues of British seizures of naval stores on the high seas created a tempting invitation to redress the European balance of power. Others saw it as an opportunity to increase national prestige or power by becoming a third force, perhaps even mediators, in the conflict. Still others regarded British conduct toward neutrals as a moral outrage: Britain seemed to be repeating her high-handed conduct in the Seven Years' War by using brute force to dictate neutral rights on the high seas.

During the Seven Years' War, Britain could treat neutrals with a heavy hand and disregard their protests because the Royal Navy was supreme at sea. But 1778 was not 1762, and the diplomatic and military situation in Europe had changed markedly over a decade and a half. The British army was tied down in an interminable war in America, while the French army was not even engaged. The French Navy appeared capable of effectively confronting the naval power of Britain, while knowledgeable diplomatic observers saw that Spain was also slipping into war with Britain. Should that happen, the Royal Navy would be confronted, on paper at least, by enemies with overpowering naval strength. In places like Amsterdam, The Hague, Berlin, Copenhagen, Stockholm, and St. Petersburg, there were now people ready to challenge Britain's attempts to define neutral rights. It now seemed possible, as it had not been during the Seven Years' War, to force Britain to change her policies. Furthermore, in neutral capitals throughout Europe, French diplomats, French money, and French power secretly pressed the neutrals to force Britain to embrace the policy that "free ships made free goods." As the Royal Navy unremittingly continued to seize natural ships carrying naval stores to France, the question of whether or not the neutral powers might force a reversal of British policy was hotly debated in every European capital.

British seizures of naval stores presented each neutral nation with different problems or, in some cases, opportunities. For political and economic reasons, Sweden, a minor commercial and naval power but a major producer of naval stores, wanted to ship and sell naval stores to the French, but without precipitating a naval war with Britain. On 20 November 1778, Thomas Wroughton, the British ambassador to Sweden, wrote to Whitehall that he had been informed by the king of Sweden that the Baltic country "could by no means acquiesce" in the seizure of naval stores on Swedish merchant ships bound to France, acts contrary to various treaties between Sweden and Britain. Moreover, the Swedish economy would be greatly hurt because naval stores were the country's major exports. If the trade in naval stores was stopped, Sweden would have no way to pay for imports. British payment for seized Swedish cargoes would result in great losses to Swedish merchants and shipowners because these sums would not cover the entire cost of the voyages.[22] In other dispatches from Stockholm written in the autumn and winter of 1778, Wroughton told the British government that Swedish merchants were outraged and confused by the British seizures because they were un-aware of the true policy of the British government. Britain now defined contraband naval stores broadly, using the term to mean just about anything. To the Swedes, including in this definition goods such as tar, iron, and timber meant that "There is an end at once to the principal productions of this Kingdom." The Swedes also complained that British privateers were taking their ships "without the least shadow of justice."[23] On 2 March 1779, Wroughton reported that discussions of Anglo-Swedish relations with the Swedish authorities broke down because "naval stores is the Rock on which we always split, as he [the king of Sweden] says it would be equal to shutting up the ports of the Kingdom, and consequently [is something] to which the King would never acquiesce."[24]

It is clear that during the winter of 1778–79, either the Swed-ish merchants and government were unaware of the British policy of preemptive buying of naval stores or did not understand the program. The Swedes' economic problems were quickly settled. On 19 February 1779, Wroughton was directed to inform the Swedes that they should ship their naval stores directly to En-gland, where "no better market can surely exist during a state of hostilities like the present."[25] The sale of naval stores in British markets and the British policy of preemptive buying apparently satisfied Swedish merchants, for on 15 June 1779, Wroughton reported from Stockholm "that the merchants of this place are extremely pleased & contented with the manner that judgement has been passed upon some of their ships & cargoes lately by the Count of Admiralty." Economics and merchants, however, are one thing—kings and national prestige are another. In the same dispatch, Wroughton informed London that the king of Sweden had disregarded the statements of Swedish merchants and informed the British diplomat that the seizures of Swedish merchant ships by the Royal Navy were matters of "principle" and "that he had reason to complain."[26]

Throughout the winter and spring of 1779, Wroughton re-ported to London many conflicting bits of intelligence about the Swedish government's likely reaction to the British government's policy of seizing naval stores on Swedish merchant ships bound to French ports. There was talk in Stockholm of the Baltic or north-ern powers forming some kind of association to protect merchant ships from seizure.[27] There were reports that Swedish merchant ships planned to use fake papers to mask their real destinations and their cargoes' ownership.[28] There were also many reports that the Swedes were going to use warships to convoy their merchant ships to France, their objective being "to protect the commerce, and navigation of the trading subjects against any power who should endeavor to circumscribe the independency of the Swedish flag." Wroughton believed the French had subsidized the equipment of warships to escort Swedish trade.[29] The use of convoys to protect Swedish merchant ships bound to France was a clever ploy requiring nerve, but it also entailed dangers. It was not considered an act of war for the British to search a merchant ship on the high seas for contraband, but if the Royal Navy stopped and searched a warship legally commissioned by the king of Sweden, this would be an outright act of war against Sweden. It might be argued that it was already an act of war for the British to use superior force to stop, search, and seize Swedish merchant ships carrying contraband under the protection of the Swedish navy. National honor could lead to war.

In 1779 the Swedish government had to decide between war or peace. On 14 May, Lord Weymouth, a British secretary of state, directed Wroughton to inform the Swedish government that Britain would not permit neutrals to ship naval stores to France under any circumstances.[30] Writing from Stockholm on 20 July, Wroughton reported that it was his considered opinion that if the Royal Navy used force against a Swedish warship to maintain the blockade against the French, the Swedes "would take a decided part with the House of Bourbon who have animated them to this equipment and according to many appearances have contributed to the expense of it."[31] On 31 August 1779, Wroughton was ordered to inform the Swedish government that, with or without convoy, Britain would not permit Swedish merchant ships to carry naval stores to France.[32]

British resolve and Swedish nerve were put to the test on 5 December 1779, when the Swedish frigate *Trolle* and two Swedish merchant ships loaded with naval stores bound to French ports arrived in The Downs. Rear Adm. Francis William Drake, the commander of the squadron in The Downs, seized the merchant ships, and the captain of the Swedish frigate sent an officer onboard Drake's flagship to demand that the British admiral release the two merchant vessels. The Swedish officer then informed Drake that if the two ships were not released, the captain of the *Trolle* "must take such steps, as the orders from his Court have pointed out for him to pursue; which Adm. Drake understands to [be] use [of] Force, to attain his purpose." Drake then told the Swedish officer that his orders would not permit him to release the two merchantmen.

After the Swedish officer left his flagship, Drake sent an express dispatch to the Admiralty explaining the situation. At 5 A.M. on 8 December, he received instructions from the Admiralty not to release the two Swedish merchant ships and to repel force with force. On no account, however, was the admiral to fire the first shot. Drake then sent an officer onboard the *Trolle* to inform the Swedish captain of his instructions. At the same time, the secretary to the Swedish ambassador to the Court of St. James's arrived onboard the *Trolle* with orders for the Swedish warship not to attempt to regain possession of the two merchantmen. Shortly thereafter, the *Trolle* departed from The Downs, leaving behind the pair of merchant ships.[33] It is unknown whether the captain of the *Trolle* acted on his own or whether the Swedes staged the whole incident to see if the British were prepared to go to war over the question of the shipment of naval stores to France. The Swedes came closer to war than they perhaps realized at the time, for on 19 November 1779 the British government had decided to stop Dutch merchant ships from carrying naval stores to the French, even if it resulted in a war.[34] During the course of the *Trolle* incident, the British clearly convinced the Swedes that they were prepared to go to any lengths to prevent the shipment of naval stores to France. The Swedes backed down because they did not want war and because it appeared then that diplomacy might be a better way of obtaining their objectives.

Because of geography, politics, and greed, the Dutch, unlike the Swedes, were not given the opportunity to choose between war and peace. Politically, economically, and militarily, the Netherlands were caught between Britain and France. In 1778 the Dutch were a minor military and naval power with the second largest merchant marine in Europe. If the Dutch did not appease the French, the French army might invade their country. However, if the Dutch made an enemy of England, the British might use the Royal Navy to conquer Dutch colonies and destroy the Dutch economy through blockade and attacks on the nation's merchant marine and fishing fleets.

In 1674 and 1678 the British and the Dutch concluded two

treaties designed to regulate each nation's conduct if one became involved in a war. Unfortunately, the treaties were in some respects contradictory. The Anglo-Dutch Commercial and Maritime Treaty of 1674 specifically stated that naval stores were not contraband and that if one power was at war, the other had the right to trade with both the warring powers. Only warlike materials, narrowly defined as arms and munitions, were considered contraband and subject to seizure. But the Anglo-Dutch Alliance of 1678 required the Dutch to aid Great Britain with six thousand troops and twenty warships should the British become involved in a war.[35]

With the Anglo-French naval war with France of 1778, it became British policy to seize all Dutch merchant ships carrying naval and warlike stores to French ports but not to demand that the Dutch supply the troops and warships called for under the Anglo-Dutch Alliance of 1678. It was acceptable to the British for the Dutch to carry on trade as in peacetime so long as they did not ship naval or warlike stores to the French. If the Dutch did not ship naval stores to the French, they could continue to enjoy all the other advantages of the Treaty of 1674 and bear none of the burdens of the Alliance of 1678.[36] On 1 September 1778, the British ambassador to The Hague, Sir Joseph Yorke, informed the stadtholder of the Netherlands that Dutch merchant ships were transporting naval stores to France and that the Royal Navy had orders to seize any such Dutch ships.[37] Further, if a Dutch ship was found to carry naval stores to France, the whole matter would be turned over to the High Court of Admiralty, where it would be handled, in the words of Yorke, "with the most impartial justice."[38] On the other hand, if a Dutch merchant ship was stopped and found to be free of naval or warlike stores for France, the ship and cargo would be immediately released even if it carried French goods between French ports.[39] To strengthen this policy and to ensure that both the Dutch and the commanders of British warships understood British policy in regard to Dutch shipping, an order in council on 14 December 1778 directed all British warships not to seize any Dutch merchant ships except those carrying warlike or naval stores to French ports.[40] This precaution did not placate Dutch merchants and shipowners, whose protests intensified as the Royal Navy put this policy into effect.[41]

To avoid the possibility of seizure by the British in the English Channel, several hundred merchant ships had taken shelter in the Texel. This great mass of shipping was to be escorted down the

English Channel by nine Dutch warships. Nearly all of the merchant ships carried innocent cargoes, but there were at least fifteen ships loaded with naval stores intermixed with the convoy. These had not been given instructions and signals by the commander of the escort,[42] and hence, according to British law, they were not legally a part of the convoy even though they were physically part of the group.[43] There were also a number of merchant vessels that had received instructions and signals from the escort commander that carried mixed cargoes of innocent goods and naval stores. The British were not ready for a showdown with the Dutch in the autumn of 1778, so they permitted this convoy to pass down the Channel unmolested although they realized this meant that some naval stores would reach French ports.[44]

This was, however, the first and the last Dutch convoy of merchant ships that the British allowed to pass unmolested down the Channel. While the Dutch government was deciding whether to permit ships carrying naval stores to be escorted by Dutch warships, Yorke informed the Dutch authorities that in the future the British would not permit Dutch ships to carry naval stores to France under any circumstances.[45] On 3 November, the British ambassador assured Suffolk that if the British stood firm, the Dutch would forbid naval stores to be convoyed to France and would, in the end, "let their merchants clamor on, till they sink into an acquiescence. . . . In this manner your objective will be obtained, tho' with bad grace."[46] Several days later, Suffolk informed Yorke that what the Dutch did was of no real importance, for "if the Dutch push us to the wall, and, like Shylock in the play, will be contented with nothing but their bond, the moderation and forbearance we wish to show must be superseded by a less scrupulous conduct."[47]

While British, French, and Dutch politicians, diplomats, and merchants spent 1779 arguing over such things as limited and unlimited convoys, the rights of neutrals, and the nature of contraband during 1779, the Royal Navy's squadron in The Downs hunted enemy cruisers, convoyed British trade, and stopped, searched, and seized neutral merchant ships carrying naval and warlike stores to Britain's enemies. This operation was a dirty, dangerous, and frustrating assignment, but when carried out correctly, paid big dividends. On many occasions, intelligence (largely from British diplomats) enabled Drake to deploy ships and vessels to intercept a particular neutral ship or group of ships carrying contraband. For example, on 15 March 1779, Drake reported to the Admiralty that he had directed HM cutter *Wells* and two hired armed cutters to cruise between the South Sand and Calais to intercept a neutral ship loaded with cannon bound for Toulon.[48] Drake's dispatches to the Admiralty contain scores of accounts of the interception and seizure of neutral merchant ships carrying contraband down the Channel to enemy ports.[49]

Intercepting neutral merchant ships was just one of the many tasks of The Downs squadron. Ships also had to be deployed to escort vessels carrying flaxseed from Dutch ports to Ireland and Scotland[50] and merchant ships on their way to either London or Spithead.[51] Furthermore, escorts had to be supplied to British merchant ships proceeding to neutral ports on the Channel.[52] Another task of the squadron was hunting down enemy cruisers operating in English coastal waters and in the Channel, for, as Drake noted, "the sea hereabouts swarms with French privateers."[53] On 23 February 1779 Drake had to dispatch HMS *Amphitrite* and the cutters *Fortune* and *Peggy* as far north as Flamborough Head to hunt for a French privateer thought to be operating in that region. On 10 June 1779 the admiral had to order the cutters *Jackall* and *Sprightly* to Margate in order to capture or drive away a French dogger and shallop that were chasing colliers into Margate Road.[54] Armed vessels also had to be deployed to guard the anchorage at The Downs to prevent small French craft from crossing the Channel at night and cutting out and capturing British merchant ships within sight of Drake's flagship.[55]

Another function of The Downs squadron was obtaining intelligence about enemy naval forces in French channel ports. For example, on 25 July 1779, Drake sent HM cutter *Robert and Jane* to Ostend to pick up the latest reports from the British consul in that port, while another cutter was ordered to sail along the French coast seeking intelligence. On 2 September 1779 the cutter *Robert and Jane* was sent to look into Dunkirk "to be ascertained what number of vessels are laying in that Port."[56] Even though Drake had some forty Royal Navy ships and hired armed cutters under his command at any given time, he never had enough ships.[57] Bad weather, navigational difficulties at the eastern entrance of the Channel, the need to repair damaged ships, and the number of different tasks assigned his squadron forced him to make continual requests for reinforcements.[58] The shortage of ships was

eventually overcome and The Downs squadron was able to protect British trade in the region, beat off French privateers, and
dispatch vessels to gain intelligence of enemy movements and
strengths in the eastern approaches of the English Channel. Above
all, in 1779 The Downs squadron prevented or substantially re-
tarded the movement of naval stores freighted in neutral merchant
ships through the English Channel to French ports. At the beginning of 1779, the British ambassador to The Hague, Sir Joseph
Yorke, believed that the only possible policy for the government
of the Netherlands was to "endeavor to amuse both England and
France, in order to avoid either Powers executing their threats."
The British ambassador also thought that the main objective of
French policy in the Netherlands was procurement of naval stores.
He believed that this trade's enormous potential profits would
persuade any number of Dutch merchants to assist the French in
this endeavor.[59] In a dispatch written on 1 January 1779, Yorke
pointed out to his superiors in London that the Dutch were so
weak militarily that they could not resist pressure from either the
French or the British. Moreover, the French, like a number of Dutch
merchants, did not understand British policy: even though Britain
was fighting both France and the American rebels and heading
toward war with Spain, London would never permit France to
use the protection of the Dutch flag to ship naval stores to French
ports. Yorke believed that the Anglo-Dutch Treaty of 1674 meant
that a neutral Netherlands would be of greater advantage to the
French than a Netherlands at war, with its merchant marine and
seaborne trade destroyed by the Royal Navy.[60] The French, however, apparently did not see things as Yorke did. By 19 February
1779 the British diplomat reported to London that he believed
"the Court of France will have the States [General of the Nether-
lands] comply or refuse, & nothing else will be accepted."[61] According to Yorke, French pressure was putting the Netherlands in
a position where the country would have to decide between war
with Britain or with France.

On 24 June 1778 the French government issued a decree that
embraced the concept that warlike materials such as arms and
munitions would be considered contraband when found onboard
neutral ships and would be subject to seizure. This decree was
designed to stimulate the efforts of French cruisers, for it defined
contraband to include almost anything, including naval stores.
Very quickly, the French saw that this policy was a mistake. On

26 July 1778 a new decree on prize law and contraband was issued proclaiming the principle that "free ships make free goods" with the exception of warlike materials, here narrowly defined as arms and munitions. The 26 July decree was intended to make it not only possible but also very profitable for neutrals to carry goods to French ports. In the case of the Netherlands, however, the 26 July decree was used as a weapon to force that country to insist that Britain adopt the same principle. The French scheme was very simple: reward those cities and provinces in the Netherlands willing to see force used to make Britain accept the doctrine that "free ships make free goods" and punish those that were pro-British or simply unwilling to force upon the British the new definition of neutrality.

On 23 February 1779 the British ambassador at The Hague learned that France had issued another decree calling for the seizure of all Dutch ships carrying British property with the exception of those belonging to the pro-French cities of Amsterdam and Haarlem.[62] This was the first step in the French scheme, and six days later the French government revoked the decree of 26 July 1778 and applied the prize law stated in the decree of 23 June 1778 to all Dutch ships, again excepting those from Amsterdam and Haarlem. In addition, a tax of 15 percent was laid on all Dutch ships entering French ports, again excepting those of Amsterdam and Haarlem. This policy was designed to punish the pro-British provinces of the Netherlands while rewarding Amsterdam and Haarlem (whose ships carried most of the naval stores to France) for their attempts to obtain a vote in the States General calling for the use of unlimited convoys to protect Dutch ships carrying naval stores to France.[63]

The major French diplomatic objective in the Netherlands during 1779 was to force the Dutch to provide naval escort, or what were termed "unlimited convoys," to such Dutch merchant ships. The French gave Amsterdam and Haarlem commercial advantages in the hope that other cities and provinces of the Netherlands would support the French cause in order to gain similar privileges. Yorke suggested to London that Britain might retaliate by discriminating against Amsterdam and Haarlem ships and rewarding the ships belonging to other provinces of the Netherlands. Yorke also suggested that the Royal Navy provide convoy for all Dutch merchant ships other than those belonging to Amsterdam and Haarlem.[64] Yorke's suggestions were not taken up immediately, and it remained British policy to protect the innocent from suffering any inconvenience from the war as much as possible.[65] On 30 March 1779, Yorke was directed to inform the Dutch government that "to grant Convoy indiscriminately to their Ships going to the Ports of France, such a measure can only be considered a Determination to supply them with such Materials as they may most stand in need of in the present war." Further, if the Dutch adopted the policy of limited convoys, the Dutch government would find itself "under the greatest Difficulties, in forming Instructions to their Admiralty, in the Description of such Articles as are to be excluded from the Convoy." Even if the Dutch government defined contraband exactly as the British admiralty courts did, it would be of little assistance, for a "Merchant will always contrive to evade every Regulation which does not coincide with his Interests." Yorke was also ordered to support the prince of Orange and the Dutch ministers in whatever way possible "to exert their utmost Endeavours to prevent the measure of granting Convoy, at the Instigation of those who act under the Influence of France."[66]

Seven days later, Yorke was directed to inform the Dutch government that the terms of the 1674 Treaty meant that subjects of the States General "have greater Indulgence than those of other Neutral Powers." The British government also proclaimed that "The meaning of the Word Convoy Implies an apprehension, and carries with it at least an unfriendly appearance, and in the Eyes of Europe it will be considered as a Signal to the other Maritime Powers to follow Example." Yorke was further ordered to inform the Dutch government "in the most explicit, though in the most temperate and friendly Terms," that the British would not permit "ships having Naval Stores on board, although they should be accompanied by Ships of War, to go to the Ports of France."[67] The British position was very clear and it would not change, even when Britain was threatened with invasion by the combined Franco-Spanish fleet. Under no circumstances would the Dutch be permitted to ship naval stores to France.

The Dutch reaction to British and French diplomatic threats and pressure was to stall. The pro-British stadtholder and a number of Dutch officials who saw the dangers of war with either France or Britain adopted a policy of entangling the whole question of granting convoys, limited or unlimited, in the complex machinery of the Netherlands's government. The province of

Holland made a motion in the States General that unlimited convoy be granted to Dutch merchant ships proceeding to French ports. With a one-vote majority, the stadtholder and his followers managed to get the whole question of convoys referred to the states of the various provinces, thus preventing the States General from taking any action on the question until these legislative bodies had acted upon the subject. It would thus be weeks, if not months, before the question of convoys again came before the States General.[68]

While Dutch politicians debated the convoy issue, the British prepared for the worst and increased the diplomatic pressure on the Netherlands. In the event that the Dutch government adopted a policy of convoys, on 13 April 1779 Yorke was directed to find out the size of each convoy, the strength of its escort, the instructions given to the escort, and the dates on which convoys were to sail. This would ease the tasks of the Royal Navy in intercepting them.[69] Then, on 18 May 1779 he was directed to make sure that the stadtholder, the Dutch ministers, and every member of the States General understood that authorizing convoys in any form for Dutch merchant ships bound for French ports would result in the Royal Navy stopping these convoys by force of arms, if need be, and that one could not "reflect on the probable Issue of this most necessary and indispensable order, without feeling the greatest Emotion." Yorke stated it as the opinion of the British government that this whole problem had been brought about by commercial and political connections between Amsterdam and Haarlem and France that ran contrary to the constitution of the Netherlands. If the States General voted down the motion to institute convoys, the British would treat goods and ships belonging to Amsterdam and Haarlem as if they were allies of the French, while the other cities and provinces of the Netherlands could continue to enjoy the privileges granted by the Commercial and Maritime Treaty of 1674.[70]

The Dutch were clearly caught between Britain and France. Yorke was near the truth when he informed Whitehall on 30 July 1779 that the Dutch wished "to gain time, & see [what direction] the turn of Affairs [might] take, & particularly the events of the campaign."[71] The Franco-Spanish attempt to invade England had just begun, and the Dutch knew that if the Bourbon allies succeeded, the Netherlands's problems would be at an end.

Throughout the summer and autumn of 1779, the Dutch politicians debated the convoy questions. The problem always came down to the same choices: Should the Dutch navy convoy Dutch merchant ships to French ports? If the Dutch instituted convoys, should they be limited or unlimited? The argument over convoys within the Dutch government centered on these points, with the French attempting to persuade the Dutch to choose unlimited convoys and the British hoping to persuade the Dutch to drop the idea of convoys altogether. On 22 July the British increased diplomatic pressure on the Dutch by officially requesting that the Netherlands supply the troops and warships to fight the French and Spanish under the terms of the Alliance of 1678.[72] The Dutch did nothing and the British did not press the matter, for they were merely setting up a pretext to break the Anglo-Dutch Commercial and Maritime Treaty of 1674 if necessary. In an attempt to force the pro-British inland farming provinces to support unlimited convoys, the French increased economic pressure by prohibiting the importation of Dutch cheeses into France on 18 September 1779. This measure failed because the stadtholder personally bought up one hundred thousand guilders' worth of cheese to offset the loss of the French market.[73]

During the first two weeks of November 1779, the Dutch finally resolved the convoy question. On 5 November, Yorke reported that the states of Holland had voted for a limited convoy from which ships loaded with naval stores would be "absolutely excluded." A week later, on 12 November, Yorke informed London that the States General of the Netherlands had voted for two limited convoys: one to protect Dutch merchant ships proceeding to the Mediterranean and the other for the West Indies trade.[74] Clearly, two limited convoys, supposedly banning ships carrying naval stores, fell far short of French expectations. On the other hand, the British opposed any form of Dutch convoys and considered the distinction between limited and unlimited convoys academic. On 14 September, Yorke warned London that "I have been more afraid of a concession for *Limited Convoy* than any thing else, knowing that suspicious ships would attach themselves to such a convoy, & endeavor to get thro' under convoy of it."[75] Whether a convoy was limited or unlimited, the British planned to stop it and seize any Dutch merchant ship carrying naval stores or other contraband, even if this resulted in a fight between the convoy's naval escort and ships of the Royal Navy.[76]

On 7 December 1779, Yorke reported that there were more

than fifty merchant ships loaded with naval stores in Dutch ports waiting to proceed down the English Channel.[77] By 14 December, Yorke knew that the French were going to use the cover of the Mediterranean-bound convoy to pass naval stores down the Channel to French ports. It is unclear why the Dutch government did not anticipate British reaction, for Yorke had informed them over and over again that any Dutch convoy would be intercepted by the Royal Navy. Underwriters, as usual, had a clearer understanding of the situation than the politicians. Yorke reported that those ships carrying naval stores and proceeding with the convoy could not obtain insurance, while ships sailing independently, even if loaded with naval stores, had no trouble obtaining policies.[78]

On 27 December 1779 a Dutch convoy of twenty-seven merchant ships, escorted by five Dutch warships under the command of Capt. H. B. L. Graaf van Bylandt, sailed from the Texel toward the English Channel. From the moment the Dutch ships left the Texel, they were followed by British armed cutters that supplied details of the Dutch convoy's exact movements to Drake in The Downs and to the Admiralty in London. On 12 December, knowing that the Dutch might attempt to run a convoy down the Channel, the Admiralty formed a small squadron at St. Helens under the command of Capt. Charles Feilding. Its purpose was to intercept any Dutch convoys that entered the Channel.[79] Upon receipt of orders from the Admiralty and intelligence from the British cutters that had shadowed Bylandt's convoy, Feilding's command sailed from St. Helens on the morning of 30 December to intercept the Dutch convoy and search the merchant ships for contraband.[80]

At about 3 P.M. Feilding's ships sighted the Dutch convoy between St. Alban's Head and Portland on the English side of the Channel. At 4:45 P.M., the commander of the convoy's escort requested that Feilding send an officer onboard his ship to explain to him the intentions of the British squadron. Capt. Samuel Marshall was ordered to board Bylandt's flagship and "in the most civil manner possible to beg he [the Dutch admiral] would allow [him] to visit his Convoy." Accompanied by the Dutch admiral's flag captain, Marshall soon returned with Bylandt's refusal to HMS *Namur,* Feilding's flagship. The Dutch captain explained that the merchant ships of the convoy did not have cargoes of wood for ship construction or cordage but that a number of them were bound to French ports with cargoes of hemp and iron, and that Bylandt would not permit the British to visit and search any of the merchant ships under his escort. Feilding then told the Dutch captain that his orders called for him to visit and search the Dutch merchant ships, that this would be done the next morning, and that he hoped that there would be no violence or resistance on the part of the Dutch. The Dutch captain reminded him that his admiral's orders called for the use of force against any British attempt to visit and search any of the ships under his escort.

During the night of 30–31 December, the Dutch and British ships hove to while Feilding gave the Dutch admiral time to think matters over. At 8 A.M. on 31 December, Feilding ordered searches of a number of Dutch merchant ships. As ships' boats flying British colors made their way to various Dutch merchantmen, Bylandt's flagship fired a cannon shot at one of the British boats. Thereupon, Feilding had a shot fired across the bow of the Dutch flagship. The Dutch admiral's ship and a large frigate nearby immediately answered with a broadside in the general direction of Feilding's ship. The Dutch fire was returned at once by HMS *Namur* and HMS *Valiant,* each sending twenty or thirty rounds back at the Dutch warships. Then, all the Dutch warships hauled down their colors. Feilding ordered nine Dutch merchant ships carrying hemp and iron to be seized and sent Marshall onboard the Dutch flagship with directions to inform Bylandt that he was "at liberty to do as he pleased with his squadron." After gaining Feilding's permission, salutes were exchanged and the Dutch warships rehoisted their colors. Feilding then proceeded to St. Helens with his squadron and the captured Dutch merchant ships. He was followed by two Dutch warships, for Bylandt insisted on staying with the seized Dutch merchant ships.[81]

The incident perplexed Feilding, for ten of the twenty-seven merchant ships that had sailed from the Texel with Bylandt had vanished, and the British captain could not understand why the Dutch government would use an escort of five warships for "a few small vessels" with cargoes of iron and hemp. Feilding suspected that this was a cover for moving ships with naval stores through the Channel on the French side.[82] But from the tone of Feilding's dispatches, it is clear that the British officer knew there was much more involved than just a few shiploads of naval stores. The interception of Bylandt's convoy was a major step down the road toward war with the Dutch. Perhaps Feilding could not understand why the Dutch were prepared to risk so much over a mere handful of merchant ships, for the officials in The Hague must have known that the British would have no choice other than seizing some of the ships in Bylandt's convoy. The king, after reading Feilding's dispatches, concluded that "We have done perfectly right; if we do not prevent our enemies from getting naval stores; it is impossible we can carry on the war or make a peace but on most disadvantageous terms."[83]

In the weeks following the Royal Navy's seizure of nine Dutch merchant ships, the British began to enforce their concepts of maritime neutrality upon the Netherlands systematically, seemingly without regard to the consequences. Lord George Germain, a secretary of state, summed up the British position when he wrote on 8 January 1780 that the British had given the Dutch sufficient grounds for declaring war and that the States General "must soon determine whether they will be governed by France or make common cause with us, for I think they will soon be driven out of impracticable neutrality."[84]

On 11 January 1780, Yorke was instructed to explain the British position to the Dutch authorities in strong terms. The British diplomat told the Dutch:

> We cannot suffer you to carry Naval Stores to the Enemy, because that would be suffering You to give the Enemy effectual Assistance which is not only inconsistent with every Idea of Neutrality, but directly contrary to those positive Engagements by which You are bound to take an active Part in our Defence.

However, at this time Yorke did not demand that the Dutch supply troops and ships for Britain's war with the Bourbons as required by the 1678 Anglo-Dutch Alliance. Britain did not want to appear to be pushing the Netherlands into war. The British diplomat at The Hague did, however, make it absolutely clear to the Dutch authorities that Britain would under no circumstance let the Netherlands use its status as a neutral and British ally to aid the island kingdom's enemies.[85] To drive this point home at the end of January 1780, British cruisers began seizing Dutch merchant ships carrying not only naval and warlike stores to enemy ports but also cargoes of provisions bound for the ports of France and Spain.[86] Yorke believed that the Netherlands could not withstand the pressures of both Britain and France and that any course of action the Dutch followed promised "little satisfaction." In a dispatch from The Hague dated 22 February 1780, the

British ambassador suggested that the privileges granted the Netherlands under the 1674 Treaty be withdrawn so that the Royal Navy could deal with Dutch shipping as with that of any other neutral.[87] On 14 March 1780, Yorke was directed by London to find out if the Dutch intended to fulfill the terms of the Anglo-Dutch Alliance of 1678, so that the British could know whether to treat the Netherlands "as an ally or only as a friendly neutral power."[88] When it became clear that the Netherlands would not give a satisfactory answer to this question, an order in council was issued on 17 April 1780 "suspending provisionally until further order the particular stipulations respecting the freedom of navigation of the subjects of the States General of the United Provinces."[89] With the suspension of the Anglo-Dutch treaty, the British adopted the following policy toward the Netherlands: "It is much better to leave the madness and infatuation to be cured by time, and events; and wait the operation of those cogent remedies which our cruisers will apply."[90] Britain now regarded the Netherlands as a hostile neutral power that employed its merchant shipping secretly to assist France and Spain. The Royal Navy was to be used to prevent Dutch ships from carrying anything to those enemies, and on 30 May 1780, Yorke was directed to obtain the necessary intelligence to enable the king's ships to carry out this policy.[91]

By the second week in June 1780, Yorke had concluded that the Netherlands could avoid war with either Britain or France only by joining the League of Armed Neutrality being established by Catherine II, empress of Russia.[92] For months the neutral powers of northern Europe had talked of forming some kind of league to force Britain to change, or at least moderate, its concepts of blockade and contraband. As early as 22 September 1778, Yorke reported that the Danish mission at The Hague was promoting the idea that the northern powers unite and use their combined strength to force the British to change their policies.[93] Singly, northern neutrals such as Denmark and Sweden did not pose a threat to British naval power, but together, the northern or Baltic powers, including Russia and perhaps the Netherlands, had the combined naval force to tip the scales against Britain and force a change in its stand on neutral shipping.[94] The idea of such a league, however, was little more than talk until 1780, for there was no court or political personality willing or able to run the risks involved in forming a league of neutrals to confront Britain.

At the beginning of 1780, however, all of this changed when Catherine the Great of Russia took up the cause of neutral rights on the high seas. Russia was a major military power that produced large quantities of naval stores and had almost no merchant shipping. From St. Petersburg in 1780, the diplomatic situation in the Baltic and western Europe must have looked most appealing to Catherine. Russia was between Turkish wars, Britain was at war with both France and Spain, and the small neutral nations of northern Europe were being harassed by the Royal Navy. It was British policy to gain an alliance with Russia to offset the success of French diplomacy in Europe, while it was French policy to do anything diplomatically to cause trouble for Britain. There could be no better opportunity for Catherine II to gain prestige on the European diplomatic stage than to champion the neutral nations of Europe and uphold their neutral rights on the high seas.[95]

Catherine's interest in the maritime rights of European neutrals appears to have been brought about by three separate events. In August 1778 the American privateer *General Mifflin* of Boston sank one British merchant ship and captured seven others off the North Cape of Norway. These British merchant ships were carrying Russian products from the port of Archangel, which Catherine saw as an illegal attack on Russian trade and proposed to Denmark-Norway that some joint naval action prevent similar affronts in the future. Next, Catherine believed that she had again been insulted on 10 October 1778, when the merchant ship *Jonge Prins,* loaded with flax and hemp bound to Nantes, became the first Russian ship to be seized by the British. In the next several months, Britain seized more Russian ships and Russian products onboard neutral ships. Finally, Catherine learned on 30 January 1780 that the Spanish had seized and carried into Cadiz a ship chartered by Russian merchants carrying a cargo of Russian corn to France and Italy. The empress sent a strong protest to Madrid.

By this time it appeared to Catherine that nobody—Americans, British, Spanish—respected the rights of Russia on the high seas. This was not a question of economics, for most Russian naval stores were bought by British factors in Russian ports and were either shipped to England or sold to French agents who shipped them to French ports in neutral bottoms. English factors in Russia told British diplomats which neutral ships carried naval stores to France so that the Royal Navy could seize them. A neutral shipowner might lose money if his ship were seized and condemned, but the Russian producer of naval stores received his money before the cargo had even been loaded.[96] Thus, for Catherine II, this question was not a matter of economics but one of respect and prestige.

By the middle of February 1780, Catherine concluded that she must lead the European neutrals and declare her concepts of neutral rights on the high seas to both neutrals and belligerents. Spain provided Catherine with the occasion for her diplomatic offensive on 17 February 1780, when St. Petersburg learned that the Spanish had seized another Russian merchant ship, the *St. Nicholas,* loaded with corn bound for Italy. The corn on the *St. Nicholas* was sold at Cadiz over the Russian consul's protests. The Spanish did not even attempt to determine the nationality of the ship or its cargo. On 19 February, Catherine secretly issued a *ukase* ordering the fitting out of fifteen ships of the line and five frigates.[97] This was followed on 10 March 1780 by a "Declaration of the Empress of Russia regarding the Principles of Armed Neutrality to the Courts of London, Versailles and Madrid." In this declaration, Catherine stated that the belligerents must govern their conduct toward neutral merchant ships according to the following five principles:

1. That neutral vessels may navigate freely from port to port and along the coasts of the nations at war.

2. That the effects belonging to the subjects of the said Powers at war shall be free on board neutral vessels, with the exception of contraband merchandise.

3. That, as to the specifications of the above mentioned merchandise, the Empress holds to what is enumerated in the 10th and 11th articles of her treaty of commerce with Great Britain, extending her obligations to all the Powers at war.

4. That to determine what constitutes a blockaded port, this designation shall apply only to a port where that attacking Power has stationed its vessels sufficiently near and in such a way as to render access thereto clearly dangerous.

5. That these principles shall serve as a rule for proceedings and judgements as to the legality of prizes.

The Russian declaration ended with a statement that if the belligerents did not conduct themselves according to these principles, Catherine would force them to respect the commerce of her subjects by force of arms.[98] On 3 April 1780 the Russian government presented to the States General of the Netherlands and to the courts of Copenhagen, Berlin, Stockholm, and Lisbon a memorandum suggesting that these nations join Russia in a League of Armed Neutrality with the object of employing their combined naval forces to enforce the concepts of maritime neutrality set forth by Catherine's declaration of 10 March.[99]

There was nothing secret about the Russian memorandum of 3 April. At The Hague, Yorke knew its contents one day after it had been presented to the States General.[100] It was to the advantage of the French and Spanish for Russia to set up a league of neutral maritime powers to enforce principles like the doctrine that "free ships make free goods" and the legality of close blockade alone, for they could then continue to employ neutral shipping to import goods such as naval stores. Thus, both France and Spain quickly accepted Catherine's principles of neutrality.[101]

For Britain the problems created by Catherine's declaration and the proposed League of Armed Neutrality were much more complex. For example, how far would Russia and the other northern powers go in using force to uphold their rights on the high seas? Were the northern powers prepared to fight the British (their best buyers of naval stores) in The Downs? Was the League of Armed Neutrality a Russian diplomatic bluff or a ploy to gain prestige? Could Catherine be bought off with some kind of concessions? Then there was the problem of the Dutch, whose ships carried most of the naval stores to France and Spain. France's faction in the Netherlands was stronger than Britain's. Would Britain or Britain's enemies benefit more from a neutral Netherlands that was a member of the League of Armed Neutrality? Would it be more advantageous to Britain to have the Netherlands as a cobelligerent of France and Spain? Answering these and other questions required time and more information, so the British responded to Catherine's declaration by merely stating that His Majesty's government would conduct itself in accordance with international law.[102]

Russian policy in 1780 was perplexing and contradictory to informed observers. For example, the Swedish foreign minister on 31 March 1780 told the British ambassador that he thought "it appeared strange" for Russia to fit out a squadron of thirty warships "for the sake of protecting two or three merchant ships at the most."[103] On 11 April, Lord Stormont, the British secretary of state for the Northern Department, stated that the intentions of the Russian government "are so problematical that I know not what opinion to form." But if Catherine was really going to put into effect the policies called for in her 10 March declaration and 3 April memorandum, the British could not and would not subscribe to such a doctrine.[104]

During the spring of 1780 it became clear to Britain that the Russians were bluffing and that Catherine would not and, in fact, could not let the question of neutral rights on the high seas draw Russia into a naval war. The British ambassador to Russia, Sir James Harris, had many sources of intelligence among the officers of the Russian Baltic fleet, for many of them were British. On 26 May 1780, Harris informed London that the British commander of the Russian Baltic fleet, speaking for all the other British officers, had told Catherine that they would not serve in a conflict against their homeland.[105] In two other dispatches, dated 20 and 23 June 1780, Harris informed London that the orders of the Russian Baltic fleet ran totally contrary to the principles of the League of Armed Neutrality. Russian warships were directed to protect only Russian merchant ships, not belligerent property on neutral merchant ships or merchant ships belonging to other neutrals.[106]

Even with this intelligence, authorities in London continued to be confused. On 8 July 1780, Stormont wrote to Harris: "The more I reflect upon all that has passed of late, the more I am inclined to believe that we have not got to the bottom of this strange business."[107] The British government failed to grasp that there was no firm basis for the Russian moves and that creating the League of Armed Neutrality did not represent any such policy. Rather, it was a huge diplomatic fishing expedition by which Catherine hoped to gain diplomatic prestige as leader of the neutral maritime powers of Europe. Not understanding this, the British continued to offer concessions to gain an alliance with Russia.

At the time, the British would not give an inch when it came to the League of Armed Neutrality. On 8 August 1780, Stormont informed Harris that if the Russian government applied the provisions set forth in the League of Armed Neutrality to the Dutch, it would be "a measure little short of direct hostility and as pernicious in its consequences as actual war."[108] On the other hand, on 20 October, Harris was directed to find out from the Russian government if there was a piece of British territory that could be given to Russia in exchange for an alliance.[109] On 20 November 1780 orders were issued to all British warships to seize only those Russian merchant ships whose cargoes consisted of warlike materials such as munitions, and not naval stores and provisions.[110] Then, on 3 January 1781 the British cabinet directed Harris to offer Minorca to Russia for a "Great and Essential Service Actually performed."[111] This scheme never materialized, however, for Russia had little use for a western Mediterranean island that the Spanish thought was theirs. London's confusion about the real objectives of the League of Armed Neutrality and the lengths to which Britain was prepared to go to obtain a Russian alliance show, if nothing else, that Catherine really knew how to play along a suitor.[112]

During the summer of 1780 the courts of Copenhagen and Stockholm signed conventions with the Russian government embracing the principles of the League of Armed Neutrality. Both Denmark-Norway and Sweden, however, created diplomatic loopholes to protect themselves from the Royal Navy and, in the case of Denmark-Norway, to increase the country's share of the international carrying trade. The British resident at Copenhagen, Sir Morton Eden, negotiated a secret explanatory article to the Anglo-Danish Treaty of 1670 that specifically made naval stores contraband. This was signed on 4 July 1780, and on 9 July 1780 Denmark-Norway signed a convention with Russia that embraced the principles of the League of Armed Neutrality including the doctrine that "free ships make free goods" and the definition of contraband under the Anglo-Danish Treaty of 1670.[113] Denmark-Norway had simply squared the circle diplomatically by proclaiming that "free ships make free goods," while, unknown to the Russians, the kingdom defined naval stores as contraband of war. Copenhagen's policy was to placate both the British and the Russians by joining the League of Armed Neutrality while refraining from transporting naval stores to French and Spanish ports. Especially after the Royal Navy had driven the Dutch merchant marine from the seas, this policy substantially increased Denmark-Norway's overseas trade and the size of the country's merchant marine.[114]

Stockholm, like Copenhagen, employed legalistic, diplomatic subterfuge to avoid enraging either Britain or Russia. On 1 August 1780, Sweden signed a convention with Russia similar to the one signed by Denmark-Norway in that it upheld the principle of "free ships made free goods" while employing the vague definition of contraband in the Anglo-Swedish Treaty of 1661, which was open to various interpretations.[115]

With the exchange of the necessary notes and declarations, these conventions became a three-way alliance, begging the vital question of the transport of naval stores and calling for mutual armed assistance to protect Danish-Norwegian, Swedish, and Russian neutral rights. Another set of agreements was later signed to neutralize the Baltic and prevent all warlike acts in that sea.[116] Because these agreements either stopped the shipment of naval stores or sidestepped the issue, the way in which Denmark-Norway and Sweden joined the League of Armed Neutrality effectively settled the question of transporting naval stores in Danish-Norwegian and Swedish ships to French and Spanish ports in Britain's favor.

The Netherlands had the most to lose and perhaps the most to gain from the League of Armed Neutrality. Among the nations that received the Russian memorandum of 3 April 1780, the Dutch were the major neutral carriers of naval stores to French and Spanish ports. If the Dutch joined the League of Armed Neutrality, and this league could protect neutral merchant ships, Dutch merchants and shipowners would gain huge profits. If, however, the League of Armed Neutrality failed to protect the Dutch from the Royal Navy, the cost to the Netherlands would be huge. The Dutch could not expect naval aid from the French and Spanish because their major naval forces were stationed hundreds of miles south and west of the Netherlands at Brest and Cadiz. The British Channel Fleet stood between the Netherlands and the naval forces of the two Bourbon powers. The Netherlands also had to attend to the protection of its colonies in the East and West Indies. War with Britain would destroy the Dutch merchant marine and Dutch overseas trade.

The Dutch, however, only dimly perceived the great risk of an Anglo-Dutch war when they attempted to join the League of Armed Neutrality. On 24 April 1780, one week after the British withdrew the privileges the Dutch enjoyed under the Anglo-Dutch Treaty of 1674, the States General of the Netherlands passed a resolution endorsing the principles of neutrality proclaimed by the empress of Russia in her declaration of 10 March and her memorandum of 3 April. Two days later, on 26 April, the French government issued a declaration to the Dutch approving of the armed neutrality.[117] If the Dutch had joined the League of Armed Neutrality immediately, the British would have been unable to forestall this action, but the Dutch stalled, hoping to negotiate a

Russian pledge to protect the Netherlands's East and West Indian possessions.[118] From the beginning the Dutch misinterpreted the situation. First, they failed to see that the League of Armed Neutrality was designed to gain prestige for Catherine not to protect neutral maritime rights. Second, they ignored the fact that the Russians lacked both the means and the desire to protect Dutch colonies against British attack. On 12 September the Russian empress informed the Dutch that under no condition would she guarantee Dutch overseas possessions and that the Dutch could not expect such a guarantee merely for joining the League of Armed Neutrality.[119]

By August 1780, however, it had become just a question of time before Great Britain declared war on the Netherlands. While Dutch diplomats in St. Petersburg negotiated vainly with the Russians over the Netherlands's terms for joining the League of Armed Neutrality, the British warned authorities at The Hague that such a step would likely result in an Anglo-Dutch war. Stormont thought that if the Dutch joined the league they would "leave us no alternative and must be treated as the secret enemies of that nation with which they ought to be the firmest friends."[120] Under no circumstances would the British government permit the Dutch to transport naval stores to the ports of France and Spain. By August 1780 the question of the Dutch joining Denmark-Norway, Sweden, and Russia in the league was largely academic. On 11 August 1780, Yorke reported from The Hague that the French had requested that the States General remove the taxes on exporting naval stores from the Netherlands because they were developing means to transport naval stores through the Netherlands and Belgium to French Channel ports by means of a complex system of inland waterways.[121] Ten days later the Admiralty learned that the French canal system had progressed so far that the French could move naval stores from the Netherlands to the port of Nantes on the Bay of Biscay.[122] The French ability to transport naval stores from the Netherlands to French ports by inland routes destroyed the effectiveness of the British blockade in the English Channel. Dutchmen, acting secretly as French purchasing agents, could buy naval stores in Baltic ports and ship these naval stores as Dutch property on Dutch merchant ships to the Netherlands. On reaching a Dutch port, the naval stores could be sent to France. There were no legal grounds for the Royal Navy to seize a neutral Dutch merchant ship carrying Dutch property from a neutral Baltic port to the Netherlands. The British blockade of the English Channel had been outflanked by French engineering. On 1 September 1780, Yorke reported to London that "an immense quantity of Masts" would be shipped from the Netherlands to French naval bases by means of inland canals. Some weeks later Yorke reported that there was no longer talk of instituting convoys for Dutch shipping and that "conveying of naval stores thro' the Low Countries to France continues."[123] The only way that Britain could now prevent naval stores from reaching the French was to declare war on the Netherlands and extend the blockade of the English Channel to cover the Dutch coast. Such a declaration of war, however, must come before the Dutch officially became a member of the League of Armed Neutrality or diplomatic problems with the Russians would ensue. On 3 October dispatches from St. Petersburg arrived at The Hague and the States General had to decide whether to join the League of Armed Neutrality without a Russian guarantee of protection for Dutch colonies.[124] Ten days later Stormont asked Yorke for detailed intelligence on Dutch military and naval capabilities in Europe, the West Indies, and the Far East, so that the British could prepare for hostilities with the Netherlands.[125] Yorke fulfilled this request on 7 November, when he reported to Stormont that the Netherlands was "by no means prepared for war" and that the Netherlands boasted only thirty-six warships equipped for service, only sixteen of which carried fifty or more guns.[126] On 24 November 1780, Yorke reported to London that the States General of the Netherlands had voted to join the League of Armed Neutrality and that a courier would be dispatched to St. Petersburg the next day with the necessary papers to declare the Dutch accession to the league.[127] When news of the Dutch decision to join the league reached London, British authorities thought that the Netherlands was now "a secret enemy," and on 16 December, Yorke was ordered to remove himself secretly from The Hague to neutral Antwerp.[128] The British government had decided that the only way to stop the flow of naval stores to France and Spain was to declare and wage war against the Netherlands.

The official pretext for Britain's declaration of war on the Netherlands was the discovery of a draft treaty between the Americans and the city of Amsterdam. On 3 September 1780 the ship carrying American diplomat Henry Laurens was captured by a British warship. Among Laurens's papers fished out of the water by Brit-

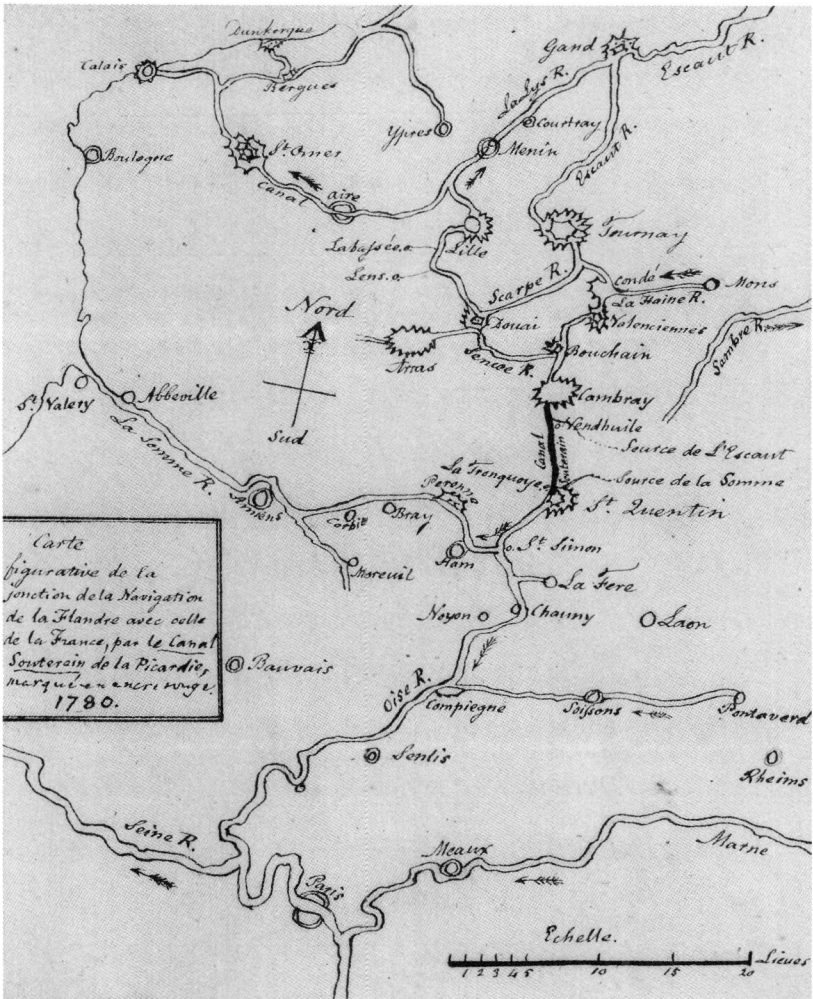

A map sent to London by Sir Joseph Yorke, British ambassador to The Hague, showing how the inland waterways of northern France and the Netherlands connected. SP 84/572, 19. Courtesy of the Public Record Office.

ish seamen was a draft treaty drawn up at Aix-la-Chapelle in 1778 by William Lee, an American diplomat, and Jean de Neufville, an agent for the city of Amsterdam. Authorities on diplomatic history and law generally agree that the unsigned treaty was void, but the British government chose to consider this document to "all intents & purposes, equivalent to actual aggression"—a declaration of war. Yorke was ordered to demand that the States General immediately punish the Amsterdam officials responsible for the Lee-de Neufville treaty.[129]

Thus, on 20 December 1780 Britain declared war against the Netherlands and issued orders in council forbidding the departure of Dutch ships and cargoes from British ports and authorizing the capture and destruction of all Dutch ships and property found on the high seas.[130] The decision to declare war was made secretly and timed to precede the Netherlands's joining the League of Armed Neutrality. At the same time, the States General would technically have just enough time to respond to the British demand that Amsterdam authorities be punished for the Lee-de Neufville treaty. When the Dutch ambassador to the Court of St. James protested the declaration of war, arguing that the Netherlands was a member of the League of Armed Neutrality, he was bluntly informed by British officials that it was impossible for the Netherlands to be a member of any league of neutrals, for the States General was a belligerent power.[131]

Britain's publicly assigned reasons for the declaration of war were the Netherlands's refusal to abide by the terms of the Anglo-Dutch Alliance of 1678, their secret assistance to the American rebels, their support of Britain's enemies in the Far East, and the draft treaty between Amsterdam and the American rebels.[132] Ostensibly, the occasion for declaring war was the Dutch decision to join the League of Armed Neutrality, but Britain's real motive was the desperate need to blockade Dutch ports to keep out the flow of naval stores that could reach French naval bases by the reported inland waterway system. On 4 January 1781 the States General of the Netherlands officially acceded to the conventions of the League of Armed Neutrality. Several days later the States General asked other members of the league to come to their aid in the war against Britain.[133] In fact, no such aid ever materialized. Yorke wrote shrewdly that when the Netherlands decided to join the League of Armed Neutrality, the Dutch only saw "security, honour, and the means of making a figure, whilst they shut their eyes & ears to every reflection which [ran] counter to their passion."[134]

The British had gambled that the League of Armed Neutrality would offer no protection to the Dutch, that Catherine's stand on the maritime rights of neutrals was talk and bluff, and that Russia would not go to war to save the Netherlands from the wrath of British sea power at the end of 1780.[135] When the British declared war on the Netherlands, no one in London could predict just what the Russians would do. On 18 February 1781, Sandwich wrote "the fact is, that we are at this moment in the most ticklish crisis with the Court of Russia, and that at this instant the giving them the least cause of complaint or entering into any altercation with them, might have the most decisive & fatal consequences."[136] Catherine, however, had achieved her goal in the League of Armed Neutrality—diplomatic prestige. The empress would not fight for a thing she described to the British ambassador to St. Petersburg as the "League of Nullity."[137]

There would also be no assistance to the Netherlands from the French and Spanish. As early as 16 May 1780, Yorke saw that an Anglo-Dutch war was not in Paris's interest, for "it would deprive France the use of the Dutch flag, which is so necessary to them."[138] When the Dutch became cobelligerents in the war against Britain, French interest in the Netherlands went by the wayside. The Dutch certainly did not have to face the Royal Navy alone, for the Americans, the French, and the Spanish were all fighting the British, but none of these powers could assist the Netherlands in the North Sea.

The ensuing Fourth Anglo-Dutch War was a disaster for the Netherlands. It had a catastrophic effect on Dutch seaborne trade. When Britain declared war, units of the Royal Navy were dispatched to blockade the Dutch coast. Day after day they patrolled the coast of the Netherlands and the eastern approaches of the English Channel, searching for intelligence and for ships attempting to carry goods to Dutch, French, and Spanish ports.[139] Some of the British ships blockading the Netherlands stayed at sea so long their crews developed scurvy and the Admiralty had to send provisions to warships in the North Sea from English east coast ports.[140] The British blockade of the coast of the Netherlands destroyed the national economy as well as Dutch seaborne trade. On 24 August 1781, an intelligence report reached the Admiralty stating that "the Harbour of Amsterdam was like a desert, &

nothing going forward either hostile or mercantile."[141] A little less than a year later, the commander of the squadron blockading the Netherlands wrote that what little Dutch seaborne trade existed was being conducted under cover of neutral flags.[142] The Dutch lacked both the ships and men needed to break the British blockade.[143]

British strategy was simple: blockade the coast of the Netherlands and the eastern approaches of the English Channel to prevent enemy shipping from entering or departing Dutch ports and prevent neutrals from carrying contraband to Britain's enemies. The blockade also greatly hindered enemy cruisers operating against British east coast shipping lanes and ships carrying naval stores to England from the Baltic. The British also formed a North Sea squadron to intercept Dutch ships attempting to reach the Netherlands by way of the North Sea and to protect British shipping from attack by enemy naval forces.[144] Whenever the Dutch appeared to be preparing to break the blockade, units of the Channel squadron were transferred to The Downs or to the coast of Holland.

During May 1781, for example, the Admiralty received intelligence reports that the Dutch navy was preparing to break the British blockade of the Netherlands.[145] On 31 May 1781, Vice Adm. Hyde Parker Sr. was ordered to proceed from Spithead with three ships of the line and four small warships. His mission was to reinforce the escorts of the British convoy proceeding from the Firth of Forth and the Thames to the Baltic and to escort the Baltic trade from Helsingör to Britain.[146] As Parker escorted the British Baltic trade to Britain on 23 July 1780, he received a dispatch from the Admiralty saying that a squadron of Dutch warships had broken out of the Texel and was escorting a number of Dutch merchant ships out of the North Sea. Parker was directed to leave the convoy with a small escort and intercept the Dutch. Parker hesitated to reduce the strength of the convoy's escort when there was a Dutch squadron at large in the North Sea,[147] but on the morning of 5 August, Parker intercepted the Dutch convoy and its naval escort on Dogger Bank. The British admiral immediately dispatched his convoy to Britain under escort of several small warships while forming his own seven largest ships into a line of battle.[148] There was no maneuvering or jockeying for position by either squadron. The eight Dutch warships were in line-ahead formation as Parker's squadron approached. Neither side fired a shot until they were within "half a musquet shot" of each other. When the fighting began, it was gunport to gunport.

For three hours and forty minutes the British and Dutch blasted each other at point-blank range. The fighting ended only when both sides' warships were so damaged that they were unmanageable. Parker, in his official dispatch to the Admiralty, stated that "His Majesty's Officers and Men behaved with great bravery, nor did the Enemy show less gallantry." The British lost 104 men killed and 339 wounded, while the Dutch squadron commanded by Rear Adm. Johan Arnold Zoutman lost 144 men killed and 399 wounded. The next day, the British frigate HMS *Belle Poule* found what appeared to be a Dutch 74-gun ship of the line sunk in twenty-two fathoms with its topgallant masts showing above the surface of the water, a pennant still flying. The flag was the only trophy of the action. Both the British and the Dutch claimed victory. The Battle of Dogger Bank was a tactical draw, for no ships were captured and both British and Dutch convoys escaped. Strategically, the battle was a British victory, for the Dutch warships and their convoy retreated to the Texel and the Dutch fleet never left the protection of that anchorage again until the end of the war.[149]

The Battle of Dogger Bank was the only major fleet action in the North Sea between the British and the Dutch navies during the American war. For the Royal Navy, the dangerous, difficult, and unheroic work of blockading the Dutch coast and the eastern approaches of the English Channel continued until the end of the war.[150] On 14 September 1781 an intelligence report to the Admiralty stated that there were in various Dutch ports ten ships of the line and some smaller warships.[151] The Dutch navy was still a possible threat, and at various times the Admiralty received intelligence reports that the Dutch were again going to attempt to break the British blockade.[152] During 1782 the Admiralty twice ordered major units of the Channel Fleet into the North Sea to reinforce the Netherlands blockade.[153] There were no major battles to be fought in the North Sea, however, for the Dutch would not send a squadron to sea. After the Battle of Dogger Bank, the Royal Navy's main tasks in the North Sea were maintaining the blockade of the Netherlands and the eastern end of the English Channel, searching neutral merchant ships for contraband, and hunting down enemy cruisers while protecting British trade from attack.

Was the British effort to prevent naval stores from reaching enemy ports successful during the American war? There can be no doubt that thousands of tons of naval stores were seized by the Royal Navy carrying out the blockade. But did this effort have any significant strategic effect on French and Spanish naval operations? Was the British blockade worth a great diplomatic crisis with European neutral nations and the Fourth Anglo-Dutch War? These questions and many others are difficult to answer. The interception of naval stores bound to French and Spanish ports did affect the operations of enemy naval forces in some ways.

But was the blockade strategically effective? That is, did it deprive the French and Spanish of enough naval stores to prevent or hinder seriously their naval operations? The answer here is probably not. The British were never able to cut off supplies of naval stores from French and Spanish ports. In the case of France, however, British blockades did force the expenditure of great efforts and huge amounts of money to procure the naval stores required to carry on the war.[154] The cost of subverting British blockades substantially increased the expense of carrying on the war for the French and contributed to the financial strain the war placed on the French government.[155] The real victim of British blockades and French and Russian diplomacy was the Netherlands. While the Fourth Anglo-Dutch War required the British to extend the already overtaxed resources of the Royal Navy to cover the new North Sea theater of the war, it also destroyed the Dutch merchant marine and national economy while opening the Dutch overseas empire to attack. In its efforts to prevent naval stores from reaching Britain's enemies, the Royal Navy delivered a series of blows from which the Netherlands needed years to recover.

Chapter 5

THE CHANNEL FLEET
HOLDS THE LINE, 1780–82

During the last three years of the American war, the Royal Navy could not meet its strategic commitments in European waters because of a shortage of ships. Unlike the Seven Years' War, when the French Navy had been crippled in European seas before Spain entered the conflict, the American war gave Britain no smashing victory over the French Navy, such as Quiberon Bay, and the Spanish fleet joined the war early enough to give the enemy a numerical superiority in European waters. In the years 1778–82, the Royal Navy had to fight the French, Spanish, and, after 1780, the Dutch in European seas while simultaneously trying to maintain naval superiority and seek decisive actions in such distant theaters of operations as North America and the West Indies. Ships were continually withdrawn from the Channel Fleet to reinforce squadrons in the Western Hemisphere, weakening the Channel forces so that they could not maintain control of the western approaches of the English Channel.

On 7 March 1780 the cabinet resolved that the thirty ships of the line of the Channel Fleet should be ready for service by 1 May 1780.[1] On 17 May, Adm. Sir Charles Hardy hoisted his flag onboard HMS *Victory* at Spithead. The next day, the admiral died.[2] Hardy's death confronted the government and Sandwich with the difficult task of finding a new commander from a limited pool of candidates. Most of the names on the admirals' list could be discarded as being too old, too junior, or otherwise unsuitable. A number of obvious choices also had to be ruled out: Rodney was in the West Indies; Keppel was unsuitable for political reasons; and Howe was disqualified by his politics and his habit of demanding exorbitant bribes from the government.

Sandwich's first choice was Vice Adm. Hon. Samuel

Barrington,[3] whose family had close ties with the Crown.[4] The admiral had shown great skill fighting a superior French squadron in the West Indies before his return to England in 1779, but he was an extremely difficult and "obstinate" man who believed Sandwich had sullied his honor. When the news of Barrington's action at St. Lucia in the West Indies arrived in London, Sandwich wrote a private letter congratulating the admiral and an Admiralty official later wrote Barrington an official letter. According to Barrington, he had not received adequate praise on this occasion. Later, on 5 August 1779, Sandwich drafted a second private letter cast in more fulsome terms, but this, unfortunately, arrived in the West Indies after Barrington had departed for England. Barrington viewed the Admiralty's original letter as a deliberate slight and refused to believe that Sandwich's second letter had ever been written. When a copy of the first lord's second letter was produced, Barrington declared it a forgery. Next, a backdated letter was redrafted in more laudatory terms, but Barrington declared it inadequate.[5] As a result, Barrington, the obvious choice to replace Hardy, took violent exception to Sandwich and absolutely refused to serve as Channel Fleet commander and told the first lord to appoint Keppel to the position.[6] When Barrington refused the command, Sandwich decided to appoint Adm. Francis Geary. A contemporary of Hardy's, Geary was several years older and just three places below the late commander in chief of the Channel Fleet in the admirals' list. He had served as a third in command to Hawke during the Seven Years' War but had never commanded a fleet. Indeed, he had not been to sea in years. But Geary had vast seniority, was well liked in the service, and was not involved in politics. This was crucial, for the Channel Fleet was still alive with political factions and discipline among the officers was unsatisfactory.[7] Once the appointment had been cleared with the cabinet,[8] Geary was appointed to command the Channel Fleet on 22 May, with Kempenfelt as captain of the fleet.[9] Barrington consented to be second in command of the fleet.[10]

Geary's instructions were issued on 27 May 1780. The admiral was directed to sail from Spithead and to take station to prevent the French squadrons at Toulon and Brest from joining a Spanish squadron based at Cadiz. If possible, Geary was to prevent these movements by engaging the enemy squadrons before they even met. Further, the admiral was reminded that the "safety" of Britain, Ireland, and the trade "must always be considered as very important objects of his attention." Geary was to remain at sea as long as his provisions and water permitted before putting into either Spithead or Torbay for resupply.[11]

On 8 June, Geary sailed from St. Helens with twenty-one ships of the line and several smaller warships.[12] The admiral was later joined in the Channel by HMS *Cumberland* and HMS *Alfred* from Plymouth. By 15 June the Channel Fleet had taken station off Ushant.[13] Geary remained off Ushant until 27 June, when the fleet's station was moved about a hundred miles southward into the Bay of Biscay to be able "to more effectually . . . prevent a junction of the enemy squadrons."[14] The next day, 28 June, Geary decided to move the station of the Channel Fleet farther south into the Bay of Biscay to 46°50'N and one degree west of the longitude of The Lizard. Geary believed that this position in the middle of the Bay of Biscay gave him the best chance of both blocking junction of the French and Spanish squadrons and intercepting John Paul Jones and any French ships proceeding to America. After cruising on this station, Geary intended to return northward to the latitude of Ushant to protect the homeward-bound East and West India trade.[15] Because of the government's lack of firm intelligence, Geary's instructions were vague, calling only for the interception of enemy squadrons and the protection of British merchant vessels. He had received no reliable reports of enemy deployments since putting to sea, and his decision to take the Channel Fleet southward into the middle of the Bay of Biscay was based on little more than guesswork.

In the fourth week of June intelligence arrived in London from Commodore George Johnstone, commander of a small British squadron off the coast of Portugal. This told of two Spanish squadrons cruising west of Portugal to intercept the homeward-bound British East and West India trade. One consisted of four Spanish ships of the line and two frigates and was cruising between 39°30' N and 41°30' N, some twenty to seventy leagues west of Portugal. The other squadron, consisting of seven Spanish ships of the line, three frigates, and two small warships, was reported to be operating west of Portugal between 36°30' N and 37°00' N.[16] On the basis of this information, the cabinet decided on 24 June to order Geary to detach a squadron from the Channel Fleet to go in search of the two enemy squadrons.[17]

The cabinet's orders, along with a copy of the intelligence from Johnstone, reached Geary in the Bay of Biscay on 29 July, before he had put into effect his decision to move southward. Upon receipt of the government's orders, Geary assembled a council of flag officers, which decided against dividing the fleet as called for in the government's orders.[18] Instead, the whole Channel Fleet should proceed off Ferrol, then the ships would begin to search for the Spanish ships as called for in the orders from London.[19] This decision was based in part on intelligence received during the evening of 28 June that a "French squadron sailed out of Brest."[20] Unfortunately, that intelligence was, at best, secondhand.

As the Channel Fleet proceeded southward across the Bay of Biscay toward Cape Finisterre on 3 July, it encountered a French convoy of between twenty-five and thirty ships sailing from Saint Dominique. Geary immediately ordered a general chase and, before fog ended the operation at 7 P.M., the British captured twelve merchant ships loaded with coffee, indigo, and sugar. On 10 July the Channel Fleet took up station some fifteen leagues west of Cape Finisterre.[21] For the next ten days Geary's ships cruised off Cape Finisterre, ranging as far south as 41°15' N without sighting anything.[22] Kempenfelt, for one, thought that taking station off Cape Finisterre was a waste of time, for it "is not the track of either our East or West India ships and I therefore conceive no station for the enemy to cruise in."[23] On 20 July the Channel Fleet sailed north to regain station off Ushant without having sighted the enemy.[24]

On the morning of 2 August, the Channel Fleet fell in with a large outward-bound British convoy under the escort of HMS *Ramillies* and four other warships.[25] This convoy consisted of sixty-three sail, including not only East and West India ships but also victuallers, military storeships, and transports carrying the 90th Regiment. The Channel Fleet accompanied the convoy for several hours to a point 112 leagues off the Isles of Scilly, where the two groups of ships parted company.[26] Seven days later, to the westward of Cape St. Vincent, the convoy was intercepted. All but the men-of-war and two or three merchant ships were captured by a force of thirty-two Spanish and French ships of the line from Cadiz.[27] This was a major intelligence failure, for the Admiralty did not learn of the sailing of this enemy fleet until 4 August and neither Geary nor Capt. John Moutray, commander of the convoy's escort, knew that an enemy fleet was in the area.[28] It was also a major defeat. Besides the loss of the merchant ships, 3,144 men, and goods worth £1.5 million, the convoy's capture offset Rodney's victory in the Moonlight Battle and helped derail a secret British diplomatic effort to make a separate peace with Spain.[29]

On 8 August some forty-seven leagues west of Ushant, Geary decided to return to Spithead because of a shortage of provisions and beer and an outbreak of scurvy among the ships' crews. The Channel Fleet had been at sea for more than nine weeks and more than two thousand men were sick with scurvy. Geary rejected the option of putting into Torbay instead of Spithead because the place offered neither adequate hospitals for the sick seamen nor a chance to provision the fleet quickly. Geary also decided against sending part of the fleet into Plymouth, for he did not want to divide his force: new intelligence reported a large enemy fleet from Cadiz at sea in the English Channel. As the Geary's ships proceeded up the Channel, the British intercepted a ship loaded with lemons purchased at the suggestion of a farsighted surgeon and given to the seamen of the fleet with "great effect." Two days later, on 18 August, the Channel Fleet arrived at Spithead.[30]

At this point the Channel Fleet had been at sea for seventy-six days. While a French convoy had been intercepted and twelve merchant ships captured, no enemy squadron had been sighted. The ships of the Channel Fleet had been damaged by continual service, and two thousand seamen where disabled by scurvy. Further, the British convoy escorted by HMS *Ramillies* had been captured by the enemy. Without sound intelligence on enemy movements, British strategy in the Channel during the summer of 1780 consisted mainly of letting the Channel Fleet cruise in the western approaches, off Cape Finisterre, and in the Bay of Biscay, vainly seeking for the enemy. Hawke, Geary's old commanding officer, saw the futility of this policy and suggested that it would have been better to imitate the Seven Years' War strategy of a close blockade against the French naval base at Brest.[31] However, the old plans did not match the new realities of 1780. A blockade of Brest would not affect enemy squadrons based at Cadiz and Toulon. Unable to blockade all the enemy bases as in the French Revolutionary and Napoleonic Wars, the British had little strategic choice but to use the Royal Navy to hold the western approaches, protecting the nation's overseas trade from raids and the British Isles from invasion.

To protect the homeward-bound East and West India trade, the government considered it imperative to put at least a part of the Channel Fleet to sea immediately. On 24 August the cabinet

directed that if the whole Channel Fleet could not sail, Geary must
detach a force of ten or twelve ships of the line to proceed to sea
immediately "for the protection of the East and West India fleets
that are hourly expected." In a private letter to Geary, Sandwich
explained that this was absolutely necessary because one major
convoy had already been captured by the enemy and the loss of
another convoy "would occasion such distress to this country that
no one can tell the consequences it might have."[32] Upon receiving
Admiralty orders to proceed to sea, Geary informed authorities in
London that he would detach Rear Adm. Robert Digby with ten
or twelve sail of the line to cruise to protect the trade as soon as
official directions from the Admiralty arrived. Geary considered
assigning a station for Digby's ships "a matter of too much importance in this critical juncture for myself to determine." At the
same time, Geary informed the Admiralty that the rest of the Channel Fleet would follow Digby to sea as soon as the ships were
ready.[33] As a result of Geary's request for instructions, the Admiralty directed Digby's squadron to cruise "in Mid Channel latitude not exceeding 50 leagues to the westward of Ushant," while
the remainder of the Channel Fleet would proceed to Torbay when
ready.[34]

On 27 August another command crisis erupted in the Channel Fleet. Geary wrote from Gosport to the Admiralty informing
their lordships that he was too ill to leave his bed and requesting
a leave of absence until his health was restored. The admiral's
letter enclosed a statement signed by Dr. James Lind, a navy surgeon at Haslar Hospital, setting forth the ill state of Geary's
health.[35] Geary was immediately granted a leave of absence and
the admiral went to his house at Polesden, Surrey, to recover his
strength. However, Geary's health did not improve and he resigned
his command.[36] When Barrington was ordered to take command
of the Channel Fleet, he again refused the position and informed
the Admiralty that he had turned the command of the fleet over
to the commander at Portsmouth, Adm. Sir Thomas Pye.[37]
Barrington's refusal was seen as part of a plot to place Keppel or
Howe in command of the Channel Fleet,[38] and an exasperated
king ordered Barrington to strike his flag and come ashore.[39]

On 7 September 1780, Vice Adm. George Darby was appointed
to replace Geary as commander in chief of the Channel Fleet.[40]
Several days later Darby also succeeded Vice Adm. Robert Man
as a member of the Board of Admiralty.[41] Kempenfelt was ap-

[handwritten marginal note at top: It is failure in the eyes of the haven public. Failure in... terms of leadive—not nuance... mixed given... disentri...]

pointed captain of the fleet.[42] Characterized by Horace Walpole as an "old woman,"[43] Darby has been largely forgotten by naval historians because he did not cause a political or command crisis and never fought a major battle. Apolitical, modest, and competent, Darby was the best commander of the Channel Fleet Sandwich ever appointed. According to Mulgrave, Darby was "an officer of great firmness, spirit, knowledge, and experience" who went out of his way "to make himself agreeable to those under his command without sacrificing the discipline of the service."[44] A subordinate admiral in the Channel Fleet, Darby achieved flag rank in 1778 and was from a younger generation of navy officers than Hardy, Geary, Keppel, and Howe. To appoint Darby, Sandwich had reached down into the ranks of the junior and less experienced flag officers, probably what the first lord would have been well advised to do much earlier in the American war.

On 12 September, Darby sailed from Spithead with the Channel Fleet consisting of twenty-three ships of the line[45] and arrived at Torbay the next day.[46] The orders calling for a detachment from the Channel Fleet under Digby's command had been canceled, for there was "no longer any probability of invasion or danger from the Brest fleet to our trade." Instead, Darby was directed to sail with the Channel Fleet from Torbay, taking station to prevent a junction between the Spanish squadron at Cadiz and the French ships at Brest.[47] However, the Channel Fleet did not put to sea immediately, for adverse winds and storms held it in Torbay six weeks. Ships were damaged by the weather, and Darby feared "greatly for the ships everywhere, in particular those in the Channel."[48] In the third week of October, Darby and the Channel Fleet (now down to twenty-one ships of the line) finally sailed from Torbay. Their objective was the interception of Adm. Comte Luc-Urbain Du Bouexic de Guichen's squadron as it returned to Europe from the West Indies. But the enemy ships had safely entered Cadiz before the Channel Fleet left Torbay. From 31 October to 6 December, the Channel Fleet cruised some one hundred to two hundred miles off Cape Finisterre without encountering an enemy.[49] With provisions running short, Darby returned to England, arriving at St. Helens on 21 December.[50]

At the beginning of 1781 it became apparent that Gibraltar would again have to be resupplied. On 1 January, the cabinet decided to send a relief expedition escorted by Darby with twenty-four or twenty-six ships of the line. This was considered to be "a hazardous measure," for the Channel Fleet would have to escort the convoy westward out into the Atlantic, past the French squadron at Brest, and then eastward past the Spanish fleet at Cadiz to reach the besieged fortress of Gibraltar.[51] Intelligence reaching London on 18 January told of a number of French ships as well as twenty-five Spanish ships of the line based at Cadiz.[52] Further, the dispatch of the Channel Fleet to Gibraltar would strip the western approaches of British naval forces, giving the French at Brest the opportunity to operate in the Channel or to send reinforcements to their forces overseas without fear of interception by Darby. These were risks the government was prepared to run to resupply Gibraltar. Sandwich would later argue that British forces in the West Indies and North America were thought to be strong enough to cope with any European-based French force while the Channel Fleet covered Gibraltar's relief.[53]

Darby's instructions were drawn up by the Admiralty and issued on 31 January. He was to proceed with the Channel Fleet from Spithead to Cork in Ireland, where a number of victuallers were to be picked up. Then the fleet would sail on to Gibraltar. The Admiralty was aware of the strategic dangers of withdrawing the Channel Fleet from the English Channel for an extended period, and Darby's orders on arriving at Gibraltar were:

> not to wait for the unloading of any of the storeships or victuallers, but leaving them to return to England or Ireland as opportunities may offer, avail yourself of the first favourable moment to come out of the Straits of Gibraltar . . . and make the best of your war into the English Channel.[54]

The Gibraltar relief expedition did not sail immediately, for it took almost six weeks to refit and man the ships of the Channel Fleet and to assemble all the required shipping and stores.[55] On 13 March the Channel Fleet, consisting of twenty-nine ships of the line,[56] departed from St. Helens. It escorted not only the supply ships bound for Gibraltar but also the outward-bound East and West India trade vessels.[57] When Darby arrived off Cork on 17 March, he had to wait for ten days because contrary winds and weather kept the victuallers in that port from joining him. While Darby and the Channel Fleet were off Ireland, a French force of twenty ships of the line under Adm. François Joseph Paul Comte de Grasse, bound for the West Indies, and another five ships of the line under Capt. Pierre Andre de Suffren, bound to

the Indian Ocean, sailed from Brest.[58] The unhindered sailing of
these two French squadrons produced serious consequences: de
Grasse's squadron would be instrumental in trapping Cornwallis
at Yorktown and de Suffren's ships would significantly strengthen
the French position in the Indian Ocean.

Finally, the Cork victuallers appeared and after an uneventful
voyage of some sixteen days, Darby arrived off Cape Spartal in
the entrance of the Strait of Gibraltar on 11 April.[59] Just before
Darby sailed from Spithead, the English received intelligence that
a Spanish squadron of thirty-two ships of the line and a number
of smaller warships had sortied from Cadiz "to intercept a convoy running between England and Gibraltar."[60] The king hoped
there would be a battle between the Spanish and the Channel Fleet
off Cape St. Vincent, but as the Channel Fleet approached the
straits on 11 April, it encountered only three Spanish frigates.[61]
Darby sent HMS *Alexander*, HMS *Foudroyant*, and HMS *Minerva*
to drive the frigates away, and they were chased into Cadiz, where
thirty-three Spanish ships of the line were sighted.[62]

On 12 April, Darby dispatched thirteen supply ships escorted
by HMS *Flora* and HMS *Crescent* to Minorca. At the same time,
victuallers, storeships, and thirteen merchant ships loaded with
coal were sent into Gibraltar harbor, while the bulk of the Channel Fleet remained to the south of Europa Point. As the British
ships began to enter Gibraltar, Spanish gunboats attempted to intercept them but were forced away by escorting British warships.
As the British supply ships were anchoring at 11 A.M., the Spanish
batteries opened a furious bombardment on the anchorage and
unloading area, setting the town of Gibraltar on fire. Despite the
enemy artillery fire and continual skirmishing between British naval
forces and Spanish gunboats, seamen assisted by some five hundred troops from the garrison began to unload the victuallers. To
speed the unloading of supplies and protect the anchorage, Darby
sent Rear Adm. Sir John Lockhart Ross with three ships of the
line into Gibraltar harbor on 14 April while the rest of the Channel Fleet remained off shore confronting westerly winds that prevented the warships from beginning their return voyage to England.
At the request of the governor of Gibraltar, Darby also put ashore
from his ships two thousand barrels of gunpowder, a quantity of
ship's biscuit, and "all the pitch" the ships could spare. On the
morning of 20 April, the wind came around to the east and Darby
made the signal to get under way at 9 A.M. Forty empty victuallers

were brought out of Gibraltar and placed under the escort of HM cutter *Pheasant* for the return voyage. Because of what Darby called the "usual delays, the Channel Fleet could not begin to proceed to the west out of the Strait of Gibraltar until 5 P.M.[63]

With Gibraltar resupplied, the Channel Fleet sailed out into the Atlantic to begin the voyage back to Britain. By 16 May, Darby was off the Isles of Scilly, where he received a letter from the secretary of the Admiralty informing him that a squadron of six French ships of the line under Adm. Toussaint Guillaume La Motte-Picquet had sailed from Brest.[64] Darby was commanded to detach eight ships of the line "to cruise for the protection of the homeward bound trade" and to intercept the French squadron. At the same time, Darby learned that La Motte Picquet's squadron had intercepted a homeward-bound convoy from the West Indies carrying the booty from St. Eustatius. From this convoy the French captured twenty-two merchant ships carrying cargoes said to be worth five million pounds. Darby ordered a detachment of eight ships of the line under Digby to cruise in "the outer part of the Channel" to intercept La Motte Picquet's squadron and protect British vessels, "in particular the homeward bound West India fleet from the Island of Jamaica." Digby was to remain at sea for fourteen days or until he intercepted the expected convoy from Jamaica. The Channel Fleet then proceeded to Spithead, where it arrived on 21 May.[65]

The government knew it ran a risk by sending the whole Channel Fleet southward to resupply Gibraltar but believed that the danger to the homeward-bound trade would come from small squadrons of roving French warships. Frigates were sent out to intercept the British homeward-bound trade west of Ireland and divert it north about the British Isles.[66] Although these ships failed to warn the St. Eustatius convoy before it ran into La Motte-Picquet's squadron, it did reach the Jamaica convoy in time to reroute it from the danger area in the western approaches. Such measures were attempts to patch over the fact that the Channel Fleet was too weak to check French and Spanish naval power in the eastern Atlantic. The root cause of this weakness was the government's strategy of attempting to maintain naval superiority in distant regions such as North America and the West Indies at the expense of the Channel Fleet. For example, on 1 May 1781 there were twenty-seven ships of the line assigned to the Channel Fleet and twenty-eight capital units stationed in the East and West

Indies and North America.[67] As a result, the strength of the Channel Fleet was continually sapped by demands for ships overseas.

After cruising in the western approaches to protect the homeward-bound trade, the squadron under Digby arrived at Spithead on 4 June.[68] The threat to Britain's trade was still thought to exist, and the cabinet resolved that Darby should put to sea "as soon as twenty . . . Line of Battle Ships are fit for Service."[69] On 6 June the Admiralty issued new instructions to Darby for the Channel Fleet. The admiral was directed to sail from Spithead with those ships of the fleet that were "in greater forwardness" and "to cruise for one month between the latitudes of 48° and 50° North from the longitude of Scilly as far westward as you shall judge most proper for the protection of the homeward bound and outward bound convoys." Trade convoys from Jamaica and the Leeward Islands were expected shortly in the western approaches, and the Admiralty also planned to sail convoys bound to the East Indies and North America down the Channel. Darby's mission was to protect these convoys from attack by La Motte-Picquet's squadron of seven French ships of the line and four frigates thought to have put to sea to attack British convoys.[70]

On 8 June, Darby informed the Admiralty from St. Helens that he was putting to sea and that the Channel Fleet would take station twenty to thirty leagues west of Scilly between latitudes 45° N and 49° N.[71] The next day, the fleet proceeded down the English Channel on this mission.[72] Unknown to Darby, the Jamaica convoy had already been diverted north of Britain, but on 17 June the Channel Fleet intercepted the Leeward Island convoy consisting "of 50 odd sail" and saw it safely into the English Channel.[73] In a letter to Sandwich several days later, Darby reported that the seamen of the fleet were again coming down with scurvy, which the admiral blamed on the short period of time the ships had spent in port after the relief of Gibraltar.[74] At the beginning of July, the outward-bound East India convoy was sighted; the Channel Fleet then "stretched" southward to Ushant in the hope of intercepting La Motte-Picquet. Several ships thought to be enemy frigates were sighted and an American privateer and a merchant ship were captured, but La Motte-Picquet's squadron was not seen. After regaining his station to the northward, Darby and the Channel Fleet, now reduced to nine ships of the line, were forced into Torbay on 7 July by a combination of scurvy, lack of beer, and adverse weather.[75] Two days later, the Channel Fleet arrived at Spithead.[76]

In the first days of July intelligence reached London telling of a large squadron of French ships due to sail from Brest to conduct joint operations with the Spanish. By 9 July it was known in London that eighteen sail of the line under the command of Adm. Comte de Guichen had left Brest.[77] The British did not yet know that de Guichen's Brest squadron had gone to Cadiz, arriving on 9 July to conduct joint operations with the Spanish. On 23 July the combined Franco-Spanish fleet sailed from Cadiz to cover the passage of a Spanish force through the Strait of Gibraltar bound for an invasion of Minorca. The Admiralty did not learn of de Guichen's departure for Cadiz until 28 July and remained ignorant of the planned Spanish invasion of Minorca until 20 August.[78] Since the British could not resupply Minorca or break the Spanish siege there, the king's forces on the island were forced to surrender after a siege that lasted until February 1782.[79] Once the force for Minorca was safely through the Strait of Gibraltar, the Franco-Spanish fleet of forty-nine ships of the line proceeded west into the Atlantic and then north toward the western approaches of the English Channel. Their objective, of course, was to pen the Channel Fleet in British waters during the attack on Minorca.[80]

On 10 July the Admiralty directed the Channel Fleet to "return immediately to sea" to meet de Guichen's threat. The next day the suspected presence of de Guichen's squadron prompted a suspension of the departure of all outward-bound convoys down the English Channel until the Channel Fleet could again cruise in the western approaches.[81] On 12 July the cabinet decided that the Channel Fleet should escort a small squadron, consisting of three ships of the line under Digby bound for North America, down the Channel and out into the Atlantic.[82]

Darby's instructions of 12 July called for the Channel Fleet to escort Digby's squadron 150 leagues west of The Lizard. After that, "bringing the French fleet under command of Mons de Guichen to battle are the principle object of your attention."[83] Darby remained at Spithead for several days owing to contrary winds, a shortage of sauerkraut at Portsmouth, and delays in loading beer and water on the ships. The main body of the Channel Fleet sailed from Spithead on 19 July.[84] After seeing Digby's squadron offshore, Darby intended to cruise "in the Lat of Cape Finisterre 20 leagues to the westward of there for about a month."[85] When all the ships from Plymouth and elsewhere had joined the Channel Fleet, Darby's command consisted of twenty-one ships of the line.[86]

On 31 July, Digby's squadron parted company with Darby some ninety-four leagues southwest of The Lizard, and the Channel Fleet proceeded to its cruising station off Cape Finisterre, where it arrived at the beginning of August.[87] For the next two weeks the Channel Fleet cruised west of Cape Finisterre. Nothing of importance was sighted until 17 August, when a Portuguese merchant ship was intercepted. The vessel's master informed Darby that several days before, at 47°31' N, 10°21' W, he sighted the Franco-Spanish fleet consisting of ninety sail, of which forty were thought to be ships of the line. The enemy force was steering "NE upon a wind which seems to indicate that they were intended for the English Channel." After discussing this intelligence with Rear Adm. Sir John Lockhart Ross and Commodore John Elliot, Darby decided to return to the English Channel to defend that body of water from the enemy. A warning of the approach of the Franco-Spanish fleet went to the Admiralty by HM brig *Defiance,* which also warned authorities that the Channel Fleet would approach the English coast from the southwest at Portland. During the voyage to England, the Channel Fleet obtained no new intelligence of the movements of the Franco-Spanish fleet. To avoid being forced eastward up the Channel and to spare the ships damage from the weather, the Channel Fleet put into Torbay on 24 August.[88]

When Sandwich received Darby's dispatches, the first lord of the Admiralty did not believe that the Franco-Spanish fleet was proceeding northward toward the western approaches of the Channel,[89] for recent intelligence showed the enemy fleet to be in the area of the Strait of Gibraltar.[90] During the voyage northward, Darby himself concluded that the Franco-Spanish fleet was probably escorting a Dutch convoy from Cadiz to one of the French Biscay ports.[91] Not crediting a report from a Portuguese merchant ship intercepted by Darby that it had sighted the Franco-Spanish fleet, the Admiralty ordered the Channel Fleet to put back to sea from Torbay. Its mission was protection of an expected homeward-bound convoy from Jamaica, "supposed to be the most valuable one that ever came from thence."[92]

Darby did not take the Channel Fleet to sea. Instead, he barricaded Torbay much as Barrington had fortified St. Lucia in 1778, placing his ships across the entrance of the bay in two crescent-shaped lines.[93] Darby believed that he could withstand an assault on this position by the Franco-Spanish fleet. With the wind out of the west, Torbay would be difficult to attack, and the admiral thought that the lee shore would discourage the enemy from an approach with an east wind. However, if the enemy proceeded up the Channel east of Torbay to St. Helens, Darby would have the difficult task of taking the Channel Fleet through The Needles into The Solent to defend Portsmouth and the dockyard.[94]

On 31 August the Admiralty concurred with Darby's decision to remain at Torbay and directed him to send frigates to intercept the homeward-bound trade convoys and divert them north.[95] Darby had anticipated the Admiralty's orders by dispatching frigates to the westward. One of these, HMS *Juno,* spoke with a Venetian merchant ship that had sighted the enemy force. Two more frigates, HMS *Emerald* and HMS *La Prudente,* were then sent to find the enemy and one spoke with a Swedish merchant ship that had passed through the Franco-Spanish fleet on 29 August to the west of the Isles of Scilly.[96] On 1 September, Darby received a letter from Admiral Lord Shuldham, commander at Plymouth, enclosing a copy of a letter from Capt. Benjamin Caldwell of HMS *Agamemnon.* Caldwell had been on his way to the East Indies on 30 August when he sighted the Franco-Spanish fleet some thirty leagues west of The Lizard. Before running to Plymouth to inform the authorities of the presence of the Franco-Spanish fleet, Caldwell approached close enough to the enemy force to fix its strength at between forty-four and forty-seven ships of the line. Upon receiving this intelligence, Darby ordered the frigate HMS *Monsieur* to cross over to the French coast before proceeding west to warn merchant ships of the enemy fleet as these British vessels neared the western approaches.[97] The Admiralty also dispatched a number of ships and vessels to intercept and divert the inward-bound trade to proceed north about Ireland and Scotland.[98]

The government became fully alerted to the danger on 3 September, when intelligence of the presence of the Franco-Spanish fleet west of the Isles of Scilly arrived in London. These reports put the strength of the enemy force at forty-nine ships of the line.[99] Doubt about the enemy's intentions made the strategic situation confronting the government extremely difficult, for the Channel Fleet was outnumbered almost two to one. The British discounted a possible invasion of England, assuming that the Franco-Spanish fleet planned to intercept homeward-bound convoys in the western approaches. Another objective of the enemy might be a "dissent" on Ireland or an attempt to push up the English Channel to attack the naval facilities in the Portsmouth area. Except for the squadron in the North Sea blockading the Dutch, there were no readily available ships of the line to reinforce the Channel Fleet and the government did not want to weaken the North Sea force. Therefore, the outnumbered Channel Fleet would have to confront the French and the Spanish without major reinforcements.[100]

When intelligence reached England of the possibility of an attack on Ireland by a detachment from the Franco-Spanish fleet, the king thought that Darby should put to sea and attack the enemy.[101] Middleton, on the other hand, advised Sandwich to send Darby to sea, not to fight the enemy but to exploit the superior speed of the British copper-bottomed ships to "wait for opportunities they will from circumstances of negligence and weather to be sure to meet with them and general to have in their power to turn them to advantage."[102] On 6 September, the cabinet adopted this strategy and ordered Darby and the Channel Fleet to put to sea.[103] Darby's instructions were drawn up and issued that same day. "Without waiting for any further reinforcements," the admiral was ordered to sail immediately to intercept the enemy and shadow the Franco-Spanish fleet. Darby was further directed "to avoid an Engagement with them, which your copper bottomed ships & the supposed foulness of the Spanish ships will enable you to do." Protecting the homeward-bound trade and Ireland was Darby's first objective, but if he found that the Franco-Spanish fleet was "so far weakened by detachments or by other separation," then he was to bring the enemy force to battle.[104]

The Channel Fleet did not sail immediately. It was not until 9 September that Darby received the Admiralty's orders of 6 September.[105] Kempenfelt was promoted to the rank of rear admiral of the red on 26 September 1780; he hoisted his flag on HMS *Victory* and became third in command of the fleet. Capt. Joseph Peyton replaced Kempenfelt as captain of the fleet.[106] Not until 14 September did the Channel Fleet sail from Torbay, anchoring off Berry Head because of contrary winds.[107]

The next day, 15 September, there was a "very fine breeze" and the Channel Fleet proceeded down the Channel.[108] For the next month the fleet ranged back and forth across the western approaches to the southward and southwest of Ireland. Nothing of any importance was sighted.[109] Off Cape Clear on 19 October, Darby finally received intelligence that the French fleet was proceeding to Brest, while the Spanish fleet had been "seen in Lat.

47°30' steering to the southward." At the same time, he learned that the trade coming from the West Indies had put into Cork. The threat of the Franco-Spanish fleet had vanished.[110]

The Franco-Spanish fleet had left its station west of the Isles of Scilly before Darby and the Channel Fleet left Torbay. The two enemy forces had separated on 5 September, the French going to Brest and the Spanish returning to Spain.[111] Intelligence of the French and Spanish fleets' departure from the western approaches arrived in London on 22 September. The enemy fleets were reported to be sickly and damaged and "had not made a single, capture great or small, during the whole long cruise."[112] Several days later, with the danger from the enemy's joint fleet ended, the cabinet decided that the Channel Fleet and Darby should return to port to refit for future operations.[113] Darby received these orders on 31 October, and the Channel Fleet anchored at Spithead on 5 November after an uneventful voyage of fifty-two days.[114]

In mid-October intelligence reports began to arrive in London of a French reinforcement of ships and troops that would sail from Brest to the East and West Indies. Specifically, these reports indicated that the reinforcements would consist of four ships of the line and three thousand troops for the East Indies and "a large body of troops" and "several ships of the line" for the West Indies.[115] Some reports estimated the French reinforcement for the West Indies to be as large as a train of artillery, five regiments of troops, and ten ships of the line. London believed that the reinforcement for the West Indies would be used to mount an invasion of Jamaica. At a series of meetings on 20 and 22 October, the cabinet decided to "retard" this French reinforcement by intercepting it with a detachment from the Channel Fleet.[116] The detachment would be commanded by Kempenfelt, for Darby was recovering from an illness contracted during the fleet's last cruise.[117]

On 14 November the Admiralty assigned to Kempenfelt's command fourteen ships of the line, one 50-gun ship, and seven frigates.[118] In fact, two ships of the line did not join the force,[119] and even though a fire ship[120] would be added to the command,[121] Kempenfelt considered this force unequal to the task, especially in frigates.[122] However, the government could not reinforce Kempenfelt's squadron, for there were no ships to be had: Britain's strategic commitments outstripped the available crews and vessels. While attempting to intercept a major French force departing for the Indies, the government dared not weaken the North Sea squadron or give Kempenfelt ships fitting for service in the East and West Indies.[123]

By 22 November, the day Kempenfelt's orders were issued, the size of the French force had grown in British intelligence reports to eighteen ships of the line, of which four were armed *en flute,* escorting transports carrying ten to twelve thousand troops. Kempenfelt was to put to sea with "the ships under your command or such number of them as you shall judge necessary shall be ready, & directed to proceed and cruise on such Station as you shall judge most likely for intercepting the said fleet, & to use your utmost endeavors to take or destroy it."[124] On 15 November, Kempenfelt was ordered to Spithead to make his command ready for sea,[125] but there were the usual delays in readying the ships for sea.[126] Kempenfelt's squadron did not sail until the beginning of December.[127]

At daylight on 12 December, fifty-three leagues southwest of Ushant, Capt. James Saumarez of the fire ship HMS *Tisiphone* sighted strange sails to the southeast. These belonged to the merchant ships of the convoy carrying French reinforcements to the East and West Indies. Beyond the horizon to leeward was de Guichen's naval force escorting the convoy. Kempenfelt made the signal for his "two decked ships and frigates to chase." At 9:30 A.M., the enemy ships were seen "steering large to windward." An hour later, several ships of the line were sighted on the British lee bow, forming a line of battle. On sighting the enemy warships, Kempenfelt signaled the British ships to form a line of battle, but the British admiral saw "a prospect of passing between the enemy's ships of war and the great part of their convoy. I continued a press's sail with a view of cutting them off and succeeded in part." As the British passed into the gap between the French convoy and warships, the French ship of the line *Triomphant* stood out of the convoy, proceeding across the bow of the leading British ship HMS *Edgar.* The *Triomphant* attempted to rake HMS *Edgar* with gunfire as she passed, but the *Edgar* "bore up" and fired a broadside into the passing French warship. As some of the French merchant ships began to surrender, Kempenfelt saw that some of the British warships had fallen astern of the main body of the British force, and the admiral tacked to join the ships astern to form a proper line of battle. It was dark before this maneuver was completed. During the night, the British stood on the same tack as the enemy. At daylight the British saw the French warships to leeward forming a line of battle. Kempenfelt sent the frigate *La Prudente* to reconnoiter along the enemy line of battle, sailing from van to stern just out of gunshot, and nineteen enemy ships of the line were counted. Kempenfelt was not only to windward and hence unable to open the lower deck gun ports, but also outnumbered. He "did not think it advisable to hazard a action" and stood on the opposite tack "to secure the prizes." The next day HMS *Tisiphone* was sent to the West Indies to warn of the approaching French force. The British captured nine ships out of a convoy of some one hundred sail, and in the next two days HMS *Agamemnon* captured five more stragglers from the French convoy. The captured ships carried 1,062 French soldiers and were loaded with ordnance stores. On Christmas Day, a gale scattered the French ships, forcing most of them to return to Europe: only two ships of the line and a few transports arrived in the West Indies. Kempenfelt anchored in Spithead on 20 December.[128]

Kempenfelt's interception of the French convoy and adverse weather totally disrupted the French attempts to reinforce the East and West Indies, but contemporary observers were unsatisfied. George III was "disappointed" and thought that Kempenfelt should have followed the French force and taken more ships.[129] Ignoring the consequences of weakening the Channel Fleet, Rear Adm. Sir Samuel Hood, the acting commander in chief in the Leeward Islands, argued that Kempenfelt should have taken his entire force directly to the West Indies instead of returning to England after failing to take or destroy the French convoy. Hood believed that Kempenfelt's ships would have tipped the balance of the naval war in the Leeward Islands in Britain's favor.[130] Rodney, who was in England at the time, agreed that Kempenfelt should have taken his ships to the West Indies.[131] All ignored the fact that Kempenfelt had used his inferior force with considerable skill to place the French commander in the position of being "within an ace of suffering a most ridiculous disgrace—that of having all his convoy taken from him before his face." After the event Kempenfelt believed that had he known the strength of the enemy sooner, he could have captured more ships of the convoy by continuing the general chase instead of forming a line of battle.[132] Perhaps more French ships could have been taken, but in the end it did not matter, for the weather later forced the French ships to return to Europe without reinforcing the East and West Indies.

In the House of Commons the government's naval policy was

North
Sea

Irish
Sea

Ireland

England

London •

• Calais

Portsmouth

Cork •

English Channel

• Le Harve

Lands End

Plymouth •

• Cherbourg

Scilly Islands

Atlantic Ocean

Ushant Island

• Brest

France

• Nantes

Bay of
Biscay

Cape Ortegal

Cape Finisterre

Spain

~ MDS 97 ~

The Bay of Biscay

debated and attacked. William Pitt told the House that sending Kempenfelt to sea with only twelve ships "was a measure in which the Admiralty was highly culpable." Lord Howe asked why Kempenfelt had been ordered out with such a small force to intercept a superior French squadron and claimed it was "providential" that all of Kempenfelt's ships had not been captured by the enemy. Charles James Fox, an opposition politician, went to the heart of the matter when he told the House that it was government strategy to defeat French naval power in the West Indies by attempting to be strong everywhere. As a result, Fox pointed out, the navy was weak in European seas. To Fox the government's strategy was backwards, for he believed that the best policy might be one of strength in European waters sufficient to prevent the enemy from sending naval forces to distant theaters like the West Indies.[133] By pointing to the government's apparent lack of a grand design for conducting the American war, Fox identified one of the great faults in Britain's strategic conduct of the war.

In fact, the government was weak and divided on the question of war strategy. Within the cabinet there was no overall strategic conception of how the American war should be conducted. Instead, several strategies competed for attention and adoption at various times. Lord North, indecisive and longing to resign, provided no leadership.[134] Formulation of military and naval strategy within the cabinet thus fell largely to Germain and Sandwich, who vied for control of the strategic direction of the war. Thus, the war was conducted for the most part by departments, and after 1778 it was never clear if the main effort was to be against the Bourbons or the Americans.[135] Germain, with his eyes firmly fixed on the Western Hemisphere, always demanded men, matériel, and ships for an offensive in America. On the other hand, after 1778 Sandwich focused on European seas and the navies of France and Spain. Neither Germain nor Sandwich had the political power within the cabinet to impose his strategic view on the government completely. As a result, the focus of British naval strategy tended to wander between America and European seas. In 1778 Sandwich had won the argument within the cabinet over dispatching Byron's squadron to America, but in the winter of 1781–82, Germain's views on the West Indies won out, resulting in steady reinforcement of the Leeward Islands, while the strength of the Royal Navy in European seas remained static.

The Channel Fleet's weakness in comparison to the Leeward

Islands squadron in 1782 could no longer be blamed on a shortage of ships. The Royal Navy's weakness in capital units at the beginning of the war had been largely overcome by 1782.[136] On 1 April 1782 the Royal Navy had eighty-eight ships of the line in commission.[137] Instead, the Channel Fleet's weakness was the result of the government's decision to reinforce the squadron in the Leeward Islands, looking for decisive action in that theater rather than in Europe. On 1 September 1781 the Admiralty calculated that out of a total of eighty-seven ships of the line in commission there were thirty-three in England and twenty in the Leeward Islands, while on 1 June 1782 out of ninety-six ships of the line in commission there were forty-two in the Leeward Islands and thirty-four in England.[138] Clearly naval superiority in the Leeward Islands had achieved priority within the British government over the strength of the Channel Fleet. Recognizing the weakness of the Royal Navy in European seas, Middleton developed a radically new strategy for 1782.[139] This called for a weak Channel Fleet to deter invasion, hold the North Sea, and guard the trade from the Atlantic north around Britain.[140]

Military failure in America caused the collapse of North's government on 20 March 1782 and its replacement by a new ministry headed by the marquis of Rockingham and the earl of Shelburne.[141] Keppel, raised to the peerage, replaced Sandwich as first lord of the Admiralty, while Lord Howe, now an English earl, became commander in chief of the Channel Fleet with Barrington as second in command. Darby was first offered the position of second in command of the Channel Fleet, but the admiral declined and was ordered to strike his flag and come ashore.[142] The new government was pledged to seek an early end to the war but still had to conduct the war while diplomats worked for a settlement.[143] In European seas, the new government had little choice but to continue the strategies of the North government because of the deployment of naval forces to the Leeward Islands and the resulting weakness of the Channel Fleet.

At the beginning of 1782 intelligence came to the new government in London telling of fresh enemy naval preparations and activities.[144] Not only were there the usual reports of French and Spanish naval preparations, but also rumors that the Dutch were assembling ships for a sortie into the North Sea from the Texel.[145] From this information, Keppel concluded that the French would have at least fourteen ships of the line at Brest; that the combined

Franco-Spanish fleets would number some sixty-two ships of the line; and that the Dutch fleet, including 50-gun ships, "may amount to twenty or twenty five ships." To oppose this force in European seas, the first lord of the Admiralty calculated that there were "a normal twenty ships many of them short of men" in the Channel Fleet; that the North Sea squadron fitting out at the Medway and the Thames would number about "six or seven" capital units including 50-gun ships; and that in the course of the next two months a total of thirty-two ships of the line would be available for deployment in European waters.[146] With an inferior force of ships of the line, Britain now not only had to guard the western approaches against the French and the Spanish navies, but also deploy forces into the North Sea to meet a possible Dutch attack.

To harass the French, a small squadron was stationed off Brest. Intelligence indicated that a squadron of five French ships of the line and several Spanish warships were about to escort "five or six" Dutch East Indiamen from Cadiz to L'Orient, while a "secret expedition" of ten French ships of the line and a number of merchant ships under the command of La Motte-Picquet were about to sail from Brest.[147] On 30 March the cabinet voted to send twelve ships of the line from the Channel Fleet to intercept these two enemy forces.[148]

Barrington was placed in command of this detachment from the Channel Fleet. The Admiralty issued his instructions on 5 April. Barrington was directed to take station off the French coast between the "latitude of Ushant and the latitude of Belle Isle" to intercept the enemy ships. In a private letter the next day, Keppel told Barrington that a lack of information on the movements of the enemy ships coming from Cadiz meant that the French ships departing from Brest "will probably be more your objective."[149] Barrington was also directed to avoid an engagement if the enemy proved to be of superior force. If no enemy force was encountered, he was to maintain his station until 25 April and then look into Brest. Then, in a departure from previous strategy, Barrington was directed to remain off Brest until further orders if he found a superior enemy force there. On the other hand, if the enemy force was inferior, Barrington was to leave a squadron of "four or five" ships of the line off the enemy naval base until the arrival of further orders.[150] While this was still a strategy of detachments, the new government was beginning to think in terms of blockading Brest.

On 13 April, Barrington sailed from Spithead in a gale of wind with twelve ships of the line[151] and several smaller vessels.[152] At 1 P.M. on 20 April, Barrington was some twenty-three leagues southwest of Ushant when he sighted an enemy fleet at a great distance. Barrington ordered a general chase. During the afternoon several British ships, led by HMS *Foudroyant,* Capt. John Jervis, drew ahead of the admiral. At sunset Barrington lost sight of the enemy and the leading British ships. The British had intercepted a French convoy bound for Ile-de-France in the Indian Ocean: eighteen merchant ships and a ship of the line armed *en flute* escorted by three warships. In the darkness HMS *Foudroyant* overhauled the French ship of the line *Pegase* and in a hard-fought action forced the French ship to surrender. That evening and the next morning, a number of French merchant ships, the ship of the line, and one thousand troops were captured. Then a gale sprang up, scattering the British ships and forcing Barrington northward. On 22 April, The Lizard was sighted and Barrington's flagship HMS *Britannia* was off St. Helens by 25 April.[153] This time, luck was with Barrington, for his intelligence proved correct and the admiral intercepted an important French convoy. This was not always the case, for intercepting enemy ships at sea to the westward of Ushant was a tricky matter.

The government intended to keep the pressure on the French at Brest. Intelligence had been received that a French force was about to put to sea from that port,[154] and on 28 April the cabinet decided to send Howe and the whole Channel Fleet to take station off Ushant, with the objective of "destroying or retarding the French force now preparing at Brest to put to sea." The Channel Fleet was to remain off Brest for forty days before putting into Torbay for resupplying; news then arrived of a threat in the North Sea. Some units of the Channel Fleet were ordered instead to blockade the Texel, while a squadron under Kempenfelt was to sail west to take station off Ushant to intercept enemy vessels. On 3 May, Kempenfelt sailed from St. Helens with seven ships of the line, a frigate, and two cutters.[155] If the wind came around from the west, Kempenfelt's squadron would position itself halfway between Ushant and The Lizard to protect British trade.[156] The squadron arrived off Ushant on 5 May and remained at sea without intercepting the enemy until 18 May, when it put into Torbay. Kempenfelt put out again until 24 May, and his squadron remained at sea in the western approaches until the end of May without intercepting anything of importance during twenty-two days at sea.[157]

On 20 April, Lord Howe hoisted his flag on HMS *Victory* at Spithead and took command of the Channel Fleet.[158] Although a difficult and taciturn man, Howe was one of the favorite admirals of the political opposition during the North ministry, and he was probably the Channel Fleet's most competent commander during the American war. Having served in America with credit during the first years of the war, Howe was the acknowledged leader of the movement within the navy to reform battle tactics and signals.[159] Immediately upon taking command of the Channel Fleet, he implemented two of Rodney's recommendations by appointing Dr. Cathbert Cahalloner physician of the Fleet and ordering locks to be fitted to HMS *Victory*'s guns.[160] At the same time, Howe began "perfecting" the signals and instructions required "for the conduct of the squadron."[161]

On 8 May, Howe received orders to put to sea and proceed east "to watch the motions of the Dutch fleet which anchored without the Texel."[162] Intelligence of Dutch preparations for a sortie from the Texel raised the possibility that the Dutch might raid the east coast coal trade or attack a Baltic convoy.[163] There were just not enough capital units of the Royal Navy in England to cover both the North Sea and the western approaches at the same time. As Keppel put it in a letter to Howe, "these quick movements with our little fleet seem to be our only recourse circumstanced as we are in point of numbers."[164] On 10 May, Howe sailed for the North Sea with nine ships of the line[165] and several smaller warships.[166]

Not long after the Channel Fleet arrived off the Dutch coast on 16 May, Howe received reports that the Dutch fleet consisted of thirteen ships of the line, of which nine were operational, and a number of smaller vessels. Further, the Dutch apparently had no intentions of leaving the Texel.[167] In light of the apparent Dutch passivity and Keppel's fears for the safety of the Channel Fleet's two largest ships in a northwest gale, the government issued orders on 25 May for Howe to return to Spithead.[168] To continue the blockade of the Texel, he left behind a force of eight ships of the line[169] commanded by Rear Adm. Sir John Lockhart Ross.[170] Keppel complained that the "Dutch war is a millstone around our necks" and informed Howe that, if necessary, Ross's squadron could be used to reinforce the Channel Fleet.[171] On 8 June, Howe arrived at Spithead with three ships of the line.[172]

Thirty-two enemy ships of the line sailed from Cadiz on 4 June. Heading north toward Ushant, the enemy encountered a British convoy proceeding to Newfoundland and Quebec and captured nineteen of its merchant ships. Before undertaking operations in the western approaches of the English Channel, the ships from Cadiz were joined off the Ile d' Ouessant on 8 July by eight French ships of the line from Brest under La Motte-Picquet.[173] The British thought that the French and Spanish fleets would probably conduct operations in the western approaches as they had done in 1781, but when the enemy ships sailed from Cadiz, London possessed little hard information about their intentions and movements. When asked by the government what he believed enemy intentions to be, Howe replied on 24 May that he lacked enough information to make "conjectures" about the movements of the Bourbon fleets.[174] On the day that the enemy sailed from Cadiz, intelligence reached London that there were twenty-seven enemy ships of the line in that port.[175] By 17 June the British knew that the combined fleet had sailed from Cadiz, and Keppel calculated that the addition of the ships from Brest would create a force of more than thirty ships of the line.[176]

To clarify the situation, the government ordered Howe to dispatch a small squadron consisting of HMS *Vigilant* and three frigates to cruise for ten days from the "Lat of 44°30' to 46°30' on or about the meridian of Cape Ortegal." This squadron was to intercept a small French convoy carrying supplies to America and gain intelligence on the movements of the enemy fleet.[177] To counter the threat posed by the combined fleet, the government reinforced the Channel Fleet to twenty ships of the line by detaching four ships from the squadron off the Dutch coast.[178] The government realized that this squadron itself had to be reinforced to contain the Dutch,[179] for the squadron at the Texel might sortie in support of the combined fleet when that force arrived in the western approaches.[180]

As the Channel Fleet sailed west from St. Helens on 2 July, Howe encountered a neutral ship that informed him that the Franco-Spanish fleet might have put into Brest. Howe notified the Admiralty that he would continue down the Channel but warned that he would return to Spithead if this intelligence proved true. On 5 July, Howe learned that the combined fleet, consisting of forty-two ships of the line, had been sighted off Ushant.[181] Southeast of the Isles of Scilly on 11 July, the Channel Fleet met HMS *Cormorant,* whose captain informed Howe that a large West India convoy was approaching from the west, expecting to make its first landfall on the Irish coast. The early morning of the next day, the Channel Fleet, twenty-five ships of the line strong, was fifteen leagues south southeast of the Isles of Scilly when it sighted the combined fleet to the westward.[182] The enemy fleet consisted of thirty-six ships of the line "besides frigates." The wind was northwest and the Franco-Spanish fleet was to windward. This meant that Howe would have to deal with a superior enemy force that lay between his fleet and the approaching West Indies convoy, which he had to protect. As the enemy ships formed a line of battle, the Channel Fleet stood to the northward, passing between Land's End and the Isles of Scilly. This maneuver required nerve and considerable seamanship. Its purpose was "to get to the westward of the enemy; both for the protection of the Jamaica convoy; and to gain that advantage of the situation for bringing them to action which the difference in our numbers renders desirable." At the same time, Howe sent HMS *Cormorant* west to warn the West India convoy of the enemy's presence and to order the merchant ships into southern Irish ports.[183] The next morning the Channel Fleet was to the northward and west of the Isles of Scilly and the Franco-Spanish fleet was nowhere in sight. The Channel Fleet then stood to the westward to intercept the West India convoy.

When news arrived in England that the combined fleet was off the Isles of Scilly, Keppel assured the king that every effort was being made to reinforce the Channel Fleet.[184] By 18 June, HMS *Panther* and HMS *Ocean* were en route to join Howe, while five other ships of the line were on the point of sailing and several others were just completing their fitting out. A shortage of seamen were "the chief obstruction" to completing these vessels.[185] Keppel thought that these reinforcements would reduce the French and Spanish advantage by four or five ships of the line, enabling Howe to seek out the enemy and bring them to battle.[186]

After eluding the Franco-Spanish fleet by passing north, the Channel Fleet waited in the track of the expected convoy from the West Indies. Howe used the opportunity to drill the ships of the Channel Fleet in battle tactics. On 27 June, failing to obtain any information on the movements of the West India convoy and forced off station by a northerly gale, Howe decided "to return to the eastward . . . to go in quest of the enemy" in hope of "attempting to draw them from their station off of Scilly." Arriving off the Isles of Scilly on 2 August, Howe discovered that the Franco-Spanish fleet had left and that the West India convoy had entered the English Channel. The Channel Fleet anchored in Torbay on 4 August and returned to Spithead ten days later.[187]

Once again the Royal Navy had failed to bring to battle a Franco-Spanish fleet. After the British fleet passed between Land's End and the Isles of Scilly, the Bourbon ships maintained their station west of Scilly until driven south by the same northerly gale that forced Howe off station. After the combined fleet left the Isles of Scilly, the British West Indian convoy passed into the English Channel. At the beginning of August, the Spanish ships of the enemy force received orders to return to Spain to oppose an expected British attempt to resupply Gibraltar.[188] The Franco-Spanish fleet's parade in the western approaches during the summer of 1782 was embarrassing for the British, but it accomplished nothing of importance. While the French and Spanish had amassed a superior fleet at the western end of the English Channel, they failed to intercept a major convoy or bring the Channel Fleet to battle and cripple British naval power in European seas.

The government's attention now turned southward. Everyone knew that the British would again have to supply the besieged fortress of Gibraltar, and Middleton and Shelburne discussed arrangements for that relief expedition as early as 12 May.[189] On 30 July, Keppel informed Howe that "the principal objects at present is how & when to relieve Gibraltar" and that the government had to choose between two courses: immediately mounting a small relief expedition with a weak escort that could be blocked by the enemy or waiting until September when the resupply of Gibraltar could be supported by the whole Channel Fleet.[190]

The whole Channel Fleet could not be spared earlier because a force of ships of the line had to be sent into the North Sea to meet a new Dutch naval threat. Keppel and other officials in the Admiralty considered it absolutely imperative that the Baltic trade return home safely and, with the possibility of a Dutch sortie from the Texel, this required a detachment from the Channel Fleet.[191]

On 6 August, the Admiralty directed Howe to detach ten ships of the line from the Channel Fleet for possible service in the North Sea.[192] At a cabinet meeting on 9 August, Howe was directed to return immediately to Spithead and prepare the Channel Fleet for further service. At the same time, it was decided to dispatch ten ships of the line to the North Sea. Howe was to stay at Spithead with a further force of twenty-three ships of the line, prepared either to sail into the North Sea or to undertake the resupply of Gibraltar.[193] As Keppel explained the plan to Howe, ten ships of the line were to sail into the North Sea to protect the Baltic trade from attack by a Dutch squadron thought to be off the Naze of Norway. If ten ships could not deal with this Dutch squadron, Howe was to enter the North Sea with reinforcements. When the Dutch threat was removed, Howe was to sail to Spithead to undertake the resupply of Gibraltar with the entire Channel Fleet.[194] On 14 August the cabinet decided that as soon as the ships of the Channel Fleet were fit for sea, Howe was to go with "twenty to thirty ships of the Line in quest of the Dutch Squadron." Howe was to seek out the Dutch, first at the Texel and then, if necessary, off the Naze of Norway. He was further directed to return to Spithead by the beginning of September to undertake the Gibraltar mission.[195]

The strategic problem confronting the British in the summer of 1782 was simple. If Gibraltar was not quickly resupplied, the fortress would fall to the Spanish. But if the Dutch threat was not contained, the British might lose naval control of the North Sea. This would cut off Britain's supplies of naval stores from the Baltic and enable the Dutch to blockade London and "every other port on the northern coast, and put an end to our coastal trade and every other branch of commerce." On 24 August, Keppel clearly stated the dilemma when he wrote Howe: "If we fail getting the ships safe from the Baltick our next years equipping the Fleet must also fail, if our relief does not get soon to Gibraltar that garrison may fall." There seemed no way to resupply Gibraltar until the ships of the Channel Fleet returned from the North Sea.[196]

On 25 August the North Sea threat disappeared when intelligence arrived in England that the Dutch fleet had returned to the Texel. Nevertheless, ten ships of the line were detached from the Channel Fleet and sent east. The squadron had orders to look into the Texel. If the Dutch fleet was in that port and did not appear likely to put to sea, the ships were to return immediately to Spithead.[197] Although the Dutch at the Texel appeared once again sunk into inactivity and the ships of the Channel Fleet had returned to Spithead on 4 September,[198] Keppel continued to fear for the safety of Britain's east coast.[199]

At Spithead, preparations went ahead for the relief of Gibraltar even while the detached ships were in the North Sea. The merchant ships needed to carry the supplies were being assembled, fitted, and loaded, and the warships of the Channel Fleet were being made ready for sea. On 29 August, HMS *Royal George* sunk at her moorings when her bottom fell out while being heeled for repairs. Some nine hundred people, including Kempenfelt, were drowned. This tragedy probably resulted from corrosion of the iron fastenings caused by the ship's copper bottom.[200]

On 30 August the Admiralty began to issue Howe's instructions for the resupply of Gibraltar. Troops of the 29th and 59th Regiments were to embark on warships for transport to Gibraltar. Howe was to use the Channel Fleet to escort not only the merchant ships carrying provisions, ordnance stores, and fuel to Gibraltar, but also the trade proceeding to the East and West Indies and a convoy to Portugal. If the Franco-Spanish fleet was encountered during the operation to resupply Gibraltar, it was left to Howe's "judgement and direction to determine what measures to pursue upon such an event." After unloading the troops and supplies at Gibraltar, Howe was to return to England. The cabinet had not entirely abandoned the North ministry's West Indian strategy: during that return voyage, six ships of the line were to be detached and sent to the Caribbean. Before arriving in England, Howe was also directed to detach "two or three" ships of the line and several frigates to cruise in the Bay of Biscay to intercept ships attempting to enter French ports.[201]

The Channel Fleet, consisting of thirty-five ships of the line, sailed from Spithead on 11 September with the supply ships bound for Gibraltar and the three trade convoys.[202] "Contrary winds & unfavorable weather" delayed the fleet's arrival off Cape St. Vincent until 9 October. Howe had intelligence that the combined enemy fleet, thought to consist of fifty ships of the line, was in Gibraltar Bay. During the evening of 10 October, a gale of wind scattered the enemy fleet, forcing many ships out of Gibraltar Bay, damaging some vessels, and driving ashore four, including the ship of the line *San Miguel*, which was captured by the British.

Early in the morning of 11 October, the Channel Fleet and the relief convoy entered the Strait of Gibraltar. The fleet was off Gibraltar by evening, giving the storeships "a favorable opportunity" to enter the anchorage without being attacked; but a "want of timely attention to the circumstances of navigation" by the merchant ships' masters meant that only four of these vessels entered Gibraltar. The remaining merchant ships as well as the warships of the Channel Fleet passed by Gibraltar and entered the Mediterranean. On 13 October the Channel Fleet was off the Spanish coast some fifty miles east of Gibraltar. Howe sent the storeships, escorted by HMS *Buffalo,* to an anchorage off the African coast to await events.

The enemy fleet "standing to the southward" was sighted during the evening of 13 October. The next morning, the Franco-Spanish force was six or seven leagues northeast of the Channel Fleet. Later in the day the wind came to the east, giving the Channel Fleet the opportunity to make for Gibraltar and enter Rosa Bay. The storeships anchored off the African coast were sent for later and also anchored in Rosa Bay. Troops, stores, and fifteen hundred barrels of gunpowder from the Channel Fleet were quickly sent ashore. Gibraltar had again been successfully resupplied.

On the morning of the 19 October, the wind was out of the east and Howe and the Channel Fleet put to sea for the return voyage to England. As the fleet left Gibraltar Bay, the Franco-Spanish fleet was sighted to the northeast. There was no room between Europa Point and Ceuta to maneuver or form a line of battle, so Howe and the Channel Fleet passed through the straits into the Atlantic, followed by the enemy. The next morning the Channel Fleet was leeward of the combined fleet of forty-five or forty-six ships, giving the enemy the opportunity to force an engagement on the British. Both fleets were in line-ahead formations, but it was sunset before the French and Spanish ships were close enough to the Channel Fleet "at a considerable distance to cannonade" the British. The fire was returned by the Channel Fleet and dilatory gunfire continued until 10 P.M., when both fleets drew apart. The British lost 68 men killed and 208 wounded in this action. The next morning the "reduced state" of the water in the ships of the Channel Fleet persuaded Howe not to chase the enemy, but rather to return to England.[203] The Channel Fleet arrived at St. Helens on 14 November, and the next day Howe received permission to come ashore and go to London.[204] This was the last major operation of the Channel Fleet, for the war was virtually over. On 13 February 1783 orders were issued ending hostilities.[205]

In the last three years of the American war, the government strategy of reinforcing the West Indies at all costs left the Channel Fleet helpless to prevent the enemy from contesting control of the western approaches of the English Channel. The combined fleets of France and Spain twice paraded in the western English Channel without being brought to battle by the Channel Fleet, and three important convoys were intercepted by the enemy. On several occasions, most notably during the second relief of Gibraltar, large enemy forces were permitted to escape from France to overseas theaters of war. Nevertheless, the outnumbered Channel Fleet successfully conducted the second and third reliefs of Gibraltar, intercepted two major enemy efforts to send reinforcements overseas, and provided a measure of protection to inward- and outward-bound trade convoys. By the narrowest of margins, the Royal Navy managed to keep the navies of France and Spain from gaining control of the western approaches of the English Channel during the American Revolutionary War.

CONCLUSION

The Definitive Treaties of Peace were signed on 3 September 1783 at Versailles by Britain and the Bourbon powers. But what were the fates of the British officials and officers charged with the conduct of the naval war in European seas? For the most part, they gradually faded from public life once hostilities ended. After leaving the Admiralty with the fall of the North government, Sandwich lived until 1792, devoting himself to music and his personal financial problems. Keppel left the Admiralty on 30 January 1783 with the fall of the Rockingham-Shelburne government, returned briefly in April, and left the office of first lord again at the end of the year. Keppel never again held public office and proved that as a first lord of the Admiralty he was, at best, inadequate. Much to the horror of his political enemies, Palliser was made governor of Greenwich Hospital by Sandwich in 1780 and remained in that position until his death in 1796. Howe was first lord of the Admiralty in the government of William Pitt for several years and then went on to beat the French on the Glorious First of June in 1794 and put down the great naval mutinies at Spithead in 1797. Rodney, the victor of the Moonlight Battle, was summarily removed from command of the squadron in the West Indies by Keppel for political reasons. Ironically, the removal came after Rodney won the Battle of the Saints but before news of that victory reached England. After returning to England, Rodney spent the rest of his life ashore. Darby never served afloat again after leaving the command of the Channel Fleet, while Barrington, Digby, and Mulgrave also remained ashore for the most part. After the American war, Middleton became one of the great reforming civil administrators of the Royal Navy and first lord of the Admiralty at the time of Trafalgar. Hyde Parker, who fought the Battle of Dogger Bank, disappeared without a trace, drowning when his ship went down on passage to India. Among the captains, several like John Jervis and James Samumarz reached the first ranks of their profession during the French Revolutionary and Napoleonic Wars. And George III, surviving madness, blindness, wars, and political crisis, outlasted them all to die in 1820.

What was the fate of the European nations involved? The great expense of the naval effort in the American war contributed substantially to the financial collapse of the French monarchy. Spain continued her slow decline as a great power, and the Dutch economy was smashed by the American war. Although Britain spent some sixty-two million pounds on her navy, she was the only belligerent to end the war financially solvent.

Had Britain gained any knowledge from the experience of her fighting ships in European waters during that war? The Royal Navy was unprepared for the American war in European seas because of a failure to mobilize the force for war. In fact, there were two mobilization failures in the months after the beginning of the fighting in America. At the outset, the North government tried to economize by deliberately failing to place orders in private shipyards for the small warships like frigates and sloops of war that could have countered America cruisers in European seas. Next, for reasons of economy and parliamentary politics, the North ministry did not make the Channel Fleet's ships of the line ready to meet the French in 1778 in a timely fashion. This was a great gamble in which the government wagered that the Americans would not fight on the high seas and that the French would not intervene in the American war. The government lost both bets, for the Americans dispatched commerce raiders to European seas, and the French joined the fray on land and sea.

When France entered the conflict, the Royal Navy was unable to meet Britain's worldwide strategic commitments. In 1778, the shortage of ships of the line forced the British to abandon the Mediterranean for the entire American war. The government was then thrown into a crisis when a French force sailed from Toulon for an unknown destination. The North ministry had to decide whether to reinforce North America promptly at the expense of the Channel Fleet. If North America was not reinforced, the British might be overwhelmed there by a superior enemy force, while a weak Channel Fleet might allow the French to seize control of the English Channel, laying the British Isles open to invasion. In the end, this strategic quandary was resolved by delaying the departure of the reinforcements for America until the destination of the French ships was known.

At the beginning of the war with France, Keppel, a member of the parliamentary opposition, was appointed to command the Channel Fleet. The first action between the Channel Fleet and the French off Ushant in the summer of 1778 was indecisive. After a futile autumn cruise in 1778, Keppel embarked on a legendary dispute with his second in command, Vice Adm. Sir Hugh Palliser. This dispute spilled over into the Houses of Parliament, setting off attacks on the government's naval policy and splitting the officer corps of the Royal Navy. Keppel was removed from command, and the uninspiring Adm. Sir Charles Hardy was appointed to command the Channel Fleet.

Spain declared war on Britain in 1779, and the French and Spanish attempted to invade England by sending a fleet of some forty-five ships of the line into the western approaches of the English Channel. The late mobilization of the Royal Navy left the British numerically inferior to the Franco-Spanish fleet in the English Channel. The Franco-Spanish attempt to invade England collapsed only because of mismanagement and sickness among the enemy crews. Luck was with the British, for the performance of Hardy and the Channel Fleet was lackluster at best during the 1779 campaign in the English Channel.

What was needed in late 1779 was a fighting admiral who could restore discipline within the officer corps of the Royal Navy and fight and win battles. The search for such a man produced Adm. Sir George Rodney, who was appointed commander in chief of the Leeward Islands squadron and ordered to resupply Gibraltar. At the end of 1779 Rodney sailed from Spithead with units of the Channel Fleet to relieve Gibraltar. Off the coast of southern Portugal, Rodney encountered a Spanish squadron of eleven sail of the line. In the ensuing battle, the British took or destroyed six Spanish ships of the line, totally defeating the Spanish squadron. After resupplying Gibraltar, Rodney sailed for the West Indies, while the ships from the Channel Fleet returned to Britain, capturing a French convoy and another ship of the line while en route to Spithead. The first relief of Gibraltar was a great victory.

British naval policy in European waters became inextricably entwined in Continental politics after France joined the war. The Royal Navy instituted a blockade of the eastern approaches of the English Channel, hoping to intercept neutral ships carrying naval stores from the Baltic to French bases along the Atlantic coast. Applying doctrines of distant blockade and "free goods do not make free ships," the British seized many neutral merchant ships, the majority Dutch. The ensuing outcry from the neutral powers of northern Europe placed the Netherlands in the middle of a conflict in which Britain and France battled for control of the foreign policy of the Dutch nation. The League of Armed Neutrality appeared to offer the Netherlands a way out of the crisis, but the British declared war on the Dutch before they could officially join the league. The Fourth Anglo-Dutch War was an economic disaster for the Dutch.

During the last three years of the American war, the Royal Navy in European seas fought the navies of France, Spain, and the Netherlands with inferior forces. Gibraltar was resupplied twice without fighting a major fleet action, and the Channel Fleet managed to protect trade convoys proceeding through the western approaches to and from Britain. Units of the Channel Fleet intercepted a number of enemy squadrons and convoys proceeding to the East and West Indies, but, on the whole, a lack of intelligence and the weakness of the Channel Fleet made it difficult to prevent the French and Spanish from sending reinforcements overseas. The overall weakness of the Channel Fleet in European seas made it impossible for the British to prevent superior enemy squadrons from making several cruises in the western approaches of the English Channel.

At the beginning of the American war, British naval weakness in European seas came from a failure to mobilize promptly for war, but in the last years of the conflict it was caused by the government's decision to reinforce the West Indies at the expense of the Channel Fleet. Clever deployments like moving ships of the line back and forth between the North Sea and the Channel and Britain's superior fighting ability in ship-to-ship terms enabled the Royal Navy to prevent the French and the Spanish from gaining total naval control of the western approaches of the English Channel in the war's last years.

The British did not ignore the fact that the Royal Navy held the western approaches of the English Channel by the narrowest of margins against the naval power of France and Spain. William Pitt never forgot the weakness of the Royal Navy in European seas during the American war. During the Nootka Sound crisis of 1789–90, the British mobilized more than enough naval power to force a settlement, and control of the western approaches of the English Channel with overpowering naval force became a cornerstone of British strategy in the French Revolutionary and Napoleonic Wars. In the American war, British statesmen had ignored the possibility that strengthening the navy in European waters would not only protect Britain and her commerce but also enable the Royal Navy to bottle up French and Spanish troop transports and warships, thus cutting off allied reinforcements for the Western Hemisphere. Instead, their shortsightedness laid the British Isles open to invasion in 1779. The Royal Navy was unable to prevent the enemy from reinforcing overseas positions and Franco-Spanish fleets were able to parade in the western approaches.

The British learned the strategic lessons of the American war. During the French Revolutionary and Napoleonic Wars, naval control of the western approaches of the English Channel was the bedrock on which British strategy rested.

NOTES

Works frequently cited have been identified by the following abbreviations:

Addit. MSS	Additional Manuscripts.
ADM	Admiralty.
BL	British Library.
CL	William L. Clements Library, University of Michigan.
G	Sir John Fortescue, ed., *The Correspondence of King George the Third from 1760 to December 1783* (London, 1972).
HMC	Historical Manuscript Commission.
NDAR	William Bell Clark and William James Morgan, eds., *Naval Documents of the American Revolution,* 10 vols. (Washington, D.C., 1964– .)
NMM	National Maritime Museum.
NRS	Navy Records Society.
NYHS	New York Historical Society.
PRO	Public Record Office.
SP	State Papers.

CHAPTER 1: THE FAILURE TO MOBILIZE FOR WAR, 1775–77

1. Piers Mackesy, *The War for America, 1775–1783* (London, 1964), 27–60.

2. Cf. David Syrett, *Shipping and the American War, 1775–83* (London, 1970).

3. Daniel A. Baugh, "The Politics of British Naval Failure, 1775–1777," *American Neptune* 52 (fall 1992): 243–44.

4. Peter D. G. Thomas, *Lord North* (New York, 1976), 95–96.

5. Bernard Donoughue, *British Politics and the American Revolution: The Path to War* (London, 1964), 253.

6. Ralph Davis, *The Rise of the English Shipping Industry in the Seventeenth and Eighteenth Centuries* (Newton Abbot, Devon, 1972), 68.

7. Baugh, "Politics of British Naval Failure," 242–43.

8. PRO, ADM 1/485, Disposition of His Majesty's Ships and Vessels in North America, 16 June 1775.

9. PRO, ADM 8/53, 1 Jan. 1777.

10. PRO, ADM 1/4129, 163f. In 1768 all British diplomats were ordered to report the arrival and departure of ships carrying suspicious cargoes to America.

11. PRO, ADM 1/4129, 169f.

12. PRO, ADM 1/4130, 72f.

13. 5 Geo. III, c. 11, s. 8; PRO, ADM 1/1430, 18f.

14. PRO, ADM 3/83, 17 Aug. 1775; *NDAR,* 2:676, 678–79.

15. E.g., PRO, ADM 2/100, 18–20, 258, 287; ADM 2/1332, 227–34; ADM 2/1333, 22–24; ADM 3/81, 10 Aug., 13 Nov. 1775; *NDAR,* 3:367, 401.

16. PRO, ADM 1/4130, 82f.; ADM 2/100, 171–72, 247–48; *NDAR,* 3:722.

17. 16 Geo. III, c. 5; *NDAR,* 3:453–54.

18. *NDAR,* 3:679–80, 684, 749–50.

19. *NDAR,* 3:525–30; 4:966–70, 974–75, 1084.

20. *NDAR,* 4:910.

21. See *NDAR,* 2:718, 744; 3:471.

22. See *NDAR,* 4:1012, 1076, 1089.

23. PRO, ADM 1/4131, 64f.; G, 1810; *NDAR,* 1:403, 409–10; Gardner W. Allen, *A Naval History of the American Revolution* (Williamstown, Mass., 1970 reprint), 2:169–97.

24. Cf. O. W. Stephenson, "The Supply of Gunpowder in 1776," *American Historical Review* 30 (Jan. 1925): 277–81.

25. NRS, *The Private Papers of John, Earl of Sandwich,* eds. G. R. Barnes and J. H. Owen (London, 1932–38), 1:223, 254.

26. PRO, ADM 1/4134, 33–34, 55, 63, 68. One authority states that 158 French ships valued at 6.5 million francs were seized by the British during 1777 and the first months of 1778. NRS, *Sandwich,* 1:204. The PRO Index to the High Court of Admiralty Prize Papers, 1776–1786, is laced with the names of French ships seized in 1777.

27. E.g., PRO, ADM 1/4130, 170f.; G, 1810; *NDAR,* 3:345.

28. PRO, PC 2/119, 151.

29. PRO, ADM 3/81, 14 Sept., 23 Oct. 1775.

30. E.g., PRO, ADM 2/100, 86–87, 128–29, 183–84; ADM 2/102, 422.

31. PRO, ADM 2/1332, 248–49; ADM 2/1333, 34–37ff.

32. PRO, ADM 1/4131, 32, 64; *NDAR,* 3:534; 4:993–94.

33. *NDAR,* 4:918–19.

34. Cf. NMM, SAN/T/6, Jackson to Sandwich, 2 Jan. 1776; SAN/T/7, Jackson to Sandwich, 29 Dec. 1776.

35. PRO, ADM 1/386, extract of a letter from the Consul at Faro . . . , dated at Faro 31 Aug. 1776.

36. Allen, *A Naval History,* 1:158, 234. For an account of one of the first American privateers in European waters, see William Richard Cutter, ed., "A Yankee Privateersman in Prison in England, 1777–1779," *New England Historical and Genealogical Register* 30 (Apr./July 1876): 175–77.

37. Francis Wharton, ed., *The Revolutionary Diplomatic Correspondence of the United States* (Washington, D.C., 1889), 3:262–63, 325–27, 329, 348, 399–400.

38. PRO, SP/78/302.

39. Wharton, *Revolutionary Diplomatic Correspondence*, 2:364–65, 377, 379–82, 388–84; See also Ruth Y. Johnston, "American Privateers in French Ports," *Pennsylvania Magazine of History and Biography* 53 (Oct. 1929): 353–74.

40. Wharton, *Revolutionary Diplomatic Correspondence*, 2:388–89.

41. For a full account of the activities of Conyngham, see R. W. Nesser, ed., *Letters and Papers Relating to the Cruises of Gustavus Conyngham: A Captain of the Continental Navy, 1777–1779* (New York, 1915).

42. E.g., PRO, ADM 2/101, 65–66, 124–25, 234–36, 336–40; ADM 2/102, 300–21, 324–25, 400–411, 423–25, 439–40, 449, 453–54, 480–83, 516, 522–23, 525–26, 530, 533, 542; ADM 2/103, 8, 22–25, 37–38, 42, 44–45, 126, 146–47, 170–71, 183, 223–24, 237–38, 300–301, 306–8, 413–14, 488–89; ADM 3/82, 2, 16, 20, 21, 23, 27 May, 4, 11, 19, 20, 28 June, 11, 17, 19, 23, 31 July, 6, 27, 28 Aug., 18 Sept., 15 Dec. 1777.

43. Cutter, "A Yankee Privateersman," 177.

44. E.g., CL, Douglas Papers, vol. 5, 16 Feb. 1777.

45. PRO, ADM 2/103, 85, 143, 151–54; ADM 3/82, 2, 10, 19, 22 July 1777.

46. E.g., PRO, ADM 2/103, 19–20, 49–50; ADM 3/83, 20 June 1777.

47. PRO, ADM 2/103, 19; ADM 3/83, 9 Dec. 1777.

48. E.g., PRO, ADM 2/103, 220–21.

49. E.g., PRO, ADM 3/83, 14, 16, 17 Oct., 12, 15 Nov. 1777.

50. E.g., PRO, ADM 2/102, 488–90, 529–30; ADM 2/103, 21; ADM 2/1332, 307–14, 330–51; ADM 3/82, 7, 16, May, 28 June 1777.

51. E.g., NRS, *Sandwich*, 1:250.

52. PRO, ADM 3/82, 16 July, 9 Aug. 1777. CL, Shelburne Papers, vol. 238, Admiralty to Navy Board, 19 Nov. 1777.

53. PRO, ADM 3/83, 25, 29 Nov. 1777; CL, Shelburne Papers, vol. 142, Admiralty to Navy Board, 28 Aug. 1777.

54. PRO, ADM 1/4134, 49f.; ADM 2/101, 284–85; HMC, *Various Collections*, 6:138.

55. PRO, ADM 2/102, 128–29, 260–69.

56. PRO, ADM 2/1332, 235–36; ADM 3/83, 25 July 1777.

57. PRO, ADM 1/4133, 146f.; ADM 2/102, 518–20; ADM 2/103, 28, 128–29, 154–56; ADM 3/83, 16, 25 May, 31 July, 21 Aug. 1777; NRS, *Sandwich*, 1:224.

58. E.g., PRO, ADM 2/102, 416–18, 357–59; ADM 2/103, 212–13, 218–19.

59. PRO, ADM 2/101, 317–20, 412: ADM 2/102, 319–21; ADM 2/103, 66–67, 108; ADM 2/104, 91–93; ADM 3/83, 26 June, 31 Dec. 1777.

60. PRO, ADM 2/101, 335–37, 346–47; ADM 2/102, 504–7; ADM 2/103, 343–44, 383–87, 483–85; ADM 2/1333, 42f.; ADM 3/82, 10 May, 4, 17 July 1777; ADM 3/83, 13, 30 Sept. 1777.

61. PRO, ADM 2/102, 318, 349–50; ADM 2/103, 93–94; ADM 3/82, 16 May, 3 July 1777.

62. PRO, ADM 2/103, 4–6, 166–67, 463–67; ADM 3/83, 23 Dec. 1777.

63. PRO, ADM 2/103, 148, 173–74, 186–87; ADM 3/82, 31 July 1777.

64. PRO, ADM 1/386, 3 Oct., 26 Dec. 1776; ADM 2/101, 345–46; ADM 2/102, 145–49, 307–10, 373–75; ADM 2/103, 187–88, 197, 317–20, 346–52, 357–59; ADM 3/82, 6, 9 Aug. 1777; ADM 3/83, 2 Oct. 1777.

65. E.g., PRO, ADM 1/4134, 14f.; ADM 3/82, 17 May, 1, 2, 8 July 1777; NRS, *Sandwich,* 1:223, 225, 227.

66. PRO, ADM 1/4134, 5f.

67. HMC, *Report on the Manuscripts of Mrs. Stopford-Sackville, of Drayton House, Northamptonshire* (London and Hereford, 1904–10), 2:73.

68. The whole subject of what numbers of ships were captured by the Americans during a given period of time is extremely complex, owing to the great number of conflicting reports and lists of captured ships. A. T. Mahan, *The Major Operations of the Navies in the War of American Independence* (New York, 1969 reprint), 61n, states that 331 British merchant ships were captured worldwide during 1777; Charles Wright and C. Ernest Fayle, *A History of Lloyd's* (London, 1928), 156–57, say that the British lost 340 merchant ships to enemy action; and Allen, *A Naval History,* 1:289–90, says that the Americans captured 464 British merchant ships in 1777. Only fifteen American privateers and warships are listed for the year 1777 in the PRO, Index to High Court of Admiralty Prize Papers, 1776–1786.

69. PRO, SP 78/304, 181f.

70. NRS, *Sandwich,* 1:242, 244–45.

71. *NDAR,* 2:379, 400; 4:1413. Guard ships are ships of the line with only 350 officers and men onboard. In theory, these ships can be rapidly made ready for sea service by merely completing their crews to full strength. *NDAR,* 6:464.

72. *NDAR,* 3:335; 5:1374.

73. *NDAR,* 3:335.

74. NRS, *Sandwich,* 1:19–23.

75. Daniel A. Baugh, "Why Did Britain Lose Command of the Sea during the War for America?" *The British Navy and the Use of Naval Power in the Eighteenth Century,* eds. Jeremy Black and Philip Woodfine (Leicester, 1988), 145.

76. Baugh, "Why Did Britain Lose Command," 155–57.

77. *NDAR,* 7:720.

78. Robert Greenhalgh Albion, *Forests and Seapower: The Timber Problem of the Royal Navy, 1652–1862.* (Cambridge, Mass., 1926), 282. American historians have not been alone in blanket criticism of Sandwich, for the great British naval historian J. K Laughton made one of the most harsh attacks on Sandwich in the *Dictionary of National Biography.* Sandwich has received the attention of a number of popular historians such as George Martelli, *Jemmy Twitcher: The Life of the Fourth Earl of Sandwich* (London, 1962). Fortunately, N. A. M. Rodger's *The Insatiable Earl: The Life of John Montagu, 4th Earl of Sandwich* (London, 1993) is a first-rate biography.

79. Horace Walpole, *Memoirs of the Reign of George III* (London, 1894), 4:170–71.

80. R. J. B. Knight, "Sandwich, Middleton and Dockyard Appointments," *The Mariner's Mirror* 57 (May 1971): 175–92.

81. R. J. B. Knight, ed., *Portsmouth Dockyard Papers, 1774–1783: The American War* (Portsmouth, 1987), xliv-xlvi.

82. Sir Lewis Namier and John Brooke, *The History of Parliament* (London, 1964), 1:311, 434.

83. I. R. Christie, *The End of North's Ministry, 1780–1782* (London, 1958), 203–8.

84. For an account of the workings of the cabinet, see Ian R. Christie, *Myth and Reality in Late-Eighteenth-Century British Politics and other Papers* (London, 1970), 55–108.

85. NRS, *Sandwich*, 2:255.

86. Ibid., 2:259.

87. David Syrett, *The Royal Navy in American Waters, 1775–1783* (Aldershot, 1989), 1–92.

88. Cf. CL, Sackville-Germain Papers, vol. 5, Germain to William Howe, 18 Oct. 1776.

89. Rodger, *Insatiable Earl*, 232–33.

90. C.f. Nicholas Tracy, *Navies, Deterrence, and American Independence: Britain Seapower in the 1760's and 1770's* (Vancouver, B.C., 1988).

91. H. M. Scott, *British Foreign Policy in the Age of the American Revolution* (Oxford, 1990), 234–35.

92. G, 1895, 1896.

93. NRS, *Sandwich*, 1:213–16.

94. G, 1918.

95. *Barfleur, Centaur, Courageux, Culloden, Egmont, Hector, Resolution, Royal Oak, Exeter, Worcester, Ocean, Albion, Torbay, Foudroyant, Boyne, Somerset, Belle Isle, Nonsuch, Raisonable, Augusta, Bedford, Monarch, Terrible, Prince of Wales, Ramillies, Ardent, Burford, Sandwich, Invincible, Prince George, Valiant, Queen, St. Albans, Bienfaisant.*

96. PRO, ADM 2/101, 381–89, 399–404, 418–20, 429.

97. PRO, ADM 8/52, 1 Dec. 1776.

98. NRS, *Sandwich*, 1:163.

99. Jonathan R. Dull, *The French Navy and American Independence: A Study in Arms and Diplomacy, 1774–1787* (Princeton, N.J., 1975), 84.

100. Scott, *British Foreign Policy*, 252.

101. G, 1974, 2049.

102. PRO, SP 78/304, 68f.

103. NRS, *Sandwich*, 1:235–38.

104. Cf. Baugh, "Why Did Britain Lose Command," 152–63; R. J. B. Knight, "The Royal Navy's Recovery after the Early Phase of the American Revolutionary War," in *The Aftermath of Defeat: Armed Forces and the Challenge of Recovery*, eds. George Andreopoulos and Harold E. Selesky (New Haven, Conn., 1994), 10–25.

CHAPTER 2: KEPPEL AND THE CHANNEL FLEET, 1778

1. PRO, SP 78/305, 173, 174, 248, 254, 262, 264.

2. PRO, SP 78/306, 45f.

3. PRO, SP 78/306, 59, 111, 124, 129, 220.

4. Scott, *British Foreign Policy*, 260.

5. G, 2150.

6. Scott, *British Foreign Policy*, 264–72.

7. Cf., Richard Pares, "American versus Continental Warfare, 1739–62," *English Historical Review* 51 (1936): 429–65.

8. NRS, *Sandwich*, 1:327–35.

9. Ibid., 1:337–39.

10. Ibid., 1:327–35, 342–43, 349–53.

11. G, 2190, 2216, 2243.

12. Scott, *British Foreign Policy*, 262–64. See also Samuel Flagg Bemis, *The Diplomacy of the American Revolution* (New York, 1935), 58–69.

13. For the origins of the peace commission of 1778, see Gerald Saxon Brown, *The American Secretary: The Colonial Policy of Lord George Germain, 1775–1778* (Ann Arbor, Mich., 1963), 139–47; C. R. Ritcheson, *British Politics and the American Revolution* (Norman, Okla., 1954), 258–80.

14. NRS, *Sandwich*, 1:361.

15. PRO, ADM 3/84, 16 Mar. 1778.

16. PRO, ADM 2/104, 236.

17. CL, Sackville-Germain Papers, Military Dispatches, 15–16.

18. PRO, ADM 1/4315, 64f.; ADM 2/1334, 54–65; CO 5/95, 95–102ff.

19. NRS, *Sandwich,* 1:293.

20. PRO, ADM 1/95, 313f.; ADM 2/104, 236.

21. John Campbell, *The Naval History of Great Britain* (London, 1818), 6:164–67.

22. Thomas Keppel, *The Life of Augustus, Viscount Keppel* (London, 1842), 2:1–2.

23. Namier and Brooke, *History of Parliament*, 3:8.

24. Ibid., 4:405.

25. Ira D. Gruber, *The Howe Brothers and the American Revolution* (New York, 1972), 64–70.

26. Rodger, *Insatiable Earl*, 241–42.

27. NRS, *Sandwich*, 2:204–5.

28. Namier and Brooke, *History of Parliament*, 3:8.

29. W. S. Lewis, Robert A. Smith, and Charles Bennett, eds., *Horace Walpole's Correspondence with Hannah Moore* (London, 1961), 193.

30. Ipswich and East Suffolk Record Office, Keppel Papers, Richmond to Keppel, 14 Nov. 1776.

31. G, 2263, 2312; NRS, *Sandwich*, 2:31–32.

32. *Worcester, Panther, Alarm.* PRO, ADM 1/387, State and Condition of His Majesty's Ships . . . in the Mediterranean, 10 Apr. 1778.

33. NRS, *Sandwich*, 1:349–50.

34. Ibid., 2:22–23. At least five ships of the line could have been obtained on 6 April 1778 if the *Trident* was not employed to carry General Cornwallis and the peace commission to New York (PRO, ADM 3/84, 15 Apr. 1778); if the *Europe* had been withdrawn from the Newfoundland squadron (PRO, ADM 2/104, 296); and if the *Asia, Belle Isle,* and *Burford* had their orders withdrawn for escorting East Indiamen (PRO, ADM 2/104, 104, 349–50; ADM 3/84, 21 Mar. 1778).

35. G, 2311.

36. A number of historians have taken Sandwich, in particular, and the government, in general, to task for not sending a squadron to the Mediterranean. A. T. Mahan, for example, calls this failure "an unpardonable fault" but does not discuss the strategic problems created by the existence of French and Spanish naval power in Europe. Mahan, *Major Operations,* 79. William B. Willcox says that Sandwich's reasons for not blocking Toulon were a "variety of red herrings" and attacks the naval authorities for caution and the failure to take risks. However, like Mahan, Willcox does not deal with the strategic threat posed to Britain by French and Spanish naval forces in Europe. William B. Willcox, "British Strategy in America, 1778," *The Journal of Modern History* 19 (1947): 100–101.

37. PRO, ADM 1/3134, 67–68, 71; NRS, *Sandwich*, 2:67.

38. NRS, *Sandwich*, 2:33–34.

39. G, 2316.

40. NRS, *Sandwich*, 2:36–37.

41. G, 2317.

42. CL, Sackville-Germain Papers, vol. 7, Memorandum by Germain, 28 Apr. 1778.

43. CL, Sackville-Germain Papers, Military Dispatches, 34–38.

44. NRS, *Sandwich*, 2:289.

45. G, 2320, 2321, 2324.

46. PRO, ADM 1/468, 94f.; ADM 3/84, 21 Mar. 1778.

47. PRO, ADM 1/94, 323f.

48. G, 2328; NRS, *Sandwich*, 2:40.

49. CL, Sackville-Germain Papers, vol. 7, 2 May 1778.

50. PRO, ADM 3/84, 3 May 1778.

51. There is a short journal kept by the king during his visit to Portsmouth covering the period 2–6 May 1778. G, 2324.

52. G, 2328.

53. PRO, ADM 1/94, 325f.

54. G, 2324.

55. G, 2325, 2330.

56. CL, Sackville-Germain Papers, vol. 7, Sandwich to Germain, 2 May 1778.

57. PRO, ADM 1/387, Duff to Stephens, 10 Apr. 1778.

58. NRS, *Sandwich,* 2:50.

59. HMC, *Stopford-Sackville,* 1:72.

60. G, 2333.

61. NRS, *Sandwich,* 2:54–56.

62. Roland G. Usher Jr., "The Royal Navy Impressment during the American Revolution," *Mississippi Valley Historical Review* 37 (Mar. 1951): 673–88.

63. NRS, *Sandwich,* 2:59.

64. PRO, ADM 3/84, 23, 28, 30 May 1778.

65. NRS, *Sandwich,* 2:57–58.

66. Ibid., 2:58. For Hood's suggestion that Byron's destination be New York, see G, 2332.

67. NRS, *Sandwich,* 2:66.

68. Ibid., 2:64, 74, 84–85.

69. Ibid., 2:65–66.

70. Ibid., 2:69.

71. PRO, ADM 2/3134, 73–77ff.

72. NRS, *Sandwich,* 2:370–71.

73. PRO, ADM 1/94, 104f.

74. NRS, *Sandwich,* 2:77–78.

75. Ibid., 2:371.

76. PRO, ADM 1/486, 104f.

77. PRO, ADM 1/94, 352–53ff.

78. NRS, *Sandwich,* 2:88–90.

79. PRO, ADM 1/486, 114f.; ADM 2/3133, 59–60; HMC, *Report on American Manuscripts in the Royal Institution of Great Britain* (London, Dublin, and Hereford, 1904–9), 1:261.

80. NRS, *Sandwich,* 2:90n.

81. PRO, ADM 1/94, 354, 357, 370.

82. Keppel, *Keppel,* 2:25–26.

83. Marie Martel Hach, ed., "Letters of Captain Sir John Jervis to Sir Henry Clinton, 1774–1782," *American Neptune* 7 (Apr. 1951): 95.

84. PRO, ADM 1/94, 372–74ff.

85. PRO, ADM 1/94, 375–80ff.

86. Scott, *British Foreign Policy,* 264.

87. NRS, *Sandwich,* 2:94, 97.

88. Ipswich and East Suffolk Record Office, Keppel Papers, Palliser to Keppel, 20 June 1778.

89. PRO, ADM 1/94, 377f.

90. Ibid., 381–86ff.

91. Ibid., 391–402ff.

92. Ipswich and East Suffolk Record Office, Keppel Papers, Palliser to Keppel, 21 June 1778.

93. NRS, *Sandwich*, 2:99–100.

94. PRO, ADM 1/94, 406f.

95. NRS, *Sandwich*, 2:98–99.

96. Ibid., 2:105.

97. Ibid., 2:108.

98. HMC, *Various Collections*, 6:144.

99. PRO, ADM 1/94, 439f.

100. Ibid., 421–22, 432–34.

101. Ibid., 443, 447–49.

102. NRS *Sandwich*, 2:126.

103. *Dauphin Royal, Duc de Bourgogne, Alexandre, Bien-Aime, Couronne, Palmier, Saint-Michel, Indien, Glorieux, Amphion, Vengeur, Reflechi, Ville de Paris, Actif, Magnifique, Bretagne, Fendant, Eeveille, Actionnaire, Orient, Artesien, Sphinx, Robuste, Roland, Fier, Zodiaque, Saint-Esprit, Intrepide, Triton, Solitaire, Conquerant, Diademe.* Frigates: *Junon, Sibylle, Fortunee, Resolue, Sensible, Nymphe, Surveillante, Danae, Iphigenie.* Corvettes: *Sylphide, Hirondelle, Lunette, Cruieuse, Favorite.* Luggers: *Espiegle, Chasseur.*

104. *Monarch, Hector, Center, Exeter, Duke, Queen, Shrewsbury, Cumberland, Berwick, Stirling Castle, Courageux, Thunderer, Vigilant, Sandwich, Valiant, Victory, Foudroyant, Prince George, Bienfaisant, Vengeance, Worcester, Elizabeth, Defiance, Robust, Formidable, Ocean, America, Terrible, Egmont,* and *Ramillier.* Frigates: *Arethusea, Fox, Milford, Proserpine.* Fire ships: *Pluto, Vulcan.*

105. PRO, ADM 1/94, 455–57ff.

106. Ipswich and East Suffolk Record Office, Keppel Papers, Keppel to Shuldham, 24 July 1778.

107. PRO, ADM 51/169, 23–28 July 1778; ADM 51/220, 23–28 July 1778; ADM 51/303, 23–28 July 1778; ADM 51/365, 23–28 July 1778; ADM 51/372, 23–28 July 1778; ADM 51/609, 23–28 July 1778; ADM 51/649, 23–28 July 1778; ADM 51/790, 23–28 July 1778; ADM 51/840, 23–28 July 1778; ADM 51/1036, 23–28 July 1778; ADM 51/1037, 23–28 July 1778.

108. PRO, ADM 1/94, 467f.

109. Ibid., 464–66ff.

110. Keppel, *Keppel*, 2:51.

111. NRS, *Sandwich*, 2:128.

112. *London Gazette Extraordinary*, 3 Aug. 1778.

113. NRS, *Sandwich*, 2:142.

114. PRO, ADM 3/88, 2 Aug. 1778.

115. HMC, *Various Collections,* 6:149.

116. PRO, ADM 1/94, 480, 488–90.

117. CL, Sackville-Germain Papers, vol. 7, Hon. Augustus Keppel, 25 Apr.–26 Oct. 1778.

118. NRS, *Sandwich,* 2:319.

119. PRO, ADM 1/94, 510, 521, 523–24.

120. NRS, *Sandwich,* 2:156.

121. PRO, ADM 1/94, 529–56, 563–70.

122. NRS, *Sandwich,* 2:168.

123. Ibid., 2:160n.

124. PRO, ADM 1/94, 599–600ff.

125. NRS, *Sandwich,* 2:169, 192.

126. PRO, ADM 1/94, 593f.

127. NRS, *Letters Written by Sir Samuel Hood in 1781–2–3,* ed. David Hannany (London, 1895), 2.

128. PRO, ADM 3/86, 27 Oct. 1778.

129. NMM, Sandwich Papers, Keppel to Sandwich, 26 Oct. 1778.

130. NRS, *Sandwich,* 2:184–85, 205.

131. Ibid., 2:206.

132. Robert M. Hunt, *The Life of Sir Hugh Palliser, Bart.* (London, 1844), 2:28–30.

133. Rodger, *Insatiable Earl,* 246.

134. Hunt, *Palliser,* 234.

135. NRS, *Sandwich,* 2:210n.

136. Hunt, *Palliser,* 1–200.

137. NRS, *Sandwich,* 2:206.

138. Ipswich and East Suffolk Record Office, Keppel Papers, Palliser to Keppel, 3 Nov. 1778.

139. Keppel, *Keppel,* 2:78.

140. Hunt, *Palliser,* 235.

141. Keppel, *Keppel,* 2:82.

142. *London Evening Post, London Chronicle, London Morning Post, The Morning Intelligencer,* and *The Gazetteer.*

143. Hunt, *Palliser,* 235–45.

144. NRS, *Sandwich,* 2:207–10.

145. Ipswich and East Suffolk Record Office, Keppel Papers, Richmond to Keppel, 15 Nov. 1778.

146. Hach, "Letters," 97.

147. A. Francis Steuart, ed., *The Last Journal of Horace Walpole during the Reign of George III from 1771 to 1783* (London, 1910), 2:208–9.

148. Namier and Brooke, *History of Parliament,* 1:138–45.

149. Ibid., 3:604.

150. Cf. Syrett, *Royal Navy,* 1–91.

151. Rodger, *Insatiable Earl,* 158–59.

152. Peter O. Hutchinson, ed., *Diary and Letters of His Excellency Thomas Hutchinson* (London, 1883), 2:210.

153. *The Parliamentary Register: Or History of the Proceedings and Debates of the House Commons* (London, 1779), 11:89–90.

154. NRS, *Sandwich,* 2:193.

155. PRO, ADM 3/86, 9 Dec. 1778.

156. Steuart, *Last Journal,* 2:223–26.

157. Hach, "Letters," 98.

158. *Parliamentary Register,* 11:151–52.

159. Ibid., 11:180–81, 191–93.

160. NMM, Sandwich Papers, cabinet minutes, 19 Dec. 1778.

161. *Parliamentary Register,* 11:192.

162. G, 2470, 2485, 2486.

163. For an account of the negotiations to make Howe first lord of the Admiralty, see Gruber, *Howe Brothers,* 330–36.

164. NRS, *Sandwich,* 2:193–94.

165. Ibid., 2:210.

166. PRO, ADM 3/86, 24 Dec. 1778.

167. NRS, *Sandwich,* 2:217n.

168. Ibid., 2:194, 214–24. There are many contemporary accounts of the trial. For a partial list, see NRS, *Sandwich,* 2:x–xiv. For the official minutes, see PRO, ADM 1/5312.

169. PRO, ADM 3/87, 21 Feb. 1779.

170. Keppel, *Keppel,* 2:183–84, 190–91, 196–97, 206–7, 212–13.

171. Hunt, *Palliser,* 303–4.

172. NRS, *Sandwich,* 2:228–30.

173. G, 2547, 2548, 2549, 2550, 2551.

174. *Parliamentary Register,* 11:249–52.

175. Hunt, *Palliser,* 305–6.

176. NRS, *Sandwich,* 2:196, 241.

177. *Parliamentary Register,* 14:190–231.

178. Hunt, *Palliser,* 307–90; NRS, *Sandwich,* 2:x–xiv, 197–98. For the official proceedings, see PRO, ADM 1/5313.

179. NRS, *Letters and Papers of Charles, Lord Barham,* ed. Sir John Knox Laughton (London, 1907–11), 1:267.

180. *Parliamentary Register,* 12:274–308.

181. Ibid., 14:251–52.

182. For an account of the inquiry into the conduct of the war in America, see Gruber, *Howe Brothers*, 324–50.

183. For the cult of the independent country gentleman, see Namier and Brooke, *History of Parliament*, 1:145–49.

184. *Parliamentary Register*, 12:46.

185. NRS, *Sandwich*, 2:243.

186. Ibid., 3:201.

187. NRS, *Letters and Papers of Admiral of the Fleet Sir Thos. Byam Martin. G.C.B.*, ed. Hamilton Sir Richard Vesey (London, 1898–1903), 3:292n.

CHAPTER 3: THE ATTEMPTED FRANCO-SPANISH INVASION AND THE FIRST RELIEF OF GIBRALTAR, 1779–80

1. G, 2565, 2570.

2. PRO, ADM 3/87, 12, 18, March 1779.

3. G, 2460.

4. PRO, ADM 3/87, 19 Mar. 1779.

5. NRS, *Sandwich*, 2:236; 3:3.

6. Ibid., 2:242.

7. Ibid., 3:3.

8. G, 2209. This letter is dated by Fortescue as 9 March 1778, when it is clearly 9 March 1779.

9. Ake Lindwall, "The Kempenfelt Family," *The Mariner's Mirror 57* (Nov. 1971): 379–83.

10. NRS, *Sandwich*, 3:3–4; NRS, *Signals and Instructions, 1776–1794*, ed. Julian S. Corbett (London, 1904), 3, 6, 7, 17–48, 117–18.

11. PRO, ADM 3/88, 2 Apr. 1779; NRS, *Sandwich*, 3:43.

12. PRO, ADM 3/87, 24 Mar. 1779.

13. G, 2209.

14. Maurer Maurer, "Coppered Bottoms for the Royal Navy: A Factor in the Maritime War of 1778–1783," *Military Affairs* 14 (1950): 57–58.

15. R. J. B. Knight, "Introduction of Copper Sheathing into the Royal Navy, 1779–1786," *The Mariner's Mirror* 59 (Aug. 1973): 300.

16. Knight, "Copper Sheathing," 300–3.

17. Brian Lavery, *The Arming and Fitting of English Ships of War 1600–1815* (London, 1987), 62–65.

18. Knight, *Portsmouth Dockyard Papers*, lii, lvi.

19. Dull, *French Navy*, 176n.

20. NRS, *Sandwich*, 4:201.

21. Mackesy, *War for America*, 322.

22. Knight, "Copper Sheathing," 306–9.

23. NRS, *Barham*, 1:290–91.

24. PRO, ADM 3/88, 30 July, 5 Aug. 1779.

25. Brian Lavery, *The Ship of the Line* (Annapolis, Md., 1983), 1:117.

26. PRO, PC 2/124, 59.

27. PRO, ADM 3/88, 29 June, 10, 15 July 1779.

28. NRS, John B. Hattendorf et al., eds., *British Naval Documents, 1200–1960* (London, 1993), 496–98.

29. PRO, ADM 106/2207, 18 Dec. 1780.

30. NRS, *British Naval Documents*, 499.

31. NMM, SAN/T/6, Ships in Commission, 15 Jan. 1779.

32. NMM, SAN/T/6, State of Ships, 15 Jan. 1779.

33. NMM, Sandwich Papers, list of ships of the line at home with an account of the number of men actually borne on each ship, 17 Mar. 1779.

34. NRS, *The Health of Seamen*, ed. Christopher Lloyd (London, 1965), 198.

35. Christopher Lloyd and Jack L. S. Couter, *Medicine and the Navy, 1200–1960* (London, 1961), 3:124–25.

36. PRO, ADM 3/88, 14 Apr. 1779.

37. NRS, *Sandwich*, 3:16, 21.

38. PRO, ADM 3/88, 21 June 1779.

39. NRS, *Sandwich*, 3:30.

40. PRO, ADM 3/88, 30 June, 8, 19 July 1779.

41. PRO, ADM 1/4138, 40f.

42. Ibid., 85f.

43. NMM, SAN/T/6, Germain to Sandwich, 30 Mar. 1779.

44. G, 2595.

45. HMC, *Various Collections*, 6:137.

46. NRS, *Sandwich*, 2:179.

47. Scott, *British Foreign Policy*, 272–76.

48. NMM, Sandwich Papers, Arbuthnot to Sandwich, 2 May 1779.

49. CL, Sackville-Germain Papers, vol. 9, Arbuthnot to Germain, 7 May 1779.

50. CL, Sackville-Germain Papers, vol. 9, Intelligence from Paris, 6 May 1779.

51. PRO ADM 3/88, 11 May 1779. Darby's squadron consisted of *Royal George, London, Queen, Valiant, Thrumpt, Thunderer, Berwick, Hector, Monarch, Intrepid.*

52. PRO, ADM 1/95, 341f.

53. NMM, SAN/T/6, Walsingham to Sandwich, 4 June 1779; PRO, ADM 1/95, 361f.

54. NRS, *Sandwich*, 3:14.

55. PRO, ADM 2/1336, 23–29ff.

56. G, 2653.

57. PRO, ADM 1/95, 373f.; NMM, Sandwich Papers, State of Sir Charles Hardy's Force.

58. PRO, SP 42/54, Weymouth to Admiralty, 16 June 1779.

59. PRO, ADM 3/88, 16 June 1779.

60. BL, Jervis Papers, Addit. MSS 29914, 124f.

61. NRS, *Sandwich,* 2:43.

62. PRO, ADM 1/387, Duff to Stephens, 1 Apr. 1779.

63. James Pritchard, "French Strategy and the American Revolution: A Reappraisal," *Naval War College Review* 47 (fall 1994): 92.

64. Steton Conn, *Gibraltar in British Diplomacy in the Eighteenth Century* (New Haven, Conn., 1942).

65. Dull, *French Navy,* 136–43; Bemis, *Diplomacy of the American Revolution,* 75–80.

66. A. Temple Patterson, *The Other Armada: The Franco-Spanish Attempt to Invade Britain in 1779* (Manchester, 1960), 12–20, 37–58.

67. PRO, ADM 1/95, 374, 377.

68. PRO, ADM 2/1336, 30f.

69. PRO, ADM 1/95, 377f.

70. Ibid., 380–84ff.

71. PRO, WO 34/115, 24f.

72. G, 2682.

73. G, 2665; PRO, PC 2/123, 584, 590.

74. PRO, ADM 1/4139, 32, 35, 51, 53.

75. G, 2674, 2702.

76. NRS, *Sandwich,* 3:33–34, 37–38, 43–44.

77. PRO, ADM 2/1336, 36–37ff.

78. NRS, *Sandwich,* 3:40–42.

79. PRO, ADM 1/95, 389, 393.

80. Ibid., 394–398ff.

81. NRS, *Sandwich,* 3:49–51.

82. PRO, ADM 2/1336, 44–45ff.

83. G, 2729.

84. PRO, ADM 1/95, 402–3ff.

85. PRO, ADM 2/1336, 52–53ff.

86. NRS, *Sandwich,* 3:55.

87. NMM, Sandwich Papers, State of Sir Charles Hardy's Force.

88. PRO, ADM 1/95, 406, 409.

89. NRS, *Sandwich,* 3:57–60.

90. HMC, *Fourteenth Report: The Manuscripts of His Grace The Duke of Rutland, K.G., Preserved at Belvoir Castle* (London, 1888–1895), 3:17.

91. NRS, *Sandwich*, 3:60–61.

92. G, 2719, 2733.

93. G, 2741.

94. G, 2685.

95. Spanish ships of the line: *España, Mino, San Miguel, San Pablo, Arrogante, Serio, San Pedro, San Josef, Guerrero, Venoedor, San Joaquin, Santa Isabel, Septentrion, Angle de la Guarda, Rayo, San Damaso, Brillante.* Cesareo Fernandez Duro, *Armada Española desde las Union de los Reinos de Castilla y Aragon* (Madrid, 1901), 7:242–43. French ships of the line: *Le Citoyen, L'Auguste, Protee, L'Eveille, La Ville de Paris, Le Gorieux, L'Indien, La Palmier, La Victoire, Le Zodiaque, Le Scipion, Le Bien-Aime, L'Acif, La Bretagne, Le Neptune, Le Destine, La Bourgogne, Le Solitaire, L' Hercule, Le Saint-Esprit, L'Intrepide, Le Bizarre, Le Conquerant, L'Actionnaire, L'Alexandre, Le Canton, Le Rluton.* G. Lacour-Gayet, *Le Marine Militaire de la France sous le regne de Louis XVI* (Paris, 1905), 639–40.

96. Dull, *French Navy,* 136–57.

97. Patterson, *Other Armada,* 81.

98. Ibid., 82.

99. PRO, ADM 1/806, Shuldham to Stephens, 17 Aug. 1779.

100. NRS *Sandwich,* 3:64–67.

101. G, 2746.

102. PRO, WO 34/116, 230f.

103. PRO, ADM 1/806, Shuldham to Stephens, 17 Aug. 1779.

104. G. Rutherford, "The Capture of the *Ardent,*" *The Mariner's Mirror,* 27 (Apr. 1941): 106–30.

105. PRO, ADM 1/106, C. Colton to Shuldham, 18 Aug. 1779; Shuldham to Stephens, 18, 19 Aug. 1779.

106. G, 2742.

107. Warwick Record Office, Denbigh Papers, Sandwich to Denbigh, 21 Aug. 1779.

108. PRO, ADM 3/89, 18, 19 Aug. 1779.

109. PRO, ADM 2/107, 320–22; NRS, *Sandwich,* 3:73n.

110. PRO, SP 42/55, 153, 164.

111. CL, Sackville Manuscripts, Supplementary, vol. 2, Benjamin Thompson's Journal of the Fleet Commanded by Sir Charles Hardy, 17–30 Aug. 1779, 4; PRO, ADM 50/10, 12 Aug.–1 Sept. 1779. There is a gap from 12 August to 1 September 1779 during which there are no dispatches from Hardy to the Admiralty. PRO, ADM 1/95, 409–410ff.

112. NMM, SAN/T/6, State of the Fleet, 1779. There are no lists of ships or other statement of the names, number, or type of ships the Channel Fleet comprised in any of Hardy's dispatches to the Admiralty. PRO, ADM 1/95, 370–412ff.

113. CL, Sackville Manuscripts, Supplementary, vol. 2, Thompson's Journal, 4–

33; PRO, ADM 50/10, 1 Sept. 1779; NRS, *Sandwich*, 3:89–91; Patterson, *Other Armada*, 194–99.

114. PRO, ADM 1/95, 410–12ff.

115. Patterson, *Other Armada*, 205–7, 209–10; E. H. Jenkins, *A History of the French Navy* (London, 1973), 160–61; Dull, *French Navy*, 156–58.

116. PRO, ADM 3/89, 4 Sept. 1779.

117. G, 2759, 2760, 2761.

118. NRS, *Barham*, 1:293–95.

119. G, 2763.

120. Duke of Bolton; John Sawbridge, M.P.; Benjamin Keene, M.P.; Temple Simon Luttrell, M.P.

121. G, 2765, 2767.

122. PRO, ADM 1/663, Drake to Stephens, 6 Sept. 1779; NRS, *Sandwich*, 3:94–95.

123. PRO, ADM 1/4139, 102f.

124. NRS, *Sandwich*, 3:101n.

125. PRO, ADM 1/95, 416–17ff. *Courageux, Bienfaisant, Berwick, Romney, Jupiter, Apollo, Crescent, Phoenix, Ambuscade, Milford, Brilliant, Deana, Southampton, Porcupine, Cormorant, Bonetta, Helena,* and two fire ships and two cutters.

126. PRO, ADM 1/95, 434–45ff.

127. At birth, Jones was given the name John Paul, but was known to contemporary British writers as Paul Jones and to Americans as John Paul Jones.

128. *Bonhomme Richard, Alliance, Pallas, Vengeance, Cerf, Monsieur, Grenville.*

129. No other incident of the war brought forth such a flood of letters to the Admiralty as Jones's cruise. PRO, ADM 1/4139.

130. The best account of Jones's 1779 cruise is in Samuel Eliot Morison, *John Paul Jones: A Sailor's Biography* (Boston, 1959), 197–252.

131. PRO, ADM 1/4140, 40f.

132. PRO, ADM 2/1336, 62–63ff.

133. PRO, ADM 1/95, 484–85ff.; NRS, *Sandwich*, 3:9.

134. PRO, ADM 2/1336, 68–69ff.

135. PRO, ADM 1/95, 505–7ff.

136. NRS, *Barham*, 1:303–4.

137. W.S. Lewis, Grover Grown Jr., Charles H. Bennett, eds., *Horace Walpole's Correspondence with William Mason* (London, 1955), 1:453–54.

138. NRS, *Barham*, 1:293.

139. The best biography of Rodney is David Spinney, *Rodney* (London, 1969).

140. Spinney, *Rodney*, 287–97.

141. G, 2776.

142. NRS, *Barham*, 1:82–84.

143. Spinney, *Rodney,* 297.

144. PRO, ADM 3/89, 1 Oct. 1779.

145. G, 2775, 2776, 2780.

146. NRS, *Sandwich,* 3:181–82.

147. Ibid., 3:185–88.

148. NMM, SAN/T/6, Robinson to Sandwich, 27 Oct. 1779.

149. PRO, SP 42/55, 370–71ff.

150. PRO, ADM 1/311, 17f.

151. PRO, ADM 1/4140, 32f.; NMM, ADM/B/200, 10 Dec. 1779.

152. The warships under Rodney's command at the beginning of the expedition at Spithead were the ships of the line *Sandwich, Prince George, Ajax, Royal George, Alcide, Alfred, Bedford, Culloden, Cumberland, Edgar, Monarch, Montagu, Shrewsbury, Terrible, America;* the 44-gun *Phoenix;* frigates *Pearl, Greyhound, Pegasus, Triton, Hyaena, Porcupine;* cutter *Tapageur.* At Plymouth were the ships of the line *Defence, Dublin, Hector, Invincible, Marlborough, Resolution, Bienfaisant,* and the frigate *Apollo.* Spinney, *Rodney,* 437.

153. E.g., PRO, ADM 1/311, 3, 26, 27, 35.

154. NRS, *Health of Seamen,* 172–73.

155. E.g., NMM, SAN/T/6, Rodney to Sandwich, 17 Nov. 1779.

156. E.g., Marion Balderston and David Syrett, eds., *The Lost War: Letters from British Officers during the American Revolution* (New York, 1975), 195.

157. PRO, ADM 2/1336, 78–96ff.

158. NRS, *Sandwich,* 3:191.

159. CL, Sackville-Germain Papers, vol. 2, Rodney to Germain, 25 Dec. 1779.

160. PRO, ADM 1/311, 43–45ff.

161. Ship of the line: *Guipuzcoana;* frigates: *San Carlos, San Rafael, San Bruno, Santa Teresa, San Fermin, San Vicente.* PRO, ADM 1/311, 46f.

162. PRO, ADM 1/311, 46f.; ADM 51/97, 8–9 Jan. 1780; ADM 51/805, 8–9 Jan. 1780; ADM 51/905, 8–9 Jan. 1780; ADM 51/4308, 8–9 Jan. 1780.

163. PRO, ADM 1/311, 46–48ff.

164. NYHS, Rodney Order Book, 9 Jan. 1780.

165. HMS *Dublin* on 13 January lost her foremast and was sent into Lisbon accompanied by HMS *Shrewsbury.* Spinney, *Rodney,* 305.

166. PRO, ADM 1/311, 50f.; NYHS, Rodney Order Book, 10–16 Jan. 1780.

167. PRO, ADM 51/94, 17 Jan. 1780.

168. Ships of the line: *Fenix, Princesa, Diligente, Monarca, Santo Domingo, San Agustin, San Lorenzo, San Julian, San Eugenio, San Jenaro, San Fusto;* frigates: *Santa Rosalia, Santa Cecila.* Duro, *Armada Española,* 7:263.

169. NRS, *Barham,* 1:64–66. Some historians have taken Young's account at face value. E.g., W. M. James, *The British Navy in Adversity* (New York, 1970 reprint), 192.

170. PRO, ADM 1/311, 50–57ff.; ADM 51/94, 17 Jan. 1780; ADM 51/97, 17

Jan. 1780; ADM 51/235, 17 Jan. 1780; ADM 51/220, 17 Jan. 1780; ADM 51/301, 17 Jan. 1780; ADM 51/727, 17 Jan. 1780; ADM 51/4308, 17 Jan. 1780; NMM, SAN/T/6, Macbride to Rodney, 20 Jan. 1780; HMC, *Rutland*, 3:24; Spinney, *Rodney*, 306–11; Francis Vernon, *Voyages and Travels of a Sea Officer* (London, 1792), 15–20; Duro, *Armada Española*, 7:260–68; NRS, *Sandwich*, 3:191–97.

171. PRO, ADM 1/311, 65f.

172. *Guipuzcana, Princesa, Fenix, Diligente, San Eugenia, San Julian, Monarca.* The *San Julian* and *Monarca* were driven ashore after the battle and destroyed.

173. PRO, ADM 1/311, 51–52ff.

174. PRO, 30/20/10, Rodney to Jackson, 28 Jan. 1780.

175. NRS, *Sandwich*, 3:193.

176. Ibid., 3:210–11.

177. NYHS, Rodney Order Book, 13 Dec. 1779.

178. Ibid., 7 Jan. 1780.

179. Ibid., 30 Jan., 16 Feb. 1780.

180. Ships of the line *Marlborough, Defence, Invincible* and the frigate *Triton*. PRO, ADM 1/311, 68, 94–95.

181. PRO, 30/20/18, Sandwich to Rodney, 20 Dec. 1779; NRS *Sandwich*, 3:200.

182. NRS, *Sandwich*, 3:208, 210–11.

183. NYHS, Rodney Order Book, 27 Jan. 1780.

184. Couter, *Medicine and the Navy*, 45–47, 130–38.

185. PRO, ADM 1/311, 133f.

186. Ships of the line *Sandwich, Ajax, Montagu, Terrible,* and the frigates *Pegasus* and *San Vicente*.

187. NRS, *Sandwich*, 3:202; PRO, ADM 1/311, 92, 146.

188. *Prince George, Royal George, Resolution, Bedford, Cumberland, Culloden, Shrewsbury, Monarch, Alcide, Bienfaisant, Prince William, Fenix, Princesa, Monarca, Diligente,* and the frigate *Apollo*.

189. PRO, ADM 1/311, 107–8ff.

190. PRO, ADM 1/95, 530–31ff.; NRS, *Sandwich*, 3:202–5.

191. PRO, ADM 1/95, 531–532ff.; NRS, *Sandwich*, 3:204.

CHAPTER 4: NEUTRALS, NAVAL STORES, AND THE ROYAL NAVY, 1778–82

1. PRO, PC 2/122, 383–86.

2. PRO, ADM 1/4136, 60f.

3. For example, the Anglo-Dutch Commercial and Maritime Treaty of 1674 especially states that naval stores are not contraband in time of war. Daniel A. Miller, *Sir Joseph Yorke and Anglo-Dutch Relations, 1774–1780* (The Hague, 1970), 118–19.

4. Sir James Allen Park, *A System of Law of Marine Insurances, with Three*

Chapters on Bottomry, the Insurance of Lives, and Insurance against Fires (London, 1787), 290–91.

5. PRO, ADM 7/300, 29f.

6. PRO, ADM 1/3886, Gostling to Stephens, 8 May 1780; ADM 1/3887, Gostling to Stephens, 9 Feb. 1782.

7. PRO, ADM 7/300, 123f.

8. NRS, *Documents Relating to the Law and Customs of the Sea,* ed. R. G. Marsden (London, 1915–16), 2:341.

9. PRO, ADM 7/300, 202f.

10. See James Brown Scott, ed., *The Armed Neutralities of 1780 and 1800: A Collection of Official Documents, Preceded by the Views of Representative Publicists* (New York, 1918), 274.

11. PRO, SP 91/102, 511f.

12. PRO, ADM 84/562, 156–57, 236.

13. E.g., PRO, ADM 3/86, 29, 31 Oct., 4 Nov. 1778; SP 91/102, 273, 293, 304–6; SP 95/128, 25 Sept., 17 Oct. 1778.

14. PRO, SP 84/562, 8f.

15. For an example of the deployment of the squadron in The Downs, see PRO, ADM 1/663, 15 Sept., 2 Dec. 1779.

16. Park, *System of Law,* 557.

17. PRO, ADM 1/4136, 109f.

18. 19 Geo. III, c. 67. s. 41.

19. PRO, SP 84/562, 283f.

20. E.g., ADM 1/3886, Navy Board to Stephens, 21 Sept. 1779.

21. See J. F. Jameson, "St. Eustatius and the American Revolution," *American Historical Review* 8 (1903): 686–708.

22. PRO, SP 95/128, Wroughton to Suffolk, 20 Nov. 1778.

23. Ibid., 9, 16 Oct., 15 Dec. 1778; SP 95/129, 1 Jan. 1779.

24. PRO, SP 95/129, Wroughton to Suffolk, 2 Mar. 1779.

25. Ibid., Weymouth to Wroughton, 19 Feb. 1779.

26. Ibid., Wroughton to Weymouth, 15 June 1779.

27. Ibid., Wroughton to Suffolk, 16 Jan. 1779.

28. Ibid., Wroughton to Weymouth, 8 June 1779.

29. Ibid., Wroughton to Weymouth, 1, 3 Jan., 21 May 1779.

30. Ibid., Weymouth to Wroughton, 14 May 1779.

31. Ibid., Wroughton to Weymouth, 20 July 1779.

32. Ibid., Weymouth to Wroughton, 31 Aug. 1779.

33. Ibid., Admiralty to Stormont, 6 Dec. 1779; Stormont to Admiralty, 7 Dec. 1779; Drake to Admiralty, 8 Dec. 1779; Stormont to Wroughton, 21 Dec. 1779.

34. NRS, *Sandwich,* 3:106.

35. For the text of these treaties, see Miller, *Sir Joseph Yorke,* 116–19.

36. Scott, *British Foreign Policy,* 285–86.

37. PRO, SP 84/562, 18–19ff.

38. Ibid., 25–26ff.

39. Ibid., 12f.

40. PRO, PC 2/123, 151–54.

41. PRO, SP 84/562, 48, 109.

42. Ibid., 62f.

43. David Syrett, "The Organization of British Trade Convoys during the American War, 1775–83," *The Mariner's Mirror* 62 (May 1976): 173.

44. Bemis, *Diplomacy of the American Revolution,* 130–43.

45. PRO, SP 84/562, 386, 438, 441.

46. Ibid., 365f.

47. Ibid., 385f.

48. ADM 1/662, Drake to Stephens, 15 Mar. 1779.

49. E.g., PRO, ADM 1/662, Drake to Stephens, 5, 10 Aug. 1779; ADM 1/663, Drake to Stephens, 16, 21 Sept., 3, 20 Oct., 30 Nov., 2, 4, 5, 8, 17, 31 Dec. 1779.

50. PRO, SP 84/565, 120f.

51. E.g., PRO, ADM 1/662, Drake to Stephens, 20 May 1779.

52. E.g., PRO, ADM 1/661, Drake to Stephens, 10 Mar., 10 Apr. 1779; ADM 1/662, Drake to Stephens, 5 June 1779.

53. PRO, ADM 1/662, Drake to Stephens, 26 Aug. 1779.

54. PRO, ADM 1/661, Drake to Stephens, 23 Feb. 1779; ADM 1/662, Drake to Stephens, 10 June 1779.

55. E.g., PRO, ADM 1/661, Drake to Stephens, 3 Mar. 1779.

56. PRO, ADM 1/662, Drake to Stephens, 25 July 1779; ADM 1663, Drake to Stephens, 2 Sept. 1779.

57. E.g., PRO, ADM 1/663, Drake to Stephens, 1 Sept. 1779.

58. E.g., PRO, ADM 1/661, Drake to Stephens, 14 Mar. 1779; ADM 1/662, Drake to Stephens, 10, 25 July 1779; ADM 1/663, Drake to Stephens, 28 Dec. 1779.

59. PRO, SP 84/565, 55–56f.

60. Ibid., 6f.

61. Ibid., 94f.

62. Ibid., 104f.

63. Bemis, *Diplomacy of the American Revolution,* 130–43.

64. PRO, SP 84/565, 109–11, 157, 214, 316.

65. Ibid., 146–47ff.

66. Ibid., 167–71ff.

67. Ibid., 177–80.

68. Ibid., 159–61, 213.

69. Ibid., 195f.

70. Ibid., 254–57ff.

71. Ibid., 59f.

72. *The Annual Register* (London, 1779), 428.

73. Miller, *Sir Joseph Yorke*, 77.

74. PRO, SP 84/566, 320, 322.

75. Ibid., 191f.

76. Ibid., 175f; NRS, *Sandwich*, 3:106.

77. PRO, SP 84/566, 392f.

78. Ibid., 405f.

79. NRS, *Sandwich*, 3:10–11.

80. Feilding's squadron consisted of the *Namur, Centaur, Valiant, Portland, Seaford, Thunderer, Courageux, Camel, Hawke, Buffalo,* and a number of armed cutters and an armed brig. PRO, SP 84/569, 25f.

81. PRO, ADM 1/1791, 29, 31 Dec. 1779, 3 Jan. 1780.

82. PRO, SP 84/569, 191–92ff.

83. NRS, *Sandwich*, 3:114.

84. HMC, *Various Collections*, 6:165.

85. PRO, SP 84/569, 35–40ff.

86. E.g., PRO, ADM 3/90, 28 Jan. 1780; SP 84/569, 64, 99, 103.

87. PRO, SP 84/569, 156–57, 310ff.

88. Ibid., 215f.

89. PRO, SP 84/570, 241f.

90. Ibid., 37–38ff.

91. Ibid., 91f.

92. Ibid., 316–18ff.

93. PRO, SP 84/562, 120f.

94. For an account of the naval forces of the Baltic states, see Roger Charles Anderson, *Naval Wars in the Baltic, 1522–1850* (London, 1969 reprint), 236–39.

95. Russian policy and Catherine's motivations in 1780 are very difficult to comprehend. I have based most of my conclusions concerning Russian policy and Anglo-Russian relations on Isabel de Madariaga, *Britain, Russia, and the Armed Neutrality of 1780: Sir James Harris' Mission to St. Petersburg during the American Revolution* (New Haven, Conn., 1962).

96. Madariaga, *Britain, Russia, and the Armed Neutrality,* 71–72, 78, 156.

97. Ibid., 157–59.

98. Scott, *Armed Neutralities*, 273–74.

99. Ibid., 275–76.

100. PRO, SP 84/570, 212f.

101. Scott, *Armed Neutralities,* 279–80, 284–86.

102. Ibid., 282.

103. PRO, SP 95/310, Wroughton to Stormont, 31 Mar. 1780.

104. PRO, SP 91/104, 206f.

105. PRO, SP 91/105, 78–79ff.

106. Ibid., 155, 159.

107. Ibid., 197f.

108. Ibid., 225f.

109. PRO, SP 91/106, 74f.

110. Scott, *Armed Neutralities,* 238–39.

111. G, 3230, 3233.

112. For the whole confusing story of Britain's quest for a Russian alliance, see Madariaga, *Britain, Russia, and the Armed Neutrality.*

113. Scott, *Armed Neutralities,* 311–17.

114. Lauritz Pettersen, "The Influence of the American War of Independence upon Danish-Norwegian Shipping," and Herman Kellenbenz, "The Armed Neutrality of Northern Europe and the Atlantic Trade of Schleswig-Holstein and the War of Independence," in *American Revolution and the Sea* (London, 1974), 70–81.

115. Scott, *Armed Neutralities,* 311–17. Bemis, *Diplomacy of the American Revolution,* 155n.

116. The texts of all the notes, conventions, treaties, and declarations can be found in Scott, *Armed Neutralities.*

117. Scott, *Armed Neutralities,* 286–88.

118. PRO, SP 91/106, 7f.

119. Ibid., 11–12ff.

120. PRO, SP 84/571, 109, 124–25; SP 84/572, 16f.

121. PRO, SP 84/571, 153–55ff.

122. PRO, ADM 1/4143, 29, 31.

123. PRO, SP 84/572, 1, 127.

124. Ibid., 82–85ff.

125. Ibid., 167–68ff.

126. PRO, SP 84/573, 41, 43.

127. Ibid., 103f.

128. Ibid., 223f.

129. PRO, SP 84/572, 101–3, 106–24.

130. PRO, PC 2/125, 489–93, 513–15.

131. G, 2935, 3209, 3210, 3211.

132. Scott, *Armed Neutralities,* 330–34.

133. Ibid., 351–58.

134. PRO, SP 84/573, 103f.

135. PRO, SP 91/106, 201f.

136. NMM, Middleton Papers, Sandwich to Middleton, 18 Feb. 1781.

137. James Harris, *The Diaries and Correspondence of James Harris, First Earl of Malmesbury* (London, 1844), 1:335.

138. PRO, SP 84/570, 53f.

139. E.g., PRO, ADM 1/664, Drake to Stephens, 16 Feb., 2 May 1781; ADM 1/665, Drake to Stephens, 6 Apr., 18 June 1782; ADM 3/92, 1, 12 Jan., 12 Apr. 1781.

140. PRO, ADM 1/520, Stewart to Stephens, 23 Aug. 1781.

141. PRO, ADM 1/4144, 142f.

142. PRO, ADM 1/519, Ross to Stephens, 4 June 1782.

143. Charles Ralph Boxer, *The Dutch Seaborne Empire, 1600–1800* (New York, 1965), 275–76.

144. NRS, *Sandwich,* 4:83–87.

145. PRO, ADM 1/664, Drake to Stephens, 14, 21 May 1781; ADM 1/4145, 15, 17, 32.

146. *Princess Amelia, Fortitude, Bienfaisant, Buffalo, Preston, Dolphin,* and *Alert* sloop. NRS, *Sandwich,* 4:87–90.

147. PRO, ADM 1/519, Parker to Stephens, 31 July 1781.

148. *Fortitude, Bienfaisant, Berwick, Princess Amelia, Buffalo, Preston, Dolphin.* PRO, ADM 1/519, State and Condition of His Majesty's Squadron . . . 1 Aug. 1781.

149. PRO, ADM 1/519, report of the number of officers and seamen killed and wounded in the action with the Dutch fleet Sunday, 5 Aug. 1781; Parker to Stephens, 6 Aug. 1781; ADM 51/363, 4–5 Aug. 1781; W. B. Rowbotham, "The 97th Regiment at the Action on the Dogger Bank, 1781," *Journal of the Society for Army Historical Research* 19 (spring 1940):16–18; Jaap R. Bruijn, *The Dutch Navy in the Seventeenth and Eighteenth Centuries* (Columbia, S.C., 1993), 157.

150. PRO, ADM 1/520, Stewart to Stephens, 4, 18 Oct. 1781.

151. Ibid., State of the Enemy . . . the 14th September 1781.

152. E.g., PRO, ADM 1/520, Stewart to Stephens, 26 Dec. 1781; ADM 3/95, 6 May, 31 July 1781; ADM 3/96, 25 Sept. 1782.

153. PRO, ADM 1/519, Ross to Stephens, 1 June 1782; ADM 3/96, 6 Aug. 1782.

154. Paul Walden Bamford, *Forests and French Seapower, 1660–1789* (Toronto, 1956), 68–69, 152–55, 176–81.

155. Dull, *The French Navy,* 342–44.

CHAPTER 5: THE CHANNEL FLEET HOLDS THE LINE, 1780–82

1. G, 2962.

2. PRO, ADM 1/95, 516f.; ADM 3/90, 19 May 1780.

3. NRS, *Letters and Papers of Admiral the Hon. Samuel Barrington,* ed. D. Bonner-Smith (London, 1937–41), 2:337.

4. Cf., Tony Hayter, ed., *An Eighteenth-Century Secretary at War: The Papers of Viscount Barrington* (London, 1988), 3, 31–41.

5. Rodger, *Insatiable Earl,* 279–80.

6. NRS, *Barrington,* 2:338–40.

7. NRS, *Sandwich,* 3:275.

8. G, 3030.

9. PRO, ADM 3/90, 22 May 1780.

10. NRS, *Barrington,* 2:xxx.

11. PRO, ADM 2/3138, 29–31ff.

12. Ships of the line: *Victory, Britannia, Royal George, Namur, Prince George, Duke, Ocean, Queen, Edgar, Dublin, Invincible, Barfleur, Union, Princess Amelia, Alexander, Bellona, Canada, Defence, Monarch, Courageux.* Frigates: *Diana, Emerald, Ambuscade, Proserpine.* Fire ship: *Incendiary.* PRO, ADM 1/96, 11f.

13. PRO, ADM 1/96, 15, 18–20.

14. Ibid., 28–29ff.

15. Ibid., 31–32ff.

16. PRO, ADM 1/387, Johnstone to Stephens, 9 June 1780.

17. NRS, *Sandwich,* 3:284.

18. Admirals Samuel Barrington, George Darby, Robert Digby, and John Lockhart Ross and Captain Richard Kempenfelt.

19. NRS, *Barrington,* 2:342–45.

20. PRO, ADM 1/96, 33, 37.

21. Ibid., 39–40, 54, 59.

22. Ibid., 59–60ff.

23. NRS, *Barham,* 1:326.

24. PRO, ADM 1/96, 64f.

25. *Southampton, Thetis, Alarm, Buffalo, Inflexible.*

26. PRO, ADM 1/96, 67–68ff.

27. *Minutes of the Proceedings of a Court Martial Assembled for the Trial of Capt. John Moutray of His Majesty's Ship the Ramillies . . .* (New York, 1969 reprint).

28. PRO, ADM 3/93, 4 Aug. 1780.

29. Samuel Flagg Bemis, *The Hussey-Cumberland Mission and American Independence* (Princeton, N.J., 1931).

30. PRO, ADM 1/96, 72–73, 90–91, 96, 98–99.

31. Geoffrey Challender, "With the Grand Fleet in 1780," *The Mariner's Mirror* 9 (Aug./Sept. 1923): 260, 262.

32. NRS, *Sandwich,* 3:290.

33. PRO, ADM 1/96, 125–26ff.; NRS, *Sandwich,* 3:291–92.

34. PRO, ADM 2/3138, 42–43ff.

35. PRO, ADM 1/96, 310–11ff.

36. Campbell, *Naval History of Great Britain,* 6:194.

37. PRO, ADM 1/95, 714, 717.

38. NRS, *Sandwich,* 3:294–95.

39. G, 3125, 3126; PRO, ADM 1/95, 717f.

40. PRO, ADM 3/91, 7 Sept. 1780.

41. J. C. Sainty, *Admiralty Officials, 1660–1870* (London, 1975), 25.

42. G, 3132.

43. W. S. Lewis and Warren Hunting Smith, eds., *Horace Walpole's Correspondence with Sir Horace Mann* (London, 1967), 8:432.

44. NRS, *Sandwich,* 4:31.

45. *Britannia, Victory, Royal George, Prince George, Barfleur, Union, Edgar, Bellona, Alexander, Monarch, Cumberland, Courageux, Invincible, Fortitude, Marlborough, Valiant, Canada, Alfred, Defence, Inflexible, Nonsuch, Buffalo, Prince William.*

46. PRO, ADM 1/95, 52, 55.

47. PRO, ADM 2/3138, 44–45ff.

48. NRS, *Sandwich,* 3:306–7.

49. PRO, ADM 50/11, 31 Oct.–6 Dec. 1780.

50. PRO, ADM 1/95, 107–19ff.; NRS, *Sandwich,* 3:278.

51. G, 3229.

52. PRO, SP 42/55, 11–16ff.

53. NRS, *Sandwich,* 4:330–32.

54. PRO, ADM 2/3139, 1, 17–23.

55. PRO, ADM 1/95, 167–69.

56. *Britannia, Royal George, Prince George, Formidable, Ocean, Queen, Duke, Namur, Union, Marlborough, Courageux, Repulse, Canada, Defence, Nonsuch, Bellona, Bienfaisant, Foudroyant, Valiant, St. Albans, Fortitude, Lyon, Alexander, Dublin, Medway, Inflexible, Edgar, Cumberland.* BL, Addit. MSS 38682, 53–54ff.

57. PRO, ADM 1/95, 177–78, 186: BL, Darby Papers, Addit. MSS 38681, 124–25ff.

58. G. Lacour-Gayet, *Le Marine Militaire de la France,* 648–49, 653–54.

59. PRO, ADM 1/95, 180, 186.

60. PRO, ADM 1/4144, 92f.

61. NRS, *Sandwich,* 4:32.

62. PRO, ADM 1/95, 193f.

63. PRO, ADM 1/95, 193–97f.; BL, Addit. MSS 38681, 110–20ff; NRS, *Sandwich,* 4:35–36; T. H. McGuffie, *The Siege of Gibraltar, 1779–1783* (London, 1965), 94–102.

64. BL, Addit. MSS 38681, 109–10ff.

65. PRO, ADM 1/95, 202–12ff.

66. PRO, ADM 2/3139, 40–43ff.

67. PRO, ADM 8/57, 171–72ff.

68. PRO, ADM 1/95, 588f.

69. G, 3348.

70. PRO, ADM 2/3139, 93–96ff.

71. BL, Addit. MSS 38681, 104–5ff.

72. On 1 July 1780 the Channel Fleet consisted of *Britannia, Royal George, Queen, Duke, Formidable, Namur, Union, Edgar, Inflexible, Defence, Medway, Marlborough.* BL, Addit. MSS 38682, 46f.

73. PRO, ADM 1/95, 219, 221–22.

74. NRS, *Sandwich*, 4:46.

75. *Britannia, Royal George, Union, Namur, Queen, Formidable, Duke, Edgar, Inflexible.*

76. PRO, ADM 1/95, 223, 228–29, 231, 233–34, 237, 239; BL, Darby Papers, Addit. MSS 38681, 97–103ff.; NRS, *Sandwich*, 4:46–47.

77. PRO, ADM 1/4145, 72, 84.

78. Ibid., 108, 146, 314.

79. Desmond Gregory, *Minorca: The Illusory Prize. A History of the British Occupations of Minorca between 1708 and 1802* (Rutherford., N.J., 1990), 188–95.

80. Duro, *Armada Española*, 7:298–304; Lacour-Gayet, *La Marine Militaire de la France*, 375–76.

81. PRO, ADM 3/93, 10, 11, July 1781.

82. NMM, SAN/T/6, cabinet minutes, 12 July 1781.

83. PRO, ADM 2/3140, 9–10, 21.

84. PRO, ADM 1/95, 244–46, 254.

85. Ibid., 256f.

86. *Britannia, Royal George, Victory, Union, Namur, Queen, Duke, Formidable, Ocean, Foudroyant, Edgar, Valiant, Cumberland, Defence, Repulse, Inflexible, Courageux, Alexander, Marlborough, Conqueror, Medway.*

87. PRO, ADM 50/70, 31 July–1 Aug. 1781.

88. PRO, ADM 1/95, 257, 260–62, 264–65.

89. G, 3393.

90. E.g., PRO, ADM 1/4145, 133–34ff.

91. NRS, *Sandwich*, 4:49.

92. PRO, ADM 2/3140, 63–65ff.

93. Outer line: *Ocean, Victory, Union, Royal George, Duke, Britannia, Queen, Foudroyant, Formidable.* Inner Line: *Courageux, Defence, Valiant, Repulse, Marlborough, Alexander, Edgar, Conqueror, Cumberland.* BL, Addit. MSS 38682, 39–40ff.

94. NRS, *Sandwich*, 4:60.

95. PRO, ADM 2/3140, 79–80ff.

96. PRO, ADM 1/95, 279f.

97. Ibid., 280f.

98. PRO, ADM 2/3140, 81–100.

99. PRO, ADM 1/4146, 4f.; SP 42/57, 416–19ff.

100. G, 3400, 3401, 3402, 3404; NRS, *Sandwich,* 4:50–54.

101. NRS, *Sandwich,* 4:59.

102. Ibid., 4:61–62.

103. G, 3407.

104. PRO, ADM 2/3140, 101–2ff.

105. PRO, ADM 1/95, 289f.

106. Ibid.

107. Ibid., 296f.

108. On 10 September 1781 the Channel Fleet consisted of *Britannia, Ocean, Prothee, Cumberland, Marlborough, Formidable, Dublin, Conqueror, Medway, Foudroyant, Queen, Inflexible, Arrogant, Duke, Courageux, Defence, Nonsuch, Union, Alexander, Repulse, Hercules, Namue, Edgar, Valiant, Agamemnon.* BL, Addit. MSS 38682, 36f.

109. NRS, *Sandwich,* 4:70.

110. PRO, ADM 1/95, 297, 299, 300–302.

111. Lacour-Gayet, *La Marine Militaire de la France,* 375–76.

112. PRO, ADM 1/4146, 21, 32.

113. G, 3422.

114. PRO, ADM 1/95, 303–4ff.

115. PRO, ADM 1/4146, 62, 65.

116. G, 3427, 3428, 3429.

117. NRS, *Sandwich,* 4:74–75.

118. PRO, ADM 2/111, 400, 422.

119. NRS, *Sandwich,* 4:74.

120. PRO, ADM 2/111, 408.

121. Ships of the line: *Britannia, Victory, Duke, Queen, Union, Ocean, Edgar, Valiant, Courageux, Alexander, Agamemnon, Medway;* 50-gun ship: *Renown;* fire ship: *Tisiphone;* frigates: *Medea, Recovery, Arethusa, Monsieur, Tarter, La Prudente, Crocodile.*

122. NRS, *Barham,* 1:350–51.

123. NRS, *Sandwich,* 4:72–73, 226.

124. PRO, ADM 2/3140, 118–20ff.

125. PRO, ADM 2/111, 403.

126. NRS, *Sandwich,* 4:74–75.

127. PRO, ADM 1/95, 672f.

128. Ibid., 673–78ff; ADM 51/319, 12–31 Dec. 1781; ADM 51/169, 12–31 Dec. 1781; ADM 51/301, 12–31 Dec. 1781; ADM 51/649, 12–31 Dec. 1781; ADM 51/752, 12–31 Dec. 1781; ADM 51/1002, 12–31 Dec. 1781; ADM 51/1036, 12–31 Dec. 1781; NRS. *Barham*, 1:356–57; Lacour-Gayet, *Le Marine Militaire de la France*, 377–79, 425–26, 539–40; *The New Annual Register* (London, 1782), 164; J. H. Owen, "The Operations of the Western Squadron, 1781–82," *The Naval Review* 15 (1927): 36–45.

129. NRS, *Sandwich*, 4:77–78.

130. J. H. Owen, ed., "Letters from Sir Samuel Hood, 1781– 1782," *The Mariner's Mirror* 19 (Jan. 1933): 85.

131. HMC, *Stopford-Sackville*, 2:215.

132. NRS, *Barham*, 1:375.

133. *The Parliamentary History of England, from the Earliest Period to the Year 1803* (London, 1814), vols. 878–98, 929, 934–46.

134. Richard Pares, *King George III and the Politicians* (Oxford, 1953), 171–72.

135. Namier and Brooke, *History of Parliament*, 3:205.

136. Knight, "The Royal Navy's Recovery," 19–21.

137. PRO, ADM 8/58, 313ff.

138. PRO, ADM 8/57, 314–15ff.; ADM 8/58, 199–200ff.

139. CL, Shelburne Papers, vol. 151, A Plan for the Naval Campaign of 1782; Naval Campaign 1782.

140. Rodger, *Insatiable Earl*, 293.

141. All the many turns and twists of parliamentary politics leading up to the fall of the North government are delineated in Christie, *The End of North's Ministry*.

142. PRO, ADM 3/95, 1, 2, 6 Apr. 1782.

143. Scott, *British Foreign Policy*, 317.

144. E.g., PRO, ADM 1/4147, 50, 70, 79, 88.

145. PRO, ADM 1/4147, 10f.

146. Ipswich and East Suffolk Record Office, Keppel Papers, Keppel to Shelburne, 18 Apr. 1782.

147. PRO, ADM 2/1341, 85–86ff.

148. G, 3615.

149. Ipswich and East Suffolk Record Office, Keppel Papers, Keppel to Barrington, 6 Apr. 1782.

150. PRO, ADM 2/3141, 80–84ff.

151. *Britannia, Victory, Ocean, Union, Foudroyant, Alexander, Bellona, Edgar, Dublin, Fortitude, Goliath, Sampson.* G, 3619.

152. PRO, ADM 50/111, 31 Apr. 1782.

153. PRO, ADM 1/95, 730–35ff.; ADM 50/111, 20–25 Apr. 1782; James, *The British Navy in Adversity*, 366–67; Owen, "Operations of the Western Squadron," 45–51.

154. G, 3695.

155. Ships of the line: *Prince George, Goliath, Vigilant, Bellona, Sampson, Courageux, Fortitude;* frigate: *Monsieur;* cutters: *Stark, Dorset.* PRO, ADM 50/95, 3 May 1782.

156. PRO, ADM 1/97, 13–15.

157. PRO, ADM 50/95, 5 May–6 June 1782.

158. PRO, ADM 1/97, 5f.

159. There is no modern biography of Howe. However, for a study of his period of command in America, see Ira D. Gruber, *The Command of the Howe Brothers and the American Revolution* (New York, 1970). For Howe and signals see NRS, *Signals and Instructions.*

160. PRO, ADM 1/97, 4f.; ADM 3/95, 29 Apr. 1782.

161. Ibid., 18f.

162. Ibid., 18–19, 22.

163. G, 3720, 3721, 3722.

164. Ipswich and East Suffolk Record Office, Keppel Papers, Keppel to Howe, 31 May 1782.

165. *Victory, Britannia, Edgar, Ocean, Cambridge, Dublin, Alexander, Raisonable, Panther.*

166. PRO, ADM 1/97, 21f.

167. Ibid., 30–41.

168. Ipswich and East Suffolk Record Office, Keppel Papers, Keppel to Shelburne, 26 May 1782.

169. *Ocean, Cambridge, Princess Amelia, Dublin, Panther, Buffalo, Rippon, Bienfaisant.*

170. PRO, ADM 2/3141, 114–15ff.

171. Ipswich and East Suffolk Record Office, Keppel Papers, Keppel to Howe, 30 May 1782.

172. *Victory, Britannia, Edgar;* PRO, ADM 1/97, 56f.

173. Jonathan R. Dull, *French Navy,* 290.

174. PRO, ADM 1/97, 36f.

175. PRO, ADM 3/95, 4 June 1782.

176. Ipswich and East Suffolk Record Office, Keppel Papers, Keppel to Ross, 17 June 1782.

177. PRO, ADM 1/97, 57–59ff.

178. G, 3817.

179. Ipswich and East Suffolk Record Office, Keppel Papers, Keppel to Milbank, 28 June 1782.

180. G, 3829.

181. PRO, ADM 1/97, 82–83, 86–87, 91.

182. There is no list of the ships of the Channel Fleet during this operation in Howe's dispatches to the Admiralty.

183. PRO, ADM 1/97, 93–94ff.

184. G, 3850.

185. Ipswich and East Suffolk Record Office, Keppel Papers, Keppel to Shelburne, 18 July 1782.

186. G, 3855.

187. PRO, ADM 1/97, 95–100, 106.

188. Dull, *French Navy,* 290–91; James, *British Navy in Adversity,* 370.

189. NMM, Middleton Papers, Shelburne to Middleton, 11 May 1782.

190. Ipswich and East Suffolk Record Office, Keppel Papers, Keppel to Howe, 30 July 1782.

191. G, 3877.

192. PRO, ADM 3/96, 6 Aug. 1782.

193. Bedford Record Office, Grantham MSS, L. 29/661, cabinet minutes, 9 Aug. 1782.

194. Ipswich and East Suffolk Record Office, Keppel Papers, Keppel to Howe, 10 Aug. 1782.

195. G, 3880.

196. Ipswich and East Suffolk Record Office, Keppel Papers, Keppel to Howe, 24 Aug. 1782; Keppel to Shelburne, 24 Aug. 1782.

197. PRO, ADM 1/97, 115–17ff.

198. PRO, ADM 1/97, 315f.

199. Ipswich and East Suffolk Record Office, Keppel Papers, Keppel to Thomas Townshend, 6 Sept. 1782; Keppel to Howe, 7 Sept. 1782.

200. Cf. Knight, "Copper Sheathing," 304–5.

201. PRO, ADM 2/3141, 154–62ff.

202. *Ganges, Royal William, Britannia, Atlas, Ruby, Panther, Edgar, Foudroyant, Polyphemus, Suffolk, Vigilant, Courageux, Crown, Alexander, Sampson, Princess Royal, Victory, Blenheim, Aisa, Egmont, Queen, Bellona, Raisonable, Fortitude, Princess Amelia, Berwick, Bienfaisant, Dublin, Cambridge, Ocean, Buffalo, Vengeance.*

203. PRO, ADM 1/97, 141–58ff.; McGuffie, *Siege of Gibraltar,* 169–75; Mahan, *Major Operations,* 230–32.

204. PRO, ADM 1/96, 173, 183.

205. PRO, ADM PC/2/128, 181–83.

Bibliography

MANUSCRIPTS

Bedford Record Office:
Grantham MSS., L. 29/661. Transcripts of the original documents made by
Professor I. R. Christie.

British Library (BL):
Jervis Papers, Add. MSS., 29914.
Darby Papers, Add. MSS., 38681, 38682.

Ipswich and East Suffolk Record Office:
Keppel Papers.

National Maritime Museum (NMM):
ADM/B/200, Admiralty to Navy Board.
Middleton Papers.
Sandwich Papers.
SAN/T/6, 7, Transcripts of papers of the fourth earl of Sandwich made by the
Navy Records Society.

New-York Historical Society:
Rodney Order Book.

Public Record Office(PRO):
ADM 1/94, 95, 96, 97, Admiral's dispatches, Channel.
ADM 1/311, Admiral's dispatches, Leeward Islands.
ADM 1/386, 387, Admiral's dispatches, Mediterranean.
ADM 1/485, Admiral's dispatches, North America.
ADM 1/519, 520, Admiral's dispatches, Nore.
ADM 1/661, 663, 664, 665, Admiral's dispatches, Downs.
ADM 1/806, Admiral's dispatches, Plymouth.
ADM 1/3886, 3887, Letters from Doctor's Commons.
ADM 1/4129, 4130, 4131, 4133, 4134, 4135, 4136, 4138, 4139, 4140, 4143,
    4144, 4145, 4146, 4147, Letters from Secretary of State.
ADM 2/100, 101, 102, 103, 104, 107, 111, Orders and instructions.
ADM 2/1332, 1333, 1334, 1336, 1339, 1340, 1341, Secret orders.
ADM 3/81, 82, 84, 86, 89, 90, 91, 92, 93, 95, 96, Admiralty minutes.
ADM 7/300, Law officer's opinions.
ADM 8/52, 53, 57, 58, List books.
ADM 50/10, 111, 70, 95, 111, Admiral's logs
ADM 51/94, 97, 139, 169, 220, 235, 301, 303, 365, 372, 609, 649, 727, 752,
    790, 805, 840, 905, 1002, 1036, 1037, 4308, Ship's logs.
ADM 106/2207, Navy Board Papers.

CO 5/95, Military dispatches, North America.
Index to High Count of Admiralty Prize Papers, 1776–1786.
PC 2/119, 122, 123, 124, 125, 126, Privy Council.
PRO, 30/20/10, 18, Rodney Papers.
SP 42/55, 57, State Papers, naval.
SP 78/302, 305, 306, State Papers, France.
SP 84/562, 565, 566, 569, 570, 571, 572, 573, State Papers, Holland.
SP 91/102, 104, 105, 106, State Papers, Russia.
SP 95/128, 129, 130, State Papers, Sweden.
WO 34/115, 116, Amherst Papers.

Warwick Record Office:
Denbigh Papers.

William L. Clements Library, University of Michigan (CL)
Douglas Papers.
Sackville-Germain Papers.
Sackville Manuscripts, Supplementary.
Shelburne Papers.

PERIODICALS

Annual Register (London, 1779).
Gazetteer.
London Chronicle.
London Evening Post.
London Gazette Extraordinary.
Morning Intelligencer.
New Annual Register (London, 1782).

PRINTED DOCUMENTS

Balderson, Marion, and David Syrett, eds. *The Lost War: Letters from British Officers during the American Revolution.* New York: Horizon Press, 1975.
Clark, William Bell, and William James Morgan, eds. *Naval Documents of the American Revolution.* 10 vols. Washington, D.C.: U.S. Government Printing Office, 1964– .
Cutter, William Richard, ed. "A Yankee Privateersman in Prison in England, 1777–1779." *New England Historical and Genealogical Register* 30 (April/ July 1876), 175–77.
Fortescue, Sir John, ed. *The Correspondence of King George the Third from 1760 to December 1783.* 6 vols. London: Frank Cass & Co., 1972 reprint.
Hach, Marie Martel, ed. "Letters of Captain Sir John Jervis to Sir Henry Clinton, 1774–1782." *American Neptune* 7 (April 1951): 87–106.
Harris, James. *The Diaries and Correspondence of James Harris, First Earl of Malmesbury.* 4 vols. London: E. Bentley, 1844.
Hayter, Tony, ed. *An Eighteenth-Century Secretary at War: The Papers of Viscount Barrington.* London: Bodley Head, 1988.

Historical Manuscript Commission. *Fourteenth Report: The Manuscripts of His Grace The Duke of Rutland, K.G., Preserved at Belvoir Castle.* London: Printed for His Majesty's Stationery Office by Eyre and Spottiswoode, 1888–95.

———. *Report on American Manuscripts in the Royal Institution of Great Britain.* 4 vols. London, Dublin, and Hereford: Printed for His Majesty's Stationery Office by Mackie & Co., 1904–9.

———. *Report on the Manuscripts of Mrs. Stopford-Sackville, of Drayton House, Northamptonshire.* 2 vols. London and Hereford: Printed for His Majesty's Stationery Office by Eyre and Spottiswoode, 1904–10.

———. *Report on Manuscripts in Various Collections.* 8 vols. London, Dublin, and Hereford: Printed for His Majesty's Stationery Office by Mackie & Co., 1904–14.

Hutchinson, Peter O., ed. *Diary and Letters of His Excellency Thomas Hutchinson.* London: S. Low, Marston, Searle & Rivington, 1883.

Knight, R. J. B., ed. *Portsmouth Dockyard Papers, 1774–1783: The American War.* Portsmouth: City of Portsmouth, 1987.

Lewis, W. S., and Warren Hunting Smith, eds. *Horace Walpole's Correspondence with Sir Horace Mann.* London: Yale University Press, 1967.

Lewis, W. S., Grover Grown Jr., and Charles H. Bennett, eds. *Horace Walpole's Correspondence with William Mason.* London: Yale University Press, 1955.

Lewis, W. S., Robert A. Smith, and Charles H. Bennett, eds. *Horace Walpole's Correspondence with Hannah Moore.* London: Yale University Press, 1961.

Navy Records Society. *British Naval Documents, 1200–1960.* Edited by John B. Hattendorf, et al. London: Scolar Press, 1993.

———. *Documents Relating to the Law and Customs of the Sea.* Edited by R. G. Marsden. London: Navy Records Society, 1915–16.

———. *The Health of Seamen.* Edited by Christopher Lloyd. London: Navy Records Society, 1965.

———. *Letters and Papers of Admiral the Hon. Samuel Barrington.* Edited by D. Bonner-Smith. 2 vols. London: Navy Records Society, 1937–41.

———. *Letters and Papers of Admiral of the Fleet Sir Thos. Byam Martin. G.C.B.* Edited by Sir Richard Vesey Hamilton. 3 vols. London: Navy Records Society, 1898–1903.

———. *Letters and Papers of Charles, Lord Barham.* Edited by Sir John Knox Laughton. 3 vols. London: Navy Records Society, 1907–11.

———. *Letters Written by Sir Samuel Hood in 1781-2-3.* Edited by David Hannany. London: Navy Records Society, 1895.

———. *The Private Papers of John, Earl of Sandwich.* Edited by G. R. Barnes and J. H. Owen. 4 vols. London: Navy Records Society, 1932–38.

———. *Signals and Instructions, 1776–1794.* Edited by Julian S. Corbett. London: Navy Records Society, 1904.

Minutes of the Proceedings of a Court Martial Assembled for the Trial of Capt. John Moutray of His Majesty's Ship the Ramillies . . . New York: New York Times and Arno Press, 1969 reprint.

Nesser, R. W., ed. *Letters and Papers Relating to the Cruises of Gustavus Conyngham: A Captain of the Continental Navy, 1777–1779.* New York: Navy History Society, 1915.

Owen, J. H., ed. "Letters from Sir Samuel Hood, 1781–1782." *The Mariner's Mirror* 19 (Jan. 1933): 80–87.

The Parliamentary History of England, from the Earliest Period to the Year 1803. London, 1814.

The Parliamentary Register: Or History of the Proceedings and Debates of the House of Commons. London: J. Almon, 1779.

Scott, James Brown, ed., *The Armed Neutralities of 1780 and 1800: A Collection of Official Documents, Proceeded by the Views of Representative Publicists.* New York: Oxford University Press, 1918.

Steuart, A. Francis, ed. *The Last Journal of Horace Walpole during the Reign of George III from 1771 to 1783.* 2 vols. London: John Lane the Bodley Head, 1910.

Walpole, Horace. *Memoirs of the Reign of George III.* 4 vols. London: Lawrence & Bullen, 1894.

Wharton, Francis, ed. *The Revolutionary Diplomatic Correspondence of the United States.* 6 vols. Washington, D.C.: U.S. Government Printing Office, 1889.

Secondary Works

Albion, Robert Greenhalgh. *Forests and Seapower: The Timber Problem of the Royal Navy, 1652–1862.* Cambridge, Mass.: Harvard University Press, 1926.

Allen, Gardner W. *A Naval History of the American Revolution.* 2 vols. Williamstown, Mass.: Corner House Publishers, 1970 reprint.

Anderson, Roger Charles. *Naval Wars in the Baltic, 1522–1850.* London: F. Edwards, 1969 reprint.

Bamford, Paul Walden. *Forests and French Seapower, 1660–1789.* Toronto: University of Toronto Press, 1956.

Baugh, Daniel A. "Why Did Britain Lose Command of the Sea during the War for America?" In *The British Navy and the Use of Naval Power in the Eighteenth Century,* edited by Jeremy Black and Philip Woodfine. Leicester: Leicester University Press, 1988.

———. "The Politics of British Naval Failure, 1775–1777." *American Neptune* 52 (fall 1992): 221–46.

Bemis, Samuel Flagg. *The Hussey-Cumberland Mission and American Independence.* Princeton, N.J.: Princeton University Press, 1931.

———. *The Diplomacy of the American Revolution.* New York: Appleton-Century Co., 1935.

Boxer, Charles Ralph. *The Dutch Seaborne Empire, 1660–1800.* New York: Alfred A. Knopf, 1965.

Brown, Gerald Saxon. *The American Secretary: The Colonial Policy of Lord George Germain, 1775–1778.* Ann Arbor: University of Michigan Press, 1963.

Bruijn, Jaap R. *The Dutch Navy in the Seventeenth and Eighteenth Centuries.* Columbia, S.C.: University of South Carolina Press, 1993.

Campbell, John. *The Naval History of Great Britain.* 8 vols. London: Baldwyn, 1818.

Challender, Geoffrey. "With the Grand Fleet in 1780." *The Mariner's Mirror* 9 (Aug./Sept. 1923): 258–70, 290–304.

Christie, I. R. *The End of North's Ministry, 1780–1782.* London: Macmillan, 1958.

——. *Myth and Reality in Late-Eighteenth-Century British Politics and Other Papers.* London: Macmillan and Co., 1970.

Conn, Steton. *Gibraltar in British Diplomacy in the Eighteenth Century.* New Haven, Conn.: Yale University Press, 1942.

Davis, Ralph. *The Rise of the English Shipping Industry in the Seventeenth and Eighteenth Centuries.* Newton Abbot, Devon: David & Charles, 1972.

Dictionary of National Biography. 21 vols. London: Oxford University Press, 1921–22.

Donoughue, Bernard. *British Politics and the American Revolution: The Path to War.* London: Macmillan, 1964.

Dull, Jonathan R. *The French Navy and American Independence: A Study in Arms and Diplomacy, 1774–1787.* Princeton, N.J.: Princeton University Press, 1975.

Duro, Cesareo Fernandez. *Armada Española desde la Union de los Reinos de Castilla y de Aragon.* 9 vols. Madrid: Sucesores de Rivadeneya, 1901.

Gregory, Desmond. *Minorca: The Illusory Prize. A History of the British Occupations of Minorca between 1708 and 1802.* Rutherford, N.J.: Fairleigh Dickinson University Press, 1990.

Gruber, Ira D. *The Howe Brothers and the American Revolution.* New York: Atheneum, 1972.

Hunt, Robert M. *The Life of Sir Hugh Palliser, Bart.* 2 vols. London: Chapman and Hall, 1844.

James, W. M. *The British Navy in Adversity.* New York: Russell & Russell, 1970 reprint.

Jameson, J. F. "St. Eustatius and the American Revolution." *American Historical Review* 8 (1903): 686–708.

Jenkins, E. H. *A History of the French Navy.* London: MacDonald and Janes, 1973.

Johnston, Ruth Y. "American Privateers in French Ports." *Pennsylvania Magazine of History and Biography* 53 (Oct. 1929), 353–74.

Kellenbenz, Herman. "The Armed Neutrality of Northern Europe and the Atlantic Trade of Schleswig-Holstein and the War of Independence." In *American Revolution and the Sea.* London: National Maritime Museum, 1974.

Keppel, Thomas. *The Life of Augustus, Viscount Keppel.* 2 vols. London: Henry Colburn, 1842.

Knight, R. J. B. "Sandwich, Middleton and Dockyard Appointments." *The Mariner's Mirror* 57 (May 1971) 175–92.

——. "Introduction of Copper Sheathing into the Royal Navy, 1779–1786." *The Mariner's Mirror* 59 (Aug. 1973): 299–309.

——. "The Royal Navy's Recovery after the Early Phase of the American Revolutionary War." In *The Aftermath of Defeat: Armed Forces and the Challenge of Recovery,* edited by George J. Andreopoulos and Harold E. Selesky. New Haven, Conn.: Yale University Press, 1994.

Lacour-Gayet, G. *Le Marine Militaire de la France sous le regne de Louis XVI.* 4 vols. Paris: H. Champion,. 1905.

Lavery, Brian. *The Ship of the Line.* Annapolis, Md.: U.S. Naval Institute Press, 1983.

──────. *The Arming and Fitting of English Ships of War, 1660–1815*. London: Conway Maritime Press, 1987.

Lindwall, Ake. "The Kempenfelt Family." *The Mariner's Mirror* 57 (Nov. 1971): 379–83.

Lloyd, Christopher, and Jack L. S. Couter. *Medicine and the Navy, 1200–1960*. London: E. & S. Livington, 1961.

Mackesy, Piers. *The War for America, 1775–1783*. London: Longmans, 1964.

Madariaga, Isabel de. *Britain, Russia, and the Armed Neutrality of 1780: Sir James Harris' Mission to St. Petersburg during the American Revolution*. New Haven, Conn.: Yale University Press, 1962.

Mahan, A. T. *The Major Operations of the Navies in the War of American Independence*. New York: Greenwood Press, 1969 reprint.

Martelli, George. *Jemmy Twitcher: The Life of the Fourth Earl of Sandwich*. London: Jonathan Cape, 1962.

Maurer, Maurer. "Coppered Bottoms for the Royal Navy: A Factor in the Maritime War of 1778–1783." *Military Affairs* 14 (1950): 57–61.

McGuffie, T. H. *The Siege of Gibraltar, 1779–1783*. London: B. T. Batsford, 1965.

Miller, Daniel A. *Sir Joseph Yorke and Anglo-Dutch Relations, 1774–1780*. The Hague: Mouton, 1970.

Morison, Samuel Eliot. *John Paul Jones: A Sailor's Biography*. Boston: Little Brown, 1959.

Namier, Sir Lewis, and John Brooke. *The History of Parliament*. 3 vols. London: Her Majesty's Stationery Office, 1964.

Owen, J. H. "Operations of the Western Squadron, 1781–82." *Naval Review* 15 (1927): 33–53.

Pares, Richard. "American versus Continental Warfare, 1739–62." *English Historical Review* 51 (1936): 429–65.

──────. *King George III and the Politicians*. Oxford: The Clarendon Press, 1953.

Park, Sir James Allen. *A System of Law of Marine Insurances, with Three Chapters on Bottomry, the Insurance of Lives, and Insurance against Fires*. London: 1787.

Patterson, A. Temple. *The Other Armada: The Franco-Spanish Attempt to Invade Britain in 1779*. Manchester: Manchester University Press, 1960.

Pettersen, Lauritz. "The Influence of the American War of Independence upon Danish-Norwegian Shipping." In *American Revolution and the Sea*. London: National Maritime Museum, 1974.

Pritchard, James. "French Strategy and the American Revolution: A Reappraisal." *Naval War College Review* 47 (fall 1994): 83–108.

Ritcheson, C. R. *British Politics and the American Revolution*. Norman: University of Oklahoma Press, 1954.

Rodger, N. A. M. *The Insatiable Earl: The Life of John Montagu, 4th Earl of Sandwich*. London: Harper Collins, 1993.

Rowbotham, W. B. "The 97th Regiment at the Action on the Dogger Bank, 1781." *Journal of the Society for Army Historical Research* 19 (spring 1940): 16–18.

Rutherford, G. "The Capture of the *Ardent*." *The Mariner's Mirror* 27 (April 1941): 106–30.

Sainty, J. C. *Admiralty Officials, 1660–1780*. London: The Athlone Press, 1975.

Scott, H. M. *British Foreign Policy in the Age of the American Revolution.* Oxford: The Clarendon Press, 1990.

Spinney, David. *Rodney.* London: George Allen and Unwin, 1969.

Stephenson, O. W. "The Supply of Gunpowder in 1776." *American Historical Review* 30 (Jan. 1925): 277–81.

Syrett, David. *Neutral Rights and the War in the Narrow Seas, 1778–82.* Fort Leavenworth, Kans.: U.S. Army Command and General Staff College, 1985.

———. "The Organization of British Trade Convoys during the American War, 1775–83." *The Mariner's Mirror* 62 (May 1976): 169–81.

———. *The Royal Navy in American Waters, 1775–1783.* London: Scolar Press, 1989.

———. *Shipping and the American War, 1775–83.* London: The Athlone Press, 1970.

Thomas, Peter D. G. *Lord North.* New York: St. Martin's Press, 1976.

Tracy, Nicholas. *Navies, Deterrence, and American Independence: British Seapower in the 1760's and 1770's.* Vancouver, B.C.: University of British Columbia Press, 1988.

Usher, Roland G., Jr. "The Royal Navy Impressment during the American Revolution." *Mississippi Valley Historical Review* 37 (March 1951): 673–88.

Vernon, Francis V. *Voyages and Travels of a Sea Officer.* London: Wm. M'Kenzie, 1792.

Willcox, William B. "British Strategy in America, 1778." *The Journal of Modern History* 19 (1947): 84–106.

Wright, Charles, and C. Ernest Fayle. *A History of Lloyd's.* London: Macmillan, 1928.

INDEX

Index